THE LIFE AND TIMES OF

General Two-Gun Cohen

Morris Abraham Cohen—1951

THE LIFE AND TIMES

OF

General Two-Gun Cohen

✻ ✻

CHARLES DRAGE

✻ ✻

✻ ✻

New York
FUNK & WAGNALLS COMPANY
1954

1

ACKNOWLEDGMENTS

I HAVE received generous help from many quarters, but my special thanks are due to the staff of Leman Street Police Station, to Colonel W. E. Batt and the staff of Thames Magistrates Court, to the caretaker of Cannon Street Road Synagogue and of the Maccabean Branch of the British Legion; also to various ladies and gentlemen of the Borough of Stepney whose names I do not mention simply because they did not disclose them; also to Mr. J. W. Rosenthal, J.P., to Harry Cohen, Headmaster of Finnart House School, and to the family of the late Israel Ellis, the great Headmaster of Hayes Industrial School; also to Mr. C. C. Aaronfeld of the Jewish Central Information Office, to Dr. Chen of the Sino-British Cultural Bureau, to Messrs. G. E. Mitchell and G. R. Price of the China Association, and to Mr. E. E. Heppenstall of the Department of Veterans Affairs, Ottawa; also to Messrs. William Sparrow and A. H. Elston, late of the Hong Kong Police, to Sir William Shenton, Sir John Thornycroft and Brigadier-General C. R. Woodroffe.

Without the invaluable help of Mr. Gerald Clark of Montreal, the well-known Canadian journalist, this book could not have been written. Besides compiling all the narrative information used in the Canadian chapters, he himself, during a visit to Hong Kong, did much additional research and is, in his turn, indebted to His Excellency Wu Teh-chen, Secretary General of the Kuomintang, Dr. Sun Fo, Generals Li Fuk-lum and Mah Sang, and Messrs. Frank Szto and Bing Shui-lee; also to Messrs. Seymour Major and Rex Davis of the Hong Kong Police, Messrs. Mike Kendall,

ACKNOWLEDGMENTS

Graham Barrow, Findlay Andrews, Aubrey Diamond, T. B. Wilson, and Harry Graye; to Mr. and Mrs. Vivian Ferrier and Mrs. Weill.

General Cohen is personally indebted to Miss Rose Schwisber of Montreal for her help in compiling the manuscript which formed the basis of this book.

CONTENTS

ILLUSTRATIONS

THE LIFE AND TIMES OF

General Two-Gun Cohen

CHAPTER I

The East End

WE MET during the Canton Customs Crisis of Christmas 1923 when I was First Lieutenant of H.M.S. *Bluebell*, a venerable veteran of the First World War, which still carried sails and even, on occasions, used them. Morris Cohen was then a romantic and mysterious but somewhat equivocal figure in the service of the great revolutionary leader, Dr. Sun Yat-sen. We found ourselves in opposing camps, relations between which were severely strained, and our acquaintance had little chance of developing.

At our next meeting, early in 1935, the situation was very different. Morris had already become a legendary figure in the Far East, and I was newly arrived from England on an enterprise the nature of which is sufficiently indicated in Chapter XI. Japan was the common enemy, our interests were identical and our friendship ripened rapidly.

His tale was told to me over the space of seventeen years in various places and under various conditions; in Canton and Macao, in Hong Kong and Shanghai and "up-country," in river steamers and railway trains and motor cars and aircraft; sometimes when things were going well, but more often when they were going badly. It was told sometimes by his friends—and enemies—scattered over Canada, London, and China, and sometimes in written or anecdotal form, by himself. If I have used his own language, it is simply because that language expresses his personality so completely that one can think of his story in no other terms.

Accurate factual information was always a difficulty and usually came to hand in reverse chronological sequence. For instance, it was only last year that I discovered he had been born at 68 Umberston Street, Stepney, on August 3rd, 1889, the eldest son of an immigrant Jewish couple from Poland.

MY EARLIEST MEMORY—said Morris—was of a beating from my father when I was three years old for disobeying my mother. She had told me to stay indoors but I slipped out and went off to play with Yutke Klein, the little boy who lived next door. The next day I did the same thing again and he beat me twice as hard.

They were an old-fashioned, strictly orthodox couple and they kept up all the old customs. When my mother married she sheared her hair and for the rest of her life she wore a wig, the *shaitel*. My father was the churchwarden, or *gabbai*, of our synagogue and on Saturdays he would walk there along Commercial Road wearing his shiny top hat, his black cutaway coat, and low waistcoat which showed a fine expanse of starched white shirt. It was a sin for grown-ups to carry anything on the Sabbath and so I would walk beside him with the velvet bag that held his prayer-shawl, the *tallis*; and when he met his friends and said "*Sholom*," "Peace be unto you," in his deep voice, I felt very proud.

By the time I was four I'd learned to play truant from home without being caught and I used to hang about Gardiner's Corner and watch the world go by. There was plenty to look at, too: Jews from everywhere; *hasidim*, a religious sect, in their loose black coats shuffling along to the theological schools, called *Yeshivas*; Pollacks and *Litvaks*, Lithuanian Jews, and Russian and Dutch and Spanish Jews.

There were sailors from the docks and Asiatics—Chinese and Malays and Lascars—from Limehouse. Those were the days of Jack the Ripper and, when there had been another murder and it began to get dark, I'd scuttle back down Umberston Street and be glad to see my father standing in our doorway.

It was on Gardiner's Corner that I first began to want pocket money. In the winter there was an old lady who cooked potatoes in a little portable stove. I can hear her cry now—"Baked 'taters. Warm yer 'ands and fill yer belly for a penny." But there weren't many pennies to spare in our family.

When we were five Yutke Klein and I got a bit bolder. We'd venture as far as Billingsgate. There we had our first big idea. It was winter again and firewood was short. So we'd set out from home with my mother's meat-cleaver hidden under my coat and, when we got to the fish-market, Yutke Klein would keep watch while I grabbed an empty fish crate. It was heavy and awkward to handle and greasy with fish scales and slime, but somehow we'd drag it to a quiet corner and chop it into strips. Then we'd cart it from door to door—anywhere but down our own street—and shout, "Firewood oh! Firewood oh!" and it was a bad day when we didn't make sixpence apiece.

Our next idea was riskier but it worked for a bit. We made friends with the man who mended window-panes. He would wait out of sight while one of us (we'd toss up to decide which) threw a stone through a window and bolted. Then around the corner he'd stroll ringing his handbell and chanting, "Glazier, glazier. Window fixing, window fixing." He paid us a commission of a halfpenny on every pane he mended.

Then the blow fell. We were both enrolled in the kindergarten at Buckle Street School and all our fun was finished. The first day I was taken there by my sister Rose, who was two years older than me and a lot stronger, and she held my hand tight all the way, because she knew I'd bolt if I had the chance. When I got there they patted me on the head and gave me a needle and thread and told me to sew two pieces of cloth together. It was a sissy sort of job and I felt awful.

I stuck it for three days; then I found an unlocked back door and got out. Down the stone stairs I went with Yutke trailing after me yelling, "Come to the Russian war, boys! Come to the Russian war!" (I know that this was forty years after the Crimean campaign, but we stuck to old slogans in Stepney and this was still our battlecry.) It was fine to be free in the streets again and we ran around all our old haunts. That night we slept in a greengrocer's warehouse.

We were cold but comfortable enough, but I made a big mistake—I got home before my father had gone to work.

He'd been nearly off his head with worry and had spent most of the night searching the streets and the docks for me. But as soon as he saw me coming down Umberston Street he was just plain angry.

"So you will not go to school?" he shouted. "So you will not be educated? So you want to stay ignorant all your life?"

All my mother said was, "Moishe, did you have anything to eat?"

"Sure," I said proudly, "carrots and t'marters." She told Rose to take me back to school again.

I was there for about a year without giving the truant officer any trouble. I went on to the Jewish Free School in Bell Lane, which was a much more impressive and awe-inspiring place. Even at the age of seven I knew that Israel Zangwill, who wrote so many stories of my people and had just published *The King of Schnorrers*, had taught the sixth standard there a few years before.

About this time I discovered the stage. The Pavilion

Theatre seemed the most wonderful place in the world. I had a little money by now, because my father used to give me a penny a day as a bribe to attend extra classes in English and Hebrew; and most of those pennies went to pay for seats in the pit of the Pavilion, or else the Paragon Music Hall further down Commercial Road.

They were both places to be proud of. The Pavilion had been built to take the Drury Lane scenery and so the Drury Lane productions often used to come there, and they put on Yiddish plays as well. In fact, it was a rallying place for all East-End Jewry. Charities were organized there—the Pavilion Bread & Coal Society and the Pavilion Passover Society. My parents heard the Zionist cause first preached from the stage by the great Dr. Herzl.

The manager in those days was Isaac Cohen, whose daughter married a local young man called Joe Lyons. Isaac didn't think much of him then; in fact, he doubted very much whether he'd ever make a decent living for himself, so he set him up in a sort of tea-and-coffee shop called The Sussex Club. That was the beginning of all the Lyons tea-shops and Corner Houses, and Joe finished up as Sir Joseph.

The Paragon was a different sort of place, just a straightforward East-End music hall. I saw Harry Lauder and Marie Lloyd there. Harry was already earning one hundred pounds a week in the West End, but he was still working off his seven pounds a week contracts down our way. He was an honest man and he stuck to his bargains whatever happened.

It was hanging around the Pavilion pit entrance that got me into the boxing game. At eight years old I weighed ninety-two pounds and my head was too big for my body, so I looked heavy and clumsy—in fact, they called me "Fat Moishe." But I was quick on my pins and even then I packed a pretty good punch and I liked a fight. One day I picked a quarrel with a boy of twelve over our places in the queue for the first house. He was a lot taller than me and the queue thought it would be a walk-over, but just as we got down to business I heard someone shout, "I'll bet on the young 'un to beat 'im. Ten bob says it!"

That was a big bet for those days. I won all right and then I looked around for my backer. He was a character from Whitechapel, who wore a derby hat instead of the usual peaked cap. That meant he must be a man of means with an income of three pounds a week or more. I knew that and I knew too that he made most of his money betting. What I didn't know then was that the rest of it came from an occasional bit of burglary.

He took me aside and he asked me if I'd like to fight in the ring! He didn't need much sales talk to put that one over. My hero just then was "Pedlar" Palmer, who'd won the bantamweight championship of England the year before. The prospect of getting into the ring myself was the most exciting thing that had ever happened to me.

The very next Sunday I was at the People's Arcade facing another eight year old called Izzy Fink. He was boxing under the name of "Battlin' Murphy," and I was billed as "Cockney Cohen"—of course not to be confused with the famous fighter of that name of a decade or so later. Respectable Jewish families didn't see their sons as professional pugs, so we had to cover up. There must have been a crowd of two hundred—mostly touts and gamblers, of course—and I felt pretty nervous, but I stripped off and limbered up and tried to look as if I'd done it all before. Then the smoke from the Woodbines caught me by the throat and I went into a coughing jag and was nearly sick on the spot.

The referee climbed through the ropes.

"Quieeet, quieeet!" he bellowed, and the noise died down a bit. "Order now, Order! Ninety-two-pound contest of four rounds between Cockney Cohen and Battlin' Mur-

phy. On my r-r-right Cohen. On my l-l-left Murphy . . .
Seconds out of the ring. First round . . . Time!"

We came out of our corners and squared off and tried
to size each other up, but the crowd was impatient.

" 'Op to it!" they roared.

He feinted with his left and I landed a light one on
his jaw, but that wasn't good enough either.

"Now 'it 'im 'ard," they yelled. So we mixed it.

I still think that Murphy was the better man. He gave
me a bloody, swollen nose, the first real damage it ever had.
But when the final gong went, the ref held up my arm. While
I was dressing and washing my face, my backer gave me two
shillings, which he said was my cut of the gate—and that was
the biggest money I'd ever made.

I fought half a dozen times at the People's Arcade, and
always got a kick out of seeing my name on the bills.
Between whiles my backer would stage bouts for me in a
blacksmith's shop where the fights weren't advertised. The
betting was bigger and the charge for admission was sixpence. But all along I was true to my Faith and I never once
fought on the Sabbath—maybe because my father was at
home that day.

Then I got into trouble with the police, and decided
to take up a respectable occupation. I became a "shill"
(a stooge) for Harry the Gonof who sold purses. He would
stand beside his stall half-way down Petticoat Lane and
wheeze, "Step right 'ere, ladies and gents. Gen-uine purses
for sixpence apiece. And I tell you wot. Some lucky lady will
get a bob for free."

He'd pretend to drop a shilling in the purse—palming
it of course—and offer the purse all around.

"Anyone give sixpence?"

Once in a while, to whip up interest and attract customers, he would actually put the shilling inside and give

me a nod to show what he'd done. This was my cue to push forward and buy the purse quickly before anyone else could. Then I'd hold it aloft, turn it upside down, catch the shilling as it fell out, pocket it and walk off. I had to bring the purses and shillings back that night, but I got tuppence a time for my trouble.

I didn't go straight for long. In May 1900, when I was ten years of age, I was "run in" as "a person suspected of attempting to pick pockets." I appeared at the Thames Police Court before the famous magistrate Mr. Frederick Mead. He committed me to Mayford Industrial School till I reached the age of sixteen. It seemed a disaster at the time, but it was the best thing that could have happened to me.

ABOUT THE TIME when, in the streets of Stepney, Morris was whooping "Come to the Russian war!" and, in Peking, the Empress Dowager was leading her unhappy country from the disasters and humiliations of the first conflict with Japan to the crowning catastrophe of the Boxer Rebellion, some leaders of the Jewish community in London were becoming increasingly concerned with the care of juvenile delinquents of their faith.

There were, in fact, less than a score of such boys and they had hitherto been accommodated in the Industrial School at Lewisham, but the arrangement was not satisfactory and it was decided to provide them with an establishment of their own. A body of Managers was assembled, drawn from the Jewish Board of Guardians, the Spanish and Portuguese Congregations, and the United Synagogue; funds were subscribed and, in the spacious Victorian manner, the committee did not look around for a suitable house to purchase but bought instead twelve acres of orchard and park land near Hayes and proceeded to erect what, by any standards, would have been a fine building and, to the slum-bred boys who found themselves there, must have seemed a palace.

At Mayford Morris found himself one of the fifteen problem-children awaiting the inauguration and, on February 12th, 1901, his name was duly entered—No. 8 on the roll of Hayes Industrial School. His description in the register was scarcely prepossessing:

Height	4 ft. 5¼ in.
Figure	Stout
Complexion	Dark
Hair	Dark brown
Eyes	Light brown—yellowish
Nose	Broad, flat
Peculiarities	Head very large

His previous character was briefly summed up: "Has been several times previously charged and twice birched." His Educational State concludes with the ominous words "A truant," and his Mental Capacity is—surprisingly—assessed as "Slow." It was the first and last time in his life that that epithet was applied to Morris.

The School Consecration Service was held on February 17th, and the new life began. The hours were long, the holidays few, and the discipline strict. Morris was kept hard at it from 6 A.M.—"Boys rise, wash and dress"—to 8 P.M.—"Prayers and bed." The only breaks were the festivals of the New Year and Yom Kippur, the first and seventh days of Tabernacles and Passover, and the first day of Pentecost. The training emphasized drill, gymnastics, and such practical pursuits as carpentry, market-gardening, tailoring, and laundry work. The atmosphere had a semi-military tinge; at least one instructor had served in the regular army, and on state occasions the boys wore wide white Eton collars with smart pill-box hats adorned with the initials

"H.I.S." cocked rakishly, well on one side of the head, and held in place with a chin-strap.

Morris found his abundant physical energy and considerable physical gifts encouraged and directed into useful channels. He played cricket and soccer, boxed and drilled with enthusiasm, and, although the headmaster's widow (who also acted as matron) recalls that he did not shine particularly at any form of sport or athletics, he did once win an inter-school Indian-club-swinging contest.

Morris came under another influence at this time and one that he was never to forget. The school headmaster is a peculiarly English institution, and Israel Ellis was in the great tradition. Under him Hayes attained a position unique among schools of its kind and Morris was only one among hundreds of boys who, starting their lives badly, owed both happiness and success to his wisdom and understanding.

In the case of Morris it was no sudden reformation. His conduct sheet for those years reads:

Sept.	1901	Fair.
Dec.	1901	Fair.
June	1902	Implicated in theft.
Dec.	1902	Improving.
June	1903	Still improving.
Oct.	1903	Continues to improve; seems more trustworthy.
Nov.	1903	Convicted of stealing sugar from officer's room and potatoes (for baking) from Cook's Stores.
Feb.	1904	In Bad Conduct List for last three months. A food thief.
Oct.	1904	Has been very dishonest.
March	1905	Left the building to spend money without permission.

Ellis soon discovered that the one punishment Morris feared was to be barred from games and made to memorize passages from the plays of Shakespeare. It was mental torture in more ways than one, for, though the boy liked the dramatic stories and the fine, high-sounding language, he could never quite master the pronunciation of the letter "H" at the start of a word, or the letter "G" at the finish. Ellis employed drastic methods. Poor Morris stood in the school yard and hopped on his right foot while he recited ten times *"He had his hard head hammered,"* then changed to his left foot while repeating a similar phrase full of present participles. Still his memory was good and he gradually learned most of *Richard III* and *Henry VIII.*

At the annual inspection by an examiner from the London County Council, Morris's class were told to read aloud from the first-named play. His turn came and he advanced to the dais, his primer open, snapped it shut and faced the class.

"Have I a tongue to doom my brother's death
And shall that tongue give freedom to a slave?"

He paused to make sure that everyone realized he was not reading but reciting from memory, and continued to the end of the passage. The examiner was startled.
"That boy is amazing; he must be a gifted scholar!"
Ellis, who knew better, said nothing.

On his sixteenth birthday Morris returned to Stepney to face the family council in Umberston Street. They were deeply concerned and their concern was shared by the local constabulary. He had undoubtedly made good at Hayes, but it was equally undoubted that he had formerly been the unchallenged leader of the local bad boys and was only too likely to resume that position.

The council decided that the New World might offer opportunities for the unfettered development of a combination of talents which, in the restricted scope of the Old Country, would probably lead to disaster.

Josef Cohen had a friend who owned a ranch near Wapella in Saskatchewan and who could no doubt be trusted to treat his eldest son with kindness. So one morning in the autumn of 1905 Morris stood on the departure platform of Euston Station with five sovereigns and a steerage ticket to Canada in his pocket. His father stroked his beard and patted his son's shoulder.

"Moishe, you must always remember the words of the wise Rabbi Koretza: 'Five things can help us to achieve a livelihood: first, regular and earnest study; second, strict honesty; third, regular prayers for sustenance; fourth, devotion of a tithe to charity; fifth, not to be an extravagant or reckless spender.'"

If in the future Morris failed frequently to follow his father's advice, he never entirely forgot it.

CHAPTER II

The New World

WHEN I LANDED at Quebec—said Morris—I stood
five three and weighed one hundred and twenty-six. I was
chunky and husky, but I hadn't really begun to fill out.
My hair was dark brown and curly—there's not much left
of it now, but I had plenty then—I looked a bit more than
sixteen. My nose was already busted, but it's been busted a
lot worse since.

I wore a blue serge suit, a check tie, and a brown fedora hat. That was my first fedora; up to then I'd only worn
a cloth cap on Gardiner's Corner and a pill-box hat at
Hayes. I had a wooden box and on it was painted in white
capital letters:

M. A. COHEN

WAPELLA, SASK.

CANADA

I still had my five pounds, but that made up all my
worldly possessions.

Wapella is on the main C.P.R. line. It was a tiny little
township in those days with maybe a few hundred people,
wooden buildings, dirty streets, and three or four grain ele-
vators. Abe Hyam met me there with a horse and buggy and
drove me to his farm which was twelve miles out. I didn't
stay there. Although he'd told my father he would look
after me, he'd never planned to employ me himself—he'd
arranged for me to work for a man called Bob Nichelson.

Old Man Nichelson turned up after two or three days. He seemed an old man to me—he was upwards of forty, and sported a long goatee beard, a tall, lanky chap from the Eastern Provinces, and a goy.

"What's your name?" he asked.

"Moishe Cohen."

"You know anything about farming?"

"Somethin' about gardenin'."

"Know anything about horses?"

"No, but I'm willing to learn."

He looked me over, felt my muscles, turned to Hyam, and said, "He'll do." Then he asked me:

"Young man, how would you like to be a rancher and farmer?"

"I'd like it fine, sir."

"Did you ever milk a cow?"

"No, sir."

"Well, I'll give you a hundred dollars for a year's contract."

That sounded an awful lot of money to me.

As soon as we got to his farm I knew that I was going to be happy. The house was clean and cheerful and comfortable and I had a tiny bedroom to myself—for the first time in my life. Nichelson raised cattle as well as grain and employed a couple of cowhands. He had a middle-aged wife, short, stout, and jolly, and two daughters of about twenty-one. The elder, Cora, taught me to do the household chores.

I got up at five and laid and lit the fires. Then I went out to the stables and fed the eight horses. I milked the ten cows (that was something else that Cora had to teach me). I watered the horses. I went to the woodpile to saw and split wood for the winter. I had plenty to do.

The food was a revelation. I'm still a big eater; in those days I was something phenomenal. The food at home and at Hayes had been wholesome and sufficient, but I'd never before been able to eat just as much as I wanted and of dishes that were always appetizing. I'd never imagined that anything could taste quite as good as hot biscuit. At first I shied off ham and eggs because of my orthodox Jewish upbringing, but when I saw how often ham turned up on the table, I began to weaken. After I'd once tasted it, all my scruples went by the board and I dug into it like the rest.

In five or six months I grew out of my grand blue serge suit and all the other things I'd brought from England. One evening Mrs. Nichelson said, "Next time Bob goes to town, you'll have to go with him and buy yourself some new clothes."

We were eighteen miles from Wapella, even further than Abe Hyam's farm, and we didn't go in very often. But next time he took me along in the buggy, and I bought an entire new outfit that set me back eight dollars fifty.

On Sunday mornings I would hitch up the wagon and drive Mrs. Nichelson and her two daughters a mile and a half to the Methodist Chapel. Cora played the organ and the younger girl sang in the choir. I went inside out of curiosity at first. I found that I liked the singing so I used to go in and listen every Sunday. I even tried to persuade Bob Nichelson to come too, but it was no good.

I could never quite figure out his attitude. He was an honest, honorable, kindly man, a good husband, a good father, and a good boss; but he had no religion at all and he was just as strict about having no religion as other folk are about the one they've got.

Sometimes the Methodist minister would be invited to the farm for a meal and then we'd discuss theology. He often tried to get the Old Man to come to church, but never had the slightest hope of success. He even tried to convert me to Christianity and we'd argue for hours. I'd had a sound religious training and knew most of the answers, and usually got the best of it.

"Do you believe that God would give a commandment and change it?" I'd ask him. "Do you think that God can make a mistake? Do you believe in the Bible and that God's word is law?"

"Man makes mistakes," I'd finish up triumphantly, "and man does wrong; but God never changes his mind."

"I agree with you entirely," he'd say.

"Then why do you eat pork?" I'd come back at him. "The Bible forbids it."

So we'd go at it, hammer and tongs, and never get any further. If ever I cornered him, he'd wriggle out of it—or so he thought. He stuck to his opinion, and I stuck to mine.

If the Methodist minister didn't have much influence with me, there was another man who did—a cowhand called Bobby Clark. At least that was the name he liked to go by; I don't believe it was his right one. He never talked much about himself or his past, but from some of his yarns I knew that he'd been in the Yukon at the time of the Great Gold Rush. He had three strong suits—dice, cards, and pistols—and he devoted his spare time to giving me a sound grounding in all three subjects. I learned a lot.

With dice he taught me to see if they were "loaded" by dropping them in a glass of water. If the same side always came up, there was something wrong. Then he taught me the "pick-up and spin out." Supposing you want to throw a seven, you pick the bones up and hold them in your hand with the three and four uppermost. You pretend to shake them, but really hold them steady and make the rattling noise by knocking your cuff-buttons against the buttons on your coat. Then you throw them on to the table with a twist so that they spin around but don't turn over. That way

Bobby could throw any number he wanted every time he chose. It all sounds simple enough, but that trick lasted for years. It was killed eventually in big-time gambling, partly by the use of the dice-box and partly by a new rule that when the dice fell they had to bounce up clear off the table.

When it came to cards, he started me with the easier tricks like picking an ace from the bottom of the deck, or in fact dealing from the bottom whenever it suited the game. We went on to something harder like "dealing seconds," which meant dealing from underneath the top card. Then came the real difficult stuff like "bringing in a cooler," which meant switching the whole pack, after shuffling and cutting, for another in which the order of the cards had been specially arranged.

I've big hands and quick fingers and I'd always been fond of amateur conjuring, so I made an apt pupil, and the keener I got, the more he wanted to teach me.

"Now practice this," he'd say. "I'm showing you this because I like you and I want you to wisen up and protect yourself when you're a grown man."

Another whole set of tricks were tied up with "playing the glim," or using mirrors. There were the old corny maneuvers like getting your opponent to sit with a wall mirror at the right angle—the mirror behind the bar was often useful—or even getting a pal to stand behind him with a mirror in the palm of his hand. There were also more ingenious devices like having a tiny mirror in your signet ring or your cuff-links, so that you could see how you were dealing the cards. But Bobby had one trick that was peculiar to himself. He always began a game with an old corncob pipe in his mouth. Presently he'd knock it out and lay it on the table beside him. One day he showed me that it had a mirror inside the bowl—he could deal over it and see every card as it left the deck.

Above all, he taught me the philosophy of the game, or rather of the profession, because if you make your livelihood, or most of it, at gambling, then it becomes your profession.

"The difference between the producer [a sucker with an outside source of income who produces the money for the gambler to win] and the gambler is this," he said. "The gambler, when he's playing 'on the muscle' [on the square] and finds the luck running against him, will get up and quit, while the producer will stay in the game and lose his shirt. Contrariwise, if the gambler's lucky, he'll stay on till he's won the tablecloth; while if the producer finds himself forty or fifty dollars ahead, he's so thrilled that he gets up and quits and loses the rest of his lucky run."

One day he said: "If you like, I'll teach you how to handle a gun. But mind two things; never point a rod at a friend and never pull a rod out unless you mean to use it."

WHEN A MAN is fated to be known in three continents by the sobriquet of "Two-Gun," the occasion of his first meeting with the instrument of his destiny ought to be portentously described. But in fact there seems little to be said. In England he had learned to box—practically at the People's Arcade and in a more orthodox manner at Hayes. In Canada he had learned to ride. He had an inborn love of a good horse and, in the cattle-raising states, he found himself in a country where the horse was king. He had learned to handle a pair of dice and a pack of cards. Now he applied himself with the same pertinacity to the handling of a pistol.

The little spare cash at his disposal went in cartridges while, under Bob Clark's guidance, he graduated from beef cans to cigarette tins, gradually increased the range at which he was certain of a hit, and then turned to moving targets. At last Bob said:

"You'll do. You're as good now as anyone you're likely to meet in these parts. Keep out of a gunfight if you can, but if you get into one, remember the preacher's advice 'Do unto others what they would do unto you'—but do it first!"

Not long afterwards Bob left the Nichelsons' ranch. He gave no reason for going and left no word where he meant to go. Morris never heard of him again.

A year had passed since Morris landed at Quebec and he had developed into a first-class hired man who could manage cattle, harvest, and tackle any job that came up on a farm. His physical growth had been little short of prodigious. He could pick up a sack of wheat by himself and throw it on to the wagon; and he was a safe single-handed "spike-pitcher" —that is, the man who feeds the sheaves of grain into the threshing-machine—a job that usually needed two men to do it.

Abe Hyam had kept a close eye on his progress. A shrewd and rather selfish man, he had, in spite of his promise to Josef Cohen, never intended to saddle himself with an unknown boy and one who, in any case, had first to be taught his trade. Now he realized that his caution had lost him an excellent farmhand with the reputation of doing more than his fair share of work. He drove over to the Nichelsons' ranch, took Morris aside, and offered the lad two hundred and fifty dollars a year to come to him as soon as his contract had expired.

Morris was perfectly happy where he was; he knew too that Bob Nichelson, who by now regarded him almost as a son, meant to raise his pay to two hundred dollars a year for the next contract. But Hyam appealed to his family—and his Jewish—loyalty. He was Josef's friend, he had made it possible for Morris to come to Canada in the first place, and therefore he had the first claim on his services. The argument was unanswerable: Morris packed his wooden box, said goodbye to the Nichelsons, and embarked on wanderings which were destined to last a long while.

I STAYED WITH ABE HYAM just four days, Morris said. For one thing his place was all farming and no ranching; and I was a cow-hand, not a market-gardener. Besides, his food was filthy, no better than his hogs were eating. Come to that, my room wasn't much better than the sties the hogs lived in. He promised to improve things, but I didn't wait to see; I just packed up and quit.

As a matter of fact, I didn't even pack. I left my clothes behind and walked the twelve miles to Wapella in my overalls. When I got there I had seven dollars fifty in my pocket left out of my year's pay. The rest had gone on the new clothes I'd left behind me, on pistol cartridges, and on having a tooth pulled. (Those had been my only expenses; at that time I didn't smoke or drink.)

The only hotel in the township charged a dollar a day with meals and I could see that my roll wasn't going to last very long at that rate. A man in the saloon said that there were good jobs going at Virden, which was just over the border in Manitoba. When I was down to my last buck, we jumped a box-car and rode there.

The rumor was right. There were good jobs going and I got one straight away. It was in a brickyard, as pitcher to an open-air kiln at a dollar a day—real man's wages. After a bit I was promoted to one-fifty a day. I worked there for three months and saved about forty dollars. But it was the fall of the year; soon the winter freeze-up started and the factory closed down. I took the train to Winnipeg. That seemed like a big city where I was certain of a job of some sort, even in the winter.

It was an up-and-coming place when I blew in. A quarter of a century earlier, Portage Avenue, where the finest buildings now stood, had been the Great Prairie Trail between Fort Garry and Edmonton—wide enough for thirty ox-carts to drive abreast. In those days Red River carts would get bogged down in the mud in Main Street. Now both were paved thoroughfares with electric street-cars. It seemed like London to me.

That was the first time I met hotel touts. As I left the station, two of them closed in on me, one bawling "Windsor Hotel, a dollar a day," the other "Maple Leaf, one twenty-five and every luxury!" Of course I'd have chosen the cheaper place, but I never had the chance. The second man just grabbed my bag and walked off around the corner. It was only a hundred yards away, a quiet little place catering for farmers and their wives, with big shabby armchairs in the lobby and a tiny parlor upstairs for the ladies. The owner was an old man called Rosenblatt and the head bottle-washer a young man from London called Bobby Harris, who had done a bit of prize-fighting in his time and was now bartender and chef and pretty well everything else.

On my very first walk down Main Street, as I passed a little store, a man came out, took my arm and said, "Come right inside. We've got some real good bargains today."

Feeling pretty flush just then, I went in and bought a whole lot of things I didn't need, including a gold ring, which I knew must be real gold because it was stamped on the inside "14 carat"; I paid one dollar fifty for it. It soon began to turn my finger green. I guessed there must be something wrong, but I went on wearing it. A fortnight later I was broke again and sold it to a man I met in the bar for two dollars. I felt pretty pleased at myself for making fifty-cents profit and I told Bobby Harris, but he just laughed like hell.

"You can buy all you want of those for fifteen cents apiece."

"Where?"

He gave me the address of a wholesale jeweler called Levy, and I talked him into trusting me with a tray of twelve rings on tick. I'd no trouble at all in selling them for one or two dollars each. I'd walk into a saloon looking young and sad and innocent, go up to a customer, take the ring off my finger, and say:

"Listen, would you buy this ring off me? I'm broke to the wide."

I never actually said it was gold, but just let them examine it and spot the fourteen-carat stamp. I'd ask two or three dollars at first and let them beat me down to one. It hardly ever failed.

That's how I became a "hoop-merchant." It wasn't strictly legitimate and presently complaints about me began to reach the police. But by this time Eli Stodgel, the chief of the detective squad, knew me by sight and had got a chuckle out of my traffic. He never actually encouraged me, but if anyone complained, he'd have him into his office and say:

"You know damn well that if this ring was real gold, it'd be worth a whole lot more than you gave for it; and anyway Cohen would have been able to sell it in any store. You thought it was stolen and that's why you could get it cheap. So button up and beat it."

I made one friend on my rounds, Ben Zimmermann who kept a small jewelry store on Main Street. The band of the Salvation Army used to play on the sidewalk outside his window and one day a little Salvation Army lass we knew as Sallie Ann came in and asked him for a hand-out. He reached into his waistcoat pocket and gave her half a dollar.

"Oh, thank you," she gasped, "You're so generous. My, I sure do wish you were saved."

Zimmermann beckoned her to him, took her hand and said:

"Sallie Ann. What makes you a good Christian makes me a good Jew and what makes me a bad Jew, makes you a bad Christian."

Somehow that stuck in my mind.

After a while I felt I'd exhausted the hoop business and promoted myself to "super-merchant" [super-watch]. I found that I could buy for two dollars seventy-five wholesale a watch that kept quite good time. It was called the Pittsburgh Special, and if you opened the back it looked as if it was 21 jewel. My line was always much the same and it had the ring of truth:

"Got into town a couple of weeks ago with a fat roll and bought this watch and chain for twenty-seven dollars fifty. Now I'm broke again and I'll let you have it for twelve dollars fifty, because I gotta have the dough."

I got rid of plenty of Pittsburgh Specials like that. Watches were far easier to sell than rings—and I could make twenty or thirty dollars any day I really wanted to work. Soon I had a couple of hundred in my wallet, and then I found that I had friends who were ready to relieve me of some of it.

They took me on at poker and they took me on at craps, but I remembered Bobby Clark's technique and I didn't lose much. Once I got in with a wealthy bunch. A millionaire called Rod Mackenzie, the son of a big railroader, watched me roll for a bit and then started to bet "on the line" [saw that Morris would win]. I "did my best" [cheated] and made seven passes in succession. He won a couple of thousand on my dice, and even I, betting small, cleared a couple of hundred. After that there were whispers that I was pretty smart with the bones and I was invited into no more games in Winnipeg.

About the same time the super-market dried up a bit and I decided to take my watches on the road as a legitimate business man. I'd spent most of my roll as fast as I made it and I reckoned the C.P.R. was big enough to take care of itself, so, while I didn't ride box-cars any more, I "shorted caducers" [persuaded—or bribed—conductors to let him travel at half-fare] and that saved me a lot.

I travelled west and my first long stop was Moose Jaw, where I got into a new racket. I became spieler to a circus booth and pulled the crowds in to see a dwarf named Princess Ena. I was good too.

"Come in, come right in and see Princess Ena, the smallest lady that ever lived. Twenty-six years of age and weighs twenty-six pounds. She can sing, play the piano, and speak six languages—Spanish, French, Italian, Mexican, English, and Esperanto . . . Strike up the band! . . . This way, please, pass along quickly and have your money ready for your tickets."

I got ten dollars a day and the job suited me, because I was always in the middle of a mob and at quiet moments I could start shooting craps and make a bit more that way. My bankroll got fat again in no time, but after three or four weeks the circus folded and I took my tray of watches on to Saskatoon.

That saw the end of my career as a super-merchant. I'd started out with two hundred watches, but I'd stopped off at some small places in the state besides Moose Jaw and in no time at all I got rid of the lot. When I wired the wholesaler in Winnipeg for some more, he had only twelve left in stock and none on order. I had to think of something else to do.

Saskatoon was another up-and-coming town and the citizens didn't mind telling you so. The "Seven-Year-Old West-ern Wonder City" was the name they gave it. In 1903 there were only a hundred and twelve inhabitants. When I blew in there were about three thousand and the streets were still just dirt tracks, but a few years later the numbers had jumped to twelve thousand. And in those days it was wide open; the Chief of Police took protection money and so long as he was paid off, anything went.

I started serious gambling and soon got in with a bunch of "rounders," professional gamblers, who would chisel suckers out of their cash quick enough, but played on the muscle with each other. One of them was a solemn, scholarly old man of sixty or so called Hunky, who always wore blue glasses and had a quiet, dignified way of speaking. He watched me playing for a bit and said:

"I wish I knew how to put some cards in the game."

"Are they paper [marked cards]?"

"Sure."

He let me look at his cards, but there seemed nothing crooked about them to me. He explained that they were marked with phosphorus and, although in the glare of the electric light the marks were invisible, seen through his dark glasses they came up like the headlights of a car. It's an old gag now, but it was new then and I was grateful.

Another gimmick he taught me was the "Michigan Bank Roll," for when you want your wad to look bigger than it really is. You get a bundle of toilet tissue, singe the edges brown in a candle flame, and wrap a ten or twenty dollar note on the outside. I'd let the mob see that and someone would reckon that I was worth an effort and take me on at a single-handed stud game. I was quicker than him with my fingers and I could put the paper in. Old Hunky and I made some money between us.

I met someone else in Saskatoon and that meeting was to

change my whole life. Sometimes I used to eat in a chop-suey joint kept by an elderly Chinese called Mah Sam. He seemed to take a liking to me and when I was out of luck he'd stake me to a meal. Sometimes he'd even lend me money to go on gambling.

One evening I walked in hoping for a free supper and saw that there was some funny business going on. Mah Sam had a diamond ring he was very proud of. It was, say, four and a half carats and a nice little stone. But now he was looking scared and trying frantically to pull it off his finger. There was only one other customer at the counter, a tough sort of guy of about my own build, who stepped to one side keeping his hand in his pocket and his eye on me.

I saw it was a hold-up, but I wasn't heeled—that is, armed—and I had to be careful. I closed in till I was too near for him to use his rod and socked him on the jaw.

"Take care," yelled Mah. "He got gun in pocket."

I put that right and then Mah said:

"He got my money too."

The fellow was out for the count. I took all the cash he had on him and gave it back to Mah. While he was totting it up the hobo came to. I let him get on his feet, gave him a kick in the pants—maybe two kicks—and told him to beat it.

That was the first real hold-up I'd ever seen. For that matter, in spite of my nickname and my reputation, I've not seen that much rough stuff in my life. The fact is, fights come to the chap who looks for them and I've never looked for them. I talk quietly and move slowly and keep my temper. If a guy goes on like that, it's funny how much trouble he manages to duck.

After that, Mah was my friend and it wasn't long before I was made to realize what friendship means to a Chinese. I got in a poker game with a stranger and won about a hundred and twenty dollars from him. He was a tin-horn gam-

bler and wanted to get his roll back; so he went to the Chief
of Police and laid a complaint that I'd "beat" [cheated] him
out of his money. I was picked up and taken to the Police
Station, but before I knew where I was old Mah Sam had
turned up and sprung me on a bail of two thousand bucks.

I took my troubles to a lawyer and he said that I'd
nothing to worry about and that there could be no possible
charge against me. But I was in deeper than I knew. The
next thing was a visit from the man who'd lost his roll. He
spun a story about not wanting to get another gambler into
trouble. If I'd hand him back a hundred dollars, he'd leave
town before the case came on. I told him he was a dirty heel
and I'd stay right in Saskatoon.

The Chief of Police, Robinson was his name, sent me
word to jump my bail and quit the town. By this time he'd
got my goat and I took no notice and stayed put. My case
came on. The beak wouldn't listen to a word I said and I
was kangarooed—four weeks in jail for gambling in a town
that everybody knew was wide open!

When I was inside, I had time to see what the angle was.
The two thousand dollars put up by Mah Sam had gone
straight into Robinson's pocket and, if I'd jumped my
bail, it would have stayed there. Meanwhile Mah Sam was
pretty mad. He raised hell with the Police Chief and, when
he could get no change out of him, started talking to the
newspaper men. Robinson framed him too. He trumped up
a charge, got a conviction, and had him sent up for six
months.

That was as far as Robinson got. When I came out, I
found that all the Chinese in the town were solidly behind
me. They paid for a real good lawyer who got Mah Sam out
again and then appealed in my case on the grounds of fresh
evidence and got my conviction reversed. After that, Robinson let me alone. I didn't forget him. It took several years

before I could do anything about it, but I got the skids under him in the end.

After our troubles, Mah Sam and I became very close. I'd sit for hours in his back room eating Chinese chow—the real stuff, not the chop suey he sold out in front—and listening while he talked about Chinese politics. You'd never have dreamed that such a quiet, peaceable, soft-spoken old chap could be a revolutionary, but that was just what he was. He told me how, centuries ago, the Manchus had conquered China and made the men wear pigtails as a sign of their servitude and their wives bind the feet of their girl-babies so that they could never walk properly for the rest of their lives.

He had to wear a pigtail himself, he said, because if he cut it off he could never go back to China again. He took it in both hands and tugged at it to show he was speaking the truth. There were thousands of Chinese, he told me, like himself, working actively for the overthrow of the Manchus —Chinese collecting contributions to the cause, Chinese learning to be soldiers (a trade they despise as a rule), and Chinese organizing revolutionary cells and planning for the day of deliverance.

"Sounds like a good racket," I said, "but who's the boss? There must be one big brain behind it all."

"Sun Yat-sen is our leader," answered Mah, "Dr. Sun —the Great Doctor. He is No. 1 of the Revolution. He go all over the world. Sometimes he come to Canada."

I didn't quite swallow all he told me, but it stirred my imagination. I was young enough to like excitement, and his talk of soldiering and conspiracy and revolution was exciting. I'd known poverty myself and what persecution meant from things I'd heard my parents say. And though I'd never seen China, I could guess that the life of the under-dog would be a whole lot worse there than it was in the white man's world.

One day Mah said that he must go to Calgary to meet some friends: would I come along too? I couldn't understand what he wanted me for, but he made a big fuss about it, and as a Chinese never asks you for a favor unless he really means it, I agreed to go. When our train had pulled out of Saskatoon he opened up a bit and said he was going to a meeting of a Tong, a secret society—"All same Chinese Freemason" was how he described it. Just as we were running into Calgary he told me a bit more. He himself was quite a big guy in the organization and he wanted me to come with him to the meeting.

That made me think a bit. If I went to the meeting with him, I'd have to join the Tong, or I'd never come out alive; and I'd never heard of a European joining one of those outfits. Although he called them Freemasons, I guessed that it was something like the Triads and they were a tough lot. In Canada they never gave much trouble, but down in the States, especially in San Francisco, they used to stage full-size Tong wars with murders every night. Still, I knew that Mah would never lead me into a mess if he could help it and I said I was game.

That night we went to a grocery store in a back alley. There was nothing for the casual passer-by to see, but I noticed that there were men watching not only the door, but the street corners each side of it. Mah took me up the stairs; at the top there were more guards, but this bunch were armed and didn't bother to hide their rods. They had a long confabulation on the landing, but evidently I was expected, and after a while heavy double doors were thrown open and I found myself in the biggest room I'd ever seen—bigger than the main assembly hall at Hayes.

There must have been a couple of hundred Chinese there wearing their best suits and sitting silent and solemn, not chattering like Chinese usually do. The whole lot turned their heads as one man and stared at me. I stood there feeling kind of conspicuous while Mah took the floor and said his piece. I didn't understand Cantonese (they were all Southerners of course) but I could see that he was giving me a bit of a boost. When he'd finished there was some sort of a vote, and I was formally asked if I'd join the lodge.

Having agreed, I was initiated. It may sound silly, but even now I am unable to tell you how it was done. I know all this happened more than forty years ago and that books have been written about the Triads and all their rites and ceremonies described. That doesn't alter the fact that I took an oath not to reveal any of their secrets and that oath still binds me. Anyway I walked down those twisty, shabby stairs and out of that poor little grocery shop a full-blown member of the Tsing Chung-hui, pledged to devote my life to the service of Sun Yat-sen, the overthrow of the Manchu dynasty, and the liberation of the Chinese people.

I didn't take all that too seriously at the time. I wasn't much over nineteen, I'd never seen a Manchu, and China seemed a long way away. I just thought that the Chinese I'd met so far seemed good scouts and I'd like to be on their side. It was only gradually that I came to realize all that that oath meant.

Back in Saskatoon I plunged into poker-playing and bit by bit I became a real good "square card" [honest] gambler. My reputation grew and Mah Sam would always bank-roll me when I wanted to get into a game. I used to play with a lot of sharks but, as I told you before, we all played on the muscle with each other.

All except one—a middle-aged guy called Jim Fowler, who wore fancy clothes, striped pants, black jacket, a braided waistcoat, and a shirt with cuff-links, which weren't so common in those parts. He won a lot of money in Saskatoon, but I guessed he was an outsider and beating the game with his pals. I watched him a while and spotted that he was playing the glim with a little mirror in one of those cuff-links.

I kept that to myself, but one day the boys were ribbing about whether Fowler was a good player or just plain lucky and he said—he was a bit of a boaster—that he'd challenge anybody in Saskatoon to a game of single-handed stud. I'd an idea that he might say something of the sort and I was hanging around and took him up on the spot.

We sat down to a thousand dollars' worth of chips apiece (Mah Sam was staking me of course), and there must have been upwards of a dozen kibitzers. Fowler had his harness, i.e. his cuff-links, on, but although when he dealt he knew what my hole-card was, I knew that he knew and that evened matters up. And when it came to my deal, I was a good mechanic and could tell his hole-card by the peek [using sleight of hand to get a look at the cards] without using any gimmicks. Also I was the better straight player—I could tell by his play whether he was trying to bluff or held a really good hand.

We both let the cards come naturally at first, except to tell each other's hole-cards: he by the glim and me by the peek. Fowler was too smart to try to deal seconds or run up on me and with the peek I knew more or less what I was betting against. For a while the game ran neck and neck, then I put in a cooler that I'd kept tucked in beside me.

That's always a risky maneuver and you can't do it more than once, so I gave him the whole works. I dealt him kings back to back and I gave myself an ace in the hole and another outside. The end of the game went like this.

I deal him a king and myself a queen.

Fowler bets two dollars.

I deal him a ten and myself a nine.

Fowler bets ten dollars.

"Make it thirty," I say.

"Call," says Fowler.

I deal him a five and myself a jack.

Fowler bets a hundred.

"Make it five hundred," I say.

"Call."

I deal us both an ace.

Fowler looks at the table and sees an ace, king, ten, five in front of him against my ace, queen, jack, nine—and he taps himself [bets all the money he has left].

I call and I show him my two aces. . . .

There you are. It takes a cheater to cheat a cheat. Only a man with larceny in him will try to beat the game when he reckons he's the best player and will win anyway. Then along comes someone with better schooling who lets him cheat the only way he knows how. He lets him cheat up to a certain point and then he takes him for the whole of his roll.

That was one of the biggest games I played in Saskatoon and it was one of the last. I'd begun to think that there were better ways of earning one's coffee and doughnuts than sitting over a pile of poker chips. It struck me too that I might do better in a bigger town and I'd heard that things were pretty good around Edmonton, a place away west in Alberta that, not long before, had been proclaimed the provincial capital.

It had already touched the twenty thousand mark and people were flocking there from all over the place, Bluenoses from the Maritime Provinces in the east and Yanks from the two Dakotas south across the border, even British Columbians from the far side of the Rockies. Oil-prospecting had started up in the Peace River County; it was on the main line of the Canadian Northern Railway and the terminus of a branch of the C.P.R., and the Grand Trunk Pacific was said to be coming that way as well.

In fact the place was just ripe for a real estate boom. I had a few hundred dollars, so I packed my valise and took them there to try my luck. And my luck was in.

When I was on the road with my supers, I'd met a C.P.R. dining-car attendant called Bert Finch and ridden with him maybe half a dozen trips. He was around about thirty-five and obviously a go-getter who meant to end up somewhere. I'd heard that he'd left the railway and gone into real estate, but I hadn't heard how far he'd gone. When I got to Edmonton and looked him up, there he was sitting in his own posh office with his name on the door as manager of the local branch of the National Land Company. He gave me a big hand and before I walked out again I was hired as a salesman.

"All you gotta do," he said, "is find a prospect, bring him in, and let *me* talk to him."

I reckoned I was a pretty fast talker myself, and so, when I brought my prospect in, I listened carefully to what Bert had to say, and soon learned his line of spiel.

There was good money to be made in city building lots at two hundred and fifty dollars a time. I often sold four lots in a day and once or twice I handled as many as twenty in a week; at ten per cent commission that made five hundred smackers for Morris. I got Bert to agree to my selling on time, say a hundred dollars down for two lots. I had to see that the sucker—I mean the buyer—paid the rest when he said he would and till he ante'd up I only drew half my commission. But it worked well and I averaged three hundred dollars a week all the time.

After about three months Stan Shepherd, the president of the company, came up from the head office in Calgary.

He saw my results and after talking with Bert made me a proposition. I could open my own office in any city I liked to name, recruit my own salesmen, and be manager myself. He'd give me two hundred a month as salary and twelve and a half per cent commission on all the business. Of this the salesmen were to have their usual ten per cent and there was two and a half for myself.

"I'm on," I said, "but there's room for another office in Edmonton and I'd like to stay right here."

"Okay," said Stan.

Bert thought a minute and then he said "Okay" too.

I rented an office on First Street. I put in a big, solid safe to hold the cash, and I recruited ten salesmen. They were all sorts, shapes, and sizes, but the youngest of them was more than twice my age. (I was still only twenty, remember.) Some of them I'd known as rounders and I was scared they might try to dodge vagrancy charges by working for me as an alibi and go back to their old games again. The day we opened I had them all in together and gave my first pep-talk:

"Now, boys, if you wanna work here, you gotta show results. I don't want any of you lads using this office as a cover for a poker school and me finding the cops in here asking about some producer you've trimmed. If you can't sell a coupla lots a day, I just don't want you around. Now get cracking."

Some of them found it a bit strange to be in regular work, but once they'd settled down to legitimate business, they did so well they surprised themselves. Presently I thinned them out and got rid of the dead-beats and the ones left were all real good. I kept a close eye on things and I never allowed any customer to sign his contract till I'd talked to him personally, so I knew the salesmanship hadn't been too high pressure.

I went out selling myself too. "High, dry, level, and a good building lot" was my motto. At first I sold nothing that was more than a mile from the center of the town. Later on we started buying land from the nearest farmers, subdividing it, putting in roads, and selling that too. Sometimes I made a thousand a week.

Usually I spent my cash about as fast as I made it—they say that money talks, but all it ever said to me was "goodbye"—but just in this part of my life I didn't seem to be able to do that. My bank-roll began to pile up and in what seemed to be no time at all, I found myself with a wad of twenty thousand dollars and a four-carat diamond ring (a real one) as well.

I didn't forget my Chinese friends, or rather they didn't let me forget them. If any Chinese in the West thought of a deal in real estate, he'd come and consult me about it. That meant more business and good business too. I went on attending their lodge meetings as regularly as I could manage and presently I found myself giving sizeable sums, say fifty or a hundred dollars, to various revolutionary funds. I began asking other people for contributions, and that in turn started me speaking at their lodge meetings. I'd always had a pretty good line of sales talk, but to stand up and address a regular seated audience was something that I'd never tried before. Presently I got good at that too. I even started to learn one of the many local Cantonese dialects, but I must admit that I never got very far with that. Another thing I did at this time was to try my hand at recruiting and training a few amateur soldiers, again with the forthcoming Chinese Revolution always in mind. Here I found my military training at Hayes, elementary though it may have been, came in handy. I might not know much about soldiering, but I knew more than any other guy on the ground.

That was a good time for me—lots of work, lots of fun, not too much worry or responsibility, and making money hand over fist. And it went on for a couple of years. Then one day there was a rumor that Dr. Sun had arrived in Canada. He was said to have landed at Vancouver and to be coming our way. The next thing I knew he was in Edmonton—and the really important part of my life had begun. I was introduced to him at a big lodge meeting. It was all quite ordinary and commonplace.

"This is Morris Cohen," said Mah Sam, "a great friend of our revolutionary party."

"Pleased to meet you," said Dr. Sun. That was all.

It is tempting for me to start in now and tell you all that I was to learn about him in the next fifteen years—his statesmanship, his patriotism, his idealism, and all the rest of it. But to do that wouldn't give you the right picture at all. You must remember that I was still only a boy, and a good deal of a roughneck at that. I'd met plenty of people of all kinds and I'd learned to look after myself, but at that time I'd never met any great men and I'd no means of judging one—that is, except for my instinct for anything that's *good quality*.

I saw a fine-looking, straight-standing man dressed in a formal European-style frock coat. I noticed at once that he had cut off his pigtail, which of course stamped him as an open revolutionary. He wore a close-cut, rather military sort of mustache. He might easily have been the kind of distinguished soldier-retired-and-turned-politician that appears in the public life of Canada and of the Old Country too. He spoke beautiful English, better English than I've ever been able to learn in the whole of my life.

But that was all beside the point. As soon as I saw him I just knew that he was a really great man—a man that I'd be ready to follow.

He addressed the meeting in Chinese. I couldn't understand a word, but my friends whispered that he was prophesying the Revolution might break out in China at any moment and he was certain that they would sweep the board. His only concern was that there should be as little bloodshed as possible. They whispered too that the Manchu Government had just offered a new and record-breaking reward for his arrest, a million dollars for his body, dead or alive.

Later they put me on my feet, and pretty foolish I felt too, speaking after a man who, I could tell, was a great orator. I did my best and they clapped when I sat down. I suppose it wasn't too bad.

Then came my big surprise. A couple of my own friends and two others I didn't know came up to me and, without beating about the bush in the usual Chinese way, they asked me straight out if I was willing to accompany Dr. Sun on his tour of Canada and the United States and look after his safety.

My first reaction was just the same as when old Mah Sam took me to that Tong meeting in Calgary—I felt a bit scared. Don't mistake what I mean. I was big and I was tough. In those days I literally feared no man and I'd learned how to handle a rod. But when it came to watching over the safety of a man like Sun with a million dollars on his head, I could see that there was more to the game than that. I might have to deal with anything, from a highly organized big-scale kidnapping (you can get lots of organization for a million bucks) to a single-handed shooting by any down-and-out who was desperate enough to try for the reward and who'd likely be half crazy with dope as well.

I stalled for time and asked them why they'd picked on me. That finished it of course. You know just how flattering Chinese can be when they want something. By the time they'd done with me, I wouldn't only have guarded Dr. Sun,

I'd have gone and had a shot at the Emperor of China myself.

There were just four of us in that party—Sun and me and two other Chinese. It was a two months' trip. We travelled all through Western Canada, east as far as Montreal, and south to Chicago. The assignment didn't come as hard as I'd expected. I packed a Smith and Wesson when we started, and it didn't leave me night or day. There was never any call to use it. I gave the "once over" to any Chinese who wanted to see Sun privately, and I sat near him in the audience with my eyes wide open. Nothing happened at all.

Sometimes I was asked to speak and then I'd begin by apologizing for not knowing the Chinese language and explaining that I was learning it. That always went down well. They're as proud as hell of having such a difficult tongue with its ten thousand ideographs and all the rest of it.

Dr. Sun had fine old-fashioned manners and he'd always bring me into any talk that was going on. Presently he began to talk to me when we were alone. He was a wonderful listener, always making you feel you were interesting him. Without my realizing it, he must have learned just everything about me that there was to know. Towards the end of the trip he said:

"Morris, do you think that you could buy us some arms and ammunition?"

"That's a new racket for me," I said, "but I'll certainly try."

I went to a storekeeper I knew in Winnipeg, and it turned out to be dead easy.

"Say, can you sell me some guns?"

"As many as you want."

"They're going to China."

"You're sure that they're not going to Mexico? Because that means trouble with the Yanks and they're tough."

"Quite sure."

I bought five hundred second-hand reconditioned Ross rifles at five dollars each with two hundred rounds a gun, and two hundred Smith and Wesson revolvers at twelve dollars each. The rifles weren't up to much (they could hardly be at that price) but they were good enough for training and the rods were all right. As soon as I had my hands on them I turned the consignment over to the local Tong. They railed them to Vancouver and from there they were smuggled into China. That was my first deal in "sewing-machines," but it wasn't to be the last.

The tour came to an end, Dr. Sun went off to Japan and I found myself back in my branch office of the National Land Company again. But I'd changed. I was older and wiser and a lot more serious. I'd started out a happy-go-lucky rounder who thought the Chinese were a good bunch of scouts and the Chinese Revolution something vague and exciting a long way away. I came back a devoted follower of Dr. Sun, convinced that the Revolution was something vitally important and just around the corner. I'd not only met a great man, I'd enjoyed his confidence and got to know him and to see—just a little bit—how the mind of a great man works. For the first time in my life I'd met something that was right outside myself and my own people and yet had to be lived up to.

I plunged into my real estate sales again, but I gave my spare time—all my spare time—to the Chinese cause. I gave interviews on Dr. Sun to the Edmonton papers; I organized a proper Chinese cadet corps and brought its numbers up to four hundred and fifty—nearly every young Chinese man in the town.

By this time my standing with the local Chinese was real high and they brought all their troubles to me. The Chinese cooks in Alberta were having difficulties with the local labor unions and also with their employers who thought that they were just cheap Chinese labor and wouldn't pay them a fair living wage. I tried this and that and in the end I got in touch with Samuel Gompers, the organizer of the American Federation of Labor—who was the second great man I met in my life. He negotiated for them and got them admitted to the local unions. After that the hotels would come to me to find them cooks, and, as long as the wages were right, I'd help the hotels as well and see that they didn't get the bums.

About this time Stan Shepherd came to me with a new proposition. The company had bought a big tract of land in the Okanagan Valley in British Columbia that would be first-rate for fruit farms and market gardens. They reckoned that the Belgians were tops at that trade and they knew that Belgium was overcrowded. So Stan wanted me to go back home, cross over to Belgium, and sell the idea to the Belgians. I had to make up my mind at once, as the Belgian Consul for Alberta, who was keen on the scheme, was already back in Brussels and I had to catch up with him there.

I needed no time to think that over. The one idea in my head was that I hadn't seen my family for six years and now was my chance. I packed my bags the next day, turned over the office, and off I went.

When I left England I was sixteen and I had five pounds in cash and my first fedora hat. When I came back I was twenty-two and I had a four-carat diamond ring, a diamond stickpin in my tie, and a letter of credit for ten thousand dollars.

CHAPTER III

Poker and Politics

LANDING IN ENGLAND—continued Morris—was a bit of a flop. Nothing seemed to have changed. The bobbies didn't look as big as I remembered them, but then I'd grown quite a bit myself. I weighed close on two hundred pounds now. It had been raining when I left and it was still raining when I landed and it really might have been raining all those six years in between.

Nobody seemed very interested in me and, after all, there was no reason why they should be. I've landed in England a fair number of times since that one and I've got used to the sensation, but that first time I nearly took the first boat back again.

The flat feeling passed off as I got near my home, and when I saw Gardiner's Corner I felt pleased and excited. When I turned into Umberston Street I began to feel nervous and I stopped and walked back wondering what to do.

I hadn't written home very often—maybe once in six months—and I hadn't told my family that I was on the way. All of a sudden I realized what a shock my arrival would be. I thought a while and then I walked past my home and into a baker's shop at the end of the street. I recognized the owner, old Josef Greenspam, and asked him:

"Do you happen to know Josef Cohen who used to live at number sixty-eight?"

I'd thought that my big body and my tough face and

my dude clothes would be a sufficient disguise, but he took one look at me and said:

"You're Moishe Cohen!"

"Sure," I said, "but the old folk don't know I'm here and I don't want to give them too much of a shock."

I said the end of that to an empty shop. He'd nipped round the end of his counter and dashed up the street shouting:

"Mrs. Cohen, *du hast a gast!*"

I ran after him—it was all I could do—and I heard mother's voice:

"*Wemer, wemer, mein zin? Hab kuminese* from *Kanada?*"

"Yes, mama," I shouted, "it's Moishe!"

She cried for the next twenty minutes. That was a funny thing about mother; she never cried when she was sad—only when she was happy.

While she was weeping the house filled up with the family. There'd been some changes of course. Two more children—a sister called Sarah and a brother called Leslie —whom I'd never seen. Nat, Ben, Leah, and Rae were there, all six years older. But Rose, my beloved elder sister, who used to bully me and scold me and take me to Buckle Street Infant School, had married and was living in South Africa.

My father had grown a lot grayer and stooped more than he used to do. He just sat and smiled to see his first-born son home again and his family all excited. When they'd worked off some of their high spirits he said, "Come into the front parlor, son, and we'll have a talk."

Then I really felt nervous. I had plenty to be proud of —my diamond ring and my diamond tiepin and my tiddley suit by "Pinky the Stitch," the niftiest tailor in Chicago, and that letter of credit in my pocket. Even so, father would want to know the real truth and I wondered if he'd be as pleased as I hoped.

"Morris," he said, "have you made a success in life? How good is your credit?"

I thought I knew the answer to that. I put my hand in my breast pocket and out came that letter of credit for ten thousand dollars and a pretty healthy bankbook as well.

Father shook his head.

"No, Morris. I don't want to know what you are worth. I want to know how *good* is your credit. If your pockets were empty, how much would your friends lend you on your reputation alone?"

Then he questioned me very gently and tactfully on my private life and was relieved to hear that I was still single. He'd been terrified that I might have married a Gentile and kept it a secret. When I promised that, when I did marry, it would be to a good Jewish girl, his face lit up and I realized —a thing that one forgets when one is a long time abroad —just how much you matter to your own people.

"Son," he said the next day, "there is one thing that I want you to do for me. Will you?"

"Yes, father, anything you like."

"Come to the *shul*—the Cannon Street Road Synagogue—and perform the *Aliyah*."

That's a very solemn ceremony. It meant standing up in front of the whole congregation, opening the Ark of the Covenant, taking out the Scroll of the Law and reciting a prayer. When I thought of all that, I regretted my promise. I didn't know the words and I didn't know how to say them and I just couldn't see myself doing such a thing.

I had a cousin called Moishe Lifschitz who'd been to the *yeshiva*, though he'd never finished his studies there, and I got him to come every day to the Strand Palace Hotel where I had a room and work on me till I was word perfect.

I hadn't forgotten all that Israel Ellis had taught me, and I just stood in front of the big cheval mirror in my room and recited and recited while Lifschitz coached me, till I had every intonation and every gesture right. I worked hard.

The great day came and, though I say it myself, I was pretty good. In fact I may have been a bit too good. Usually the member of the congregaton who does the Aliyah is a bit nervous and self-conscious and just mumbles his way through. I stood up and declaimed as if I was still in the Shakespeare Class at Hayes—and they weren't used to it. Anyway my father was happy.

"Morris," he said, "this is the proudest day of my life."

As for me, I was so pleased with myself for saying the whole prayer right through without a single mistake that I donated fifty pounds to the synagogue—a tremendous amount for a little *shul* like that.

I didn't spend my whole holiday with the family. I stayed at the Strand Palace Hotel, and hit the high spots up West now and then. One day I went down to Hayes and got permission to take all the boys out for the day. I took four rows of stalls at the King's Theatre, Hammersmith (I can't remember for the life of me what the show was), and then gave them tea at the big Lyons shop close by. They ate the place out and I had to order more food to be sent in. I had a quiet talk to Ellis and told him that of all the things he'd taught me, the most useful had been the elocution—and was he surprised?

In no time at all my holiday was over and I had to think about the future of my family. I cashed in my ten thousand dollar credit—or what was left of it—and offered it to my father.

"No, son," he said, "you've got your way to make in the world and you'll need all of that."

I didn't argue but just took it to my mother. She wept

a bit being so happy and she took it saying, "God bless you, *mein zin*."

The family had got too big for the house in Umberston Street and so I moved them to Tredegar Square in Bow. It was a good deal further east and a much nicer neighborhood and the house faced on to a little park. I felt quite happy about leaving them there when I had to go off to Belgium.

Belgium was just what I'd expected it would be like —only more so. The Consul from Alberta, who had sponsored our scheme and was now in Brussels, had arranged for me to be met at the Gare du Nord by a Monsieur Kellermann. I was to carry a handkerchief in my hand as identification. When a little chap with a Van Dyck beard had rushed up and kissed me on both cheeks, I remembered that things like that happen on the continent, but I hadn't expected it to happen to me.

The next two months were busy. The Belgians were in earnest and my company were in earnest and so things moved fast. I learned a lot about continental business methods and, for that matter, I learned something about continental ladies as well. The agreements were signed and I was on the Atlantic and back in Edmonton.

WHILE MORRIS was in Europe, history was being made in the Far East. The year was 1911 and the various Chinese revolutionary parties were as active, as reckless, as disorganized, and as hopelessly incompetent as ever. In March Huang Hsing scored what he actually boasted to be his tenth failure with an abortive attack on the Viceroy's Yamen in Canton. It resulted only in the execution of the subsequently immortalized Seventy-two Martyrs.

In May the Railway Agreement between the Chinese Government and an international banking group roused the provinces, Szechwan burst into open revolt, the Viceroy was murdered in Chengtu, and the Manchu General was killed by his own troops. In October, in the Russian Concession at Hankow, a group of amateur anarchists blew themselves to pieces with a home-made bomb. The survivors, well aware that their own lives were forfeit, made on the famous "Double Tenth"—the tenth day of the tenth month—a desperate and apparently hopeless attack on the city. Some disaffected troops followed them, the Viceroy and the Imperial General fled, and the Revolution began.

There followed the inevitable confusion, treacheries and betrayals. Yuan Shih-kai, the great Viceroy who had been made successively Generalissimo of the Imperial forces and then Prime Minister, opened negotiations with the rebels in December; the establishment of a Republic was agreed and the Emperor abdicated. The Dragon Throne had fallen.

Meanwhile, Sun Yat-sen was hastening back from Europe. He arrived in Shanghai on Christmas Day. Three days later he was elected Provisional President of China; on New Year's Day 1912 he was formally installed in office. The Chinese Republic, from being a glittering, illusive vision of the future, had become an accomplished fact.

WHEN I GOT BACK to Canada—said Morris—things were changing so fast that it was hard to keep up with them. Everything was now open and above-board. Instead of the Tsing Chung-hui meeting secretly with all kinds of precautions in back rooms, there was the Kuomintang, a recognized political party hiring halls and advertising its rallies and conventions in the newspapers.

They were after me as soon as I landed; I was one of the first to be enrolled in Canada. I believe (though I can't be certain about it) that I'm the only European who ever became a full-blown member. I was given the title of "Foreign Secretary." That wasn't quite as important as it sounded, but it meant a lot of hard work. We travelled all over Canada (when I could get away from the office) opening new branches, collecting funds, and organizing generally.

We would arrive in a town like Toronto, collect all the Chinese together, and address them. I'd learned a very little Cantonese by now, but nothing like enough to make a speech. I'd just start with one or two Chinese sentences to get their attention and then go on in English, which would be translated for those who couldn't understand.

There was a lot of speaking to be done and a lot of explaining as well, for that matter. The proclamation of the Republic hadn't ended China's troubles; you might almost say it had just begun them, for she has certainly been in a mess ever since. Yuan Shih-kai had double-crossed Dr. Sun right away, assumed the presidency, and was intriguing to get himself made hereditary Emperor and found a new dynasty. (I know that this wasn't the whole truth of the case; things were really a lot more complicated, but that was our story and we stuck to it.) So instead of campaigning for the Tsing Chung-hui and against the Imperial House and the Manchus, we were campaigning for the Kuomintang and against Yuan Shih-kai and his mob whom we dubbed the "Northern Militarists"; and we kept pretty busy.

All this time I stuck to my job with the National Land Company and made lots of dough and I wanted to have a little fun with some of it. My old gambling buddies came around when they knew I was back and we used to sneak off to play whist and poker on the quiet. Presently getting tired of having to cover up so much, I went to see my tame lawyer.

"Is it against the law to play poker? Are we committing a crime?"

"No; there's no law against poker in Canada as long

as the 'house' doesn't take a rake-off. Once you do that, it becomes 'keeping a gaming house' and they can put you inside."

Off I went to Mayor Joe Clark (whom I'd helped to get elected) and Chief of Police Lancy, who was a friend of mine too.

"Say, I'm thinking of opening an apartment and asking my friends in to play cards. I won't charge anything of course. How do you stand about that? Can I go ahead?"

They were a bit cagey. They just smiled and said nothing; and when I pressed them for an answer all I got was, "Just be careful, my boy, and don't go breaking the law."

So I opened the game and ran it for six months with no trouble at all. Then one night the police broke in—we were in the middle of a stud-poker session—and arrested the lot of us. We were taken to the police station and sprung at once; the bail was two hundred dollars for myself and twenty-five dollars for each of the eight chaps they'd pulled in with me.

As soon as I was free I went straight round to the Mayor and the Police Chief. They swore they knew nothing about it and didn't see what evidence could be laid against me. Next day we were all up before a magistrate who'd been a cop before he got onto the bench. He convicted all of us on the charges; but the others were only fined for "frequenting," while I was found guilty of keeping a gaming house and got four months.

I appealed right away, got further bail, won my case in the Appeal Court, and got back in the clear again. Then I opened up my apartment once more and gave an invitation to the Police Department to look in and try their luck. The dick who had arrested me got a personal invitation just to show there was no ill-feeling. I kept that game going right on till the war came and I enlisted in the army.

All the same I wasn't quite happy, because somebody must have been behind that raid and that meant there was somebody about with influence with the cops and who had it in for me. Now a man's bound to make enemies and I guess I've had my share. But I don't like enemies who can put the rozzers on to me. I did some hard thinking and presently I thought of my old friend, Police Chief Robinson of Saskatoon.

I made a few discreet inquiries and soon found that he'd been behind my bit of trouble all right—and he was up to the neck in every kind of corruption as well. This time I laid for him. It's too long and involved a story to tell. To put it in a nutshell, I went to Joe Clark and I went to the Honorable C. W. Cross, the Attorney General for Alberta, and, believe me or not, it finished up with a Royal Commission investigating the charges against him. Robinson didn't even try to prove his innocence. He just bolted across the border and lay low somewhere in the States and was never heard of again.

The strangest thing of all was this. One of the principal witnesses for the prosecution against Robinson was the very hobo whom I'd caught holding up Mah Sam five years ago and kicked out of the old boy's store. And the reason he gave for squealing was just, "The Chief framed my friend, Cohen."

I was never in trouble again with the Canadian Police —never, that is, except for one occasion which was mixed up with my first romance, in fact with the only real romance I was ever to have right up to the time when I got married.

There was a Jewish family in Edmonton called Gardine who owned a big furniture store. The father and mother were much older than me, but I made friends with the two boys, Jack and Isidore, and with their kid sister, Gladys, who was a sweet little thing just rising fifteen. I hadn't seen much of girls (I mean young girls) up to then, except for my own sisters, and I hadn't thought much about them either.

One day she came in to ask me for a subscription to some Zionist organization. I wrote a check and then said I'd walk over to the Union Bank with her to cash it. On the way we passed a detective whom I didn't like because he was a heel and had pulled some fast tricks on my friends. He gave me a dirty look and I didn't mind that, but then he smirked nastily as if he thought I had ulterior motives with Gladys —and then I did get riled.

"You go on," I said to her, "I've got some business to attend to here."

As soon as she was out of earshot I said to him, "When I'm out with a young lady like that one, I don't want any of your sly looks."

"Aw, get to hell, you bastard!"

At that I hauled off and knocked him cold. He didn't say another word—just lay there taking no interest in anything. A crowd began to collect. It was lucky that Gladys had turned the corner and couldn't see what had happened.

I began to realize what a damn fool I'd been. First, I'd picked a quarrel with a dick on duty and then I'd used violence on him. I ran straight around to the police station and confessed to the Chief.

"It could be serious," he said, "you'd better see the beak right away."

Off I went to the magistrate's office and told him what I'd done.

"The best thing for you," he told me, "is to plead guilty when your case comes up. Then I'll fine you ten bucks and that'll be the end of it."

I took his advice and it worked out all right. I reckon it was the best ten bucks' worth I ever had, and half the town would have staked me to it. But when Gladys heard about it, was she mad? She wouldn't speak to me for a fortnight.

I saw her often while I was in Edmonton, but she seemed so young and so pure and somehow so different from the other girls that I never even thought of wanting to marry her. She went to Europe to study art and then there came the war and we lost touch. Years later when I was passing through San Francisco on some mission or other, I met a mutual friend who said that her family had moved to Los Angeles and she herself was now visiting in New York and staying at the Algonquin. I looked her up as soon as I got there. She'd blossomed into a beautiful young lady and I myself wasn't any longer the callow, rather rough-mannered young fellow I'd been when we first met.

I cancelled my passage to Europe, stayed on another week in New York and asked her if she'd marry me. She said "Yes!" Then I put a long-distance call through to her family in L.A. and asked their blessing and they gave it— but they said it was a long time since they'd seen me and so we ought to meet again and talk things over. I went on to Europe and on the way back to China I stopped off in L.A. and got to know them again and it was all fixed.

But you know what it was like in China all those years. There was always a civil war and just at that moment things weren't going too well for my side. I couldn't possibly take her with me and it didn't seem right to marry her and then leave her there in L.A. with her parents; and I had to get back to China pronto. We arranged that, as soon as the situation looked a bit better, I'd either come back and marry her from her own home or else send for her to join me in Shanghai.

Time went on and things in China got worse and not

better. I couldn't get away and it still didn't seem safe for her to come and join me. In the end she met someone she liked better—or at any rate she liked him a lot and he didn't lead the unsettled sort of life that I did.

She died quite young, but I've always stayed friends with her folk and whenever I'm in Hollywood, where her brother Jack is agent with a film company, I look him up and we talk about the old days. I'll always remember her and always be grateful for the happiness she gave me. A man may reckon himself pretty smart but he's not really grown-up till he's been in love.

A PHOTOGRAPH OF the Morris Cohen of this period has survived. It shows a compact, barrel-chested young man of strongly marked but regular features topped by a luxuriant head of jet-black hair with a "widow's peak" that plunged down the forehead towards the heavy eyebrows—the face, in fact, of a "tough-guy" hero of the silent films.

I HADN'T MUCH TIME for dalliance in those days. When I wasn't selling real estate or speechifying for the Kuomintang, I was electioneering. All good Canadians go into politics sooner or later and I took the plunge when I got back from my first trip to Europe. It all began by accident.

There were a couple of brothers called Lewis who owned a café on First Street. They came from Montana, and they brought in the first good coffee we ever drank in Edmonton, so they prospered and their café became the recognized hangout for what you might call the "business-cum-sporting" element. I was there most nights myself. One evening I was sitting around with the Eskimo Ice Hockey Team (they weren't real Eskimos, but they came mostly from the north of the province and that's how they got the name).

Someone told us that the Edmonton Ratepayers Association were holding a meeting that night for the nomination of the mayor and aldermen, and I said to the gang, only half seriously, "Let's all go along there and we'll put Joe Clark in."

Joe Clark was a lawyer who'd been up in the Yukon in the gold-rush days and he was a good sport. He'd always take a brief even when there was no dough in it, if it meant helping the underdog or someone who wasn't getting a square deal. He'd been a good friend to me more than once.

So into the meeting went my mob—with a good social glow on them. The chairman called us to order and addressed the assembly. The moment he sat down, I was up out of my seat:

"I take great pleasure in nominating Alderman Joseph Andrew Clark for mayor of this town."

I kicked the chap on my right and he got up and said:

"I have the honor to second the motion."

I nudged the man on my left and he jumped to his feet:

"I move that nominations now cease."

It was all as easy as that. Our "slate" was nominated; there were no other candidates and Joe was returned as mayor unopposed. The chairman didn't much like our methods and one or two of the audience were a bit bewildered, but they were quite glad to have the matter settled for them and be able to get home earlier than they'd hoped.

Once I saw how simple the political game was, I jumped in with both feet. Soon afterwards a provincial election came along; the Liberal candidates were C. W. Cross, the Attorney General for the province, and a man called A. G. Mackay. I went campaigning for Cross, not so much because I was a convinced Liberal as for the fact that he was a good guy who gave handsome hand-outs to the Eskimos Team and other organizations in which I took an interest. They were glad enough of my support because they knew I could swing the

Chinese vote, although they didn't know then quite how much I could do. For that matter, I didn't know myself. All Chinese who had taken the trouble to get themselves naturalized as Canadian citizens (not so difficult a matter in those days) had also got the franchise.

Then there came a complication. The Conservative candidates were called Ewen and Grisbeck and I didn't know much about either of them. Mrs. Ewen had done good works among the Chinese community for years past and had even run a special Sunday School for their children. We met and we talked it over and over, but one thing was plain; the Chinese wanted to support Ewen because of Mrs. Ewen and I wanted to support Cross because he was a good guy. So that was what we decided to do. If one was a Liberal and the other a Conservative, well it was just too bad.

Polling day came and I started in at dawn with four buggies and never stopped voting till the polls closed. If I found a Chinese wasn't on the voters' list, I had him sworn in on the spot (I was the Official Interpreter) and off he went and cast his vote. There was one Independent candidate, making five in all, and Cross and Ewen were second and fifth on the ballot papers. I just told my followers to vote "*Gui*" and "*Ng*," meaning "two" and "five," and that was all right.

I polled several hundred votes like that. Towards the end of the day, I found a couple of polling booths where the scrutineers were doing no challenging. I took the opportunity of obtaining the voters' list and made it my business to round up enough people to fill it. There were five or six hundred Chinese on the Register and I guess I polled just about that number.

Cross and Ewen were elected by a thumping majority. There was a bit of puzzlement in the press about "cross-voting by the Chinese community." I pointed out that it only showed that the Chinese were far above politics and voted for the best man regardless of party—which was quite true anyway.

After that the politicians knew that I could influence any election with my solid Chinese vote, and my support was in some demand. In 1913, having got myself appointed a Commissioner of Oaths and Affidavits for the Province of Alberta, I could handle Chinese applications for naturalization, put them into the proper form, and pass them on to the authorities. I made it my business to see that every single Chinese male was on the voters' list. I got busy with the politicians in the Provincial Legislature and persuaded them to bring forward an amendment to the Chinese Immigration Act, abolishing the very unfair Head Tax and permitting them, in certain cases, to bring their wives over from China to join them.

Word of what I was doing must have got through to Dr. Sun, because, in the midst of all his troubles in China, he sent a message to me to come and join him. He'd done that once before, when he was on his way back there immediately after the Revolution, but this time it was a formal invitation delivered officially through Chen See-yen, his representative in Canada, and Lin Sen, his Ambassador in the States, who later on became President of China himself.

The two of them tackled me at a party conference in San Francisco. Lin Sen was a scholarly old gentleman; he did most of the talking and it certainly seemed a tempting proposition. But it scared me. In Canada I'd made my own niche and become somebody who really mattered in Edmonton. Going to China meant throwing everything up and starting all over again in strange surroundings and among strange people. I didn't doubt Dr. Sun's friendship, but I doubted myself. I just didn't know whether I could measure up to it. Before I'd made up my mind, along came the First World War, and then to go to China would have looked like running away.

CHAPTER IV

Corporal Cohen, C.E.F.

AUGUST 4TH, 1914 came as a shock to Canada.

Although she ranged herself with the Mother Country from the very start, it took us a little time to get used to the idea of war and a little longer still to think of it as actually affecting ourselves. The Chinese realized what it meant as soon as anybody. I'd been training a little amateur army of about four hundred and fifty strong, with the vague idea of helping Dr. Sun. Now young Chinese came running into Edmonton from all over Alberta to join my boys, and by Christmas our strength had jumped to seven hundred and fifty. I called a meeting and the whole boiling lot of us volunteered for duty overseas in any capacity.

Next day I went to see an influential friend called George Massey and he drafted a letter to the Honorable Sam Hughes, the Minister for Defence, offering our services. In those days I was young and enthusiastic and I didn't know much about official channels. I thought in my innocence that we'd be dished out with rifles and uniforms the next week, sail for France the week after, and be taking pot-shots at the Germans the week after that.

That was my first meeting with officialdom. There was a long long wait. It seemed like months to me. My letter was acknowledged at last, then there was another long wait. When the reply came, it was a nice, polite letter, beautifully expressed, and it thanked the Chinese community for their patriotic proposals, but went on to explain that, owing to the peculiar diplomatic relations between China and the Entente Powers, our offer could not be accepted.

It just didn't make sense to any of us. True enough, China hadn't declared war on Germany, but nearly all my volunteers were naturalized Canadian citizens and they had a right to fight for Canada if they felt that way. It was an awful knock and quite unexpected and it set me back a lot.

There was yet another long wait while the authorities made up their minds what to do with us. Naturally, some of the best of my boys got fed up and decided that, if they couldn't fight for Canada, they'd go off to China and do a bit of fighting there. Two of them did very well too. Their names were Mah Sang and Wong Wei-lung. The next time we met they were both colonels in the Republican Army, and front-line fighting colonels at that.

Finally I got a letter saying that it had been decided to form us into a Home Defence Corps. That didn't sound much like my cup of tea, but I felt I had a responsibility to my boys, so I stayed on to see them through the reorganization that was entailed. It took me till March 1916. I felt free then to celebrate, and a few hours later found myself in Jim Cornwall's suite at the MacDonald Hotel, having a drink with him and the Attorney General. (Cornwall had been a pioneer in the Peace River country and had played a big part in opening that area up and now represented it in Parliament.) They were talking about a new infantry battalion—the 218th—being formed in Edmonton. A lot of the recruits were Irish railway construction laborers. They'd been given the local title of the Irish Guards of Edmonton and carried an Irish harp in their cap badge.

"They sound a likely bunch," said Jim Cornwall, "I guess I'll join them."

"If you enlist in the Irish Guards," I said, "I'll do the same damn thing."

We were both stone-cold-sober civilians that evening and by the next night we were both stone-cold-sober privates. Two days later Cornwall was an acting lieutenant-colonel and a fortnight later I was an acting sergeant and had been packed off to a training school for drill instructors.

Nearly all the battalion had worked on railway construction, but they weren't by any means all Irish or all laborers. Some of them were high-grade engineers and a lot were Russians, Poles, Austrians, and even Rumanians, some of whom couldn't speak a word of English. So when I came back from being polished and taught orthodox military methods, I had my hands full.

They were good boys, but once in a while (usually on some national holiday like the Greek Orthodox Christmas) they hit the bottle and, when that happened, they hit it hard. Luckily I'd met the railway construction crowd before and I'd picked up a bit of Russian—mostly pretty foul abuse —so it was easy to handle them.

"Men in military uniform speaking unknown language are smashing up a joint in Main Street," the message would come in; "Sergeant Cohen will take out a picket, pronto!"

I'd soon find the place by the shindy and the broken windows. I'd march in, hop on to the bar and shout:

"Roo-shun!"

You'd hear a click as their heels came together and they stood to attention. I'd tear off a string of Russian swear-words to show that I wasn't pleased, and we'd all march back to barracks. Some of the toughest of the lot I worked up into a demonstration platoon, and we gave displays of Manual of Arms and bayonet fighting on the stage of the leading theatre in Edmonton.

For the final part of our training we moved to Sarcee Camp just outside Calgary in Military District 13, where a lot of battalions from Western Canada were stationed. There must have been ten or twelve thousand troops. In Calgary itself was a largish and rather conspicuous German community, so the scene was set for trouble and presently we got it.

A lot of the lads laid a plot to get into Calgary together and smash up the big German-owned shops. I knew all about it and I wanted to see the fun; but I knew also that I was a pretty prominent figure myself and, in that kind of schemozzle, the guy who gets pinched is the guy the cops are certain they can recognize.

So I took precautions. I went into Calgary that night but I went to see a show and when the riot started I was in the theatre. I sauced one of the usherettes so that she'd remember me, and I kept the stub of my ticket as more evidence. By the time I got to the spot, the police were just chasing the rioters off; no one had been hurt, but there was plenty of damage to property and obviously there was going to be trouble for someone.

Sure enough, when I got back to camp an investigation had started and every soldier who'd been on liberty that night was lined up before the dicks. Sure enough too they picked on me as one of the ringleaders. The next thing was a court-of-inquiry. A detective took the stand and testified that he saw me at the back of the mob urging them on and shouting, "Come on, boys; let's give it 'em!"

I didn't contradict him; I just lay low and said nothing and waited for the court-martial. When that came along a Colonel O. M. Biggar was appointed to be prisoners' friend for all the accused, but I stood out and said I'd rather defend myself. Presently the same dick was on the stand again. When he'd given his evidence—he toned it down a bit now that he was on his oath—I asked if I could cross-examine him.

"You say that you saw me urging on the soldiers and shouting, but you couldn't hear what I was saying with all that shine going on, could you?"

"Well, not to be certain, but I could see you were shouting something."

"There was a big crowd of purely passive spectators there, too, wasn't there?"

"Yes."

"Mightn't I have been one of them—just looking on and enjoying the fun?"

A score of soldiers were being tried and I was only one of them. It looked as if I was going to be a nuisance, and there seemed no harm in his admitting that he might be mistaken over me, and maybe impressing on the court that he was an impartial witness and a stickler for the exact truth.

"That could be the case."

I'd sat down after putting my last question and he thought he was done with me, but as soon as he said that I jumped to my feet and asked Colonel Biggar to read the detective's testimony as given at the original court-of-inquiry. There was an argument as to whether this was admissible and even the prisoners' friend seemed to be against me. (I fancy he thought that I was being a bit too clever and would put the court against all the accused.) However, the president ruled that it must be read. Out came the copper's words:

"Sergeant Cohen was standing on the steps at the back of the crowd urging the soldiers on and shouting 'Come on, boys; let's give it 'em!'"

Up I got again.

"Your honor, is this witness telling the truth now or was he telling the truth at the court-of-inquiry? I know I'm not allowed to call him a liar in the court, but what else is he?"

The long and the short of it was that the court scratched their heads and reckoned that the copper's evidence was unreliable. He was the principal witness for the prosecution —and they acquitted the whole boiling lot of us.

We finished our training by the end of the year. Meanwhile, the authorities had decided to use us as technical troops; so we ceased to be infantry and became a railway construction battalion. Our change of name didn't make much difference to our behavior in Calgary, and, when we went overseas at the beginning of 1917, the town wasn't entirely sorry to see the last of us.

On February 27th we disembarked in England. It was my second return home. This time I came as a sergeant in the Canadian Army, proud of my stripes. As soon as my four days' landing leave came along, off I went to Bow to show them to the family. They were comfortable enough in their new Tredegar Square home and my father was proud to see me in uniform.

"Son," he said, "you're right to fight. We're a scattered and a persecuted people and they say we've no loyalty to any nation. But if a country treats us well and gives us a fair chance to earn our livelihood, then it's up to us to show our gratitude and the best way a man can do that is by fighting when his country is attacked."

He took me to the Synagogue and to meet his friends. One day he walked me down the Whitechapel Road and showed me the monument that the East End Jews put up to King Edward VII. But my mother took it hard. It wasn't only that I was going to France and might be killed—it went a lot deeper than that; she was an old-fashioned orthodox woman and in her world a soldier was something strange and rather terrible. She didn't cry or complain, but just sat silent and sad and nothing that I could say or do would cheer up her.

My biggest success—a bit more than I'd bargained for —was with my kid brother, Bennie, who was just sixteen. He came down to Purfleet where I was stationed, slept in the barracks for a couple of nights, and that was the last we heard of him till my mother got a letter from France. He'd gone straight from my barracks to the nearest recruiting office, lied about his age and joined up. They were short of infantry in those days and he was at the front before I got there myself.

Mother took his letter to the War Office and proved his age and he was sent back to England where they transferred him to the 38th Royal Fusiliers, an all-Jewish battalion, mostly Americans who had come rushing over, after the Balfour Declaration, to volunteer for service in Palestine under Allenby. This was before the United States declared war. These lads were going to fight for the Jewish National Home and they weren't going to do any waiting. They were a fine bunch of boys and Bennie was happy with them.

My own military career wasn't going too well just at that time. I'd been transferred to the Depot of the Canadian Railway Troops and posted to the 8th Battalion C.R.T. I hated leaving the old outfit and didn't like the new lot nearly as much. I felt that I'd come over to fight, not to sit on my backside in barracks and start all over again the same training that I'd had already in Canada. I got a bit browned off and I guess I showed what I thought. In the end I was reduced to the ranks, but this was an engineering unit so I became, not a private, but a sapper and it was as a sapper that I crossed to France on September 8th.

I'd been happy in the army in Canada, I was unhappy in England, and then in France I was happy again. Things began to break my way as soon as I landed, for in my very first batch of mail was a letter from Dr. Sun, wishing me luck and saying that if my life was spared I must visit him in China when the war was over. It was like the Doctor to remember me in the middle of all his worries and responsibilities, and it cheered me up no end.

Our job in Flanders was building and maintaining the narrow gauge railways that carried ammunition up to the front and casualties back to the rear. We spent pretty well all our time in the area round Ypres and Poperinghe.

I met the usual old friend from the other side of the world, Joe Hymans, who had been my chum at Hayes and was now serving with the Australians. We marched right past each other on the Menin Road. And I had the usual narrow escape when we were working in a railway cut and had knocked off for dinner. I crossed the tracks to get a light for my fag and a big shell splinter hit the very spot where I'd just been sitting.

Anyway I was happy. In January I got my stripes back —two of them at all events—and I was seconded to the Chinese Labour Corps. Some of the officers in those units didn't know much about the Chinese; in fact they'd only been posted to them because they weren't well liked in their own regiments. They didn't know how to handle Orientals and they showed it. Some lost their tempers and tried to throw their weight about, others were frankly frightened. I know it sounds silly to feel frightened of a Chinese coolie, but that's the way it was with them. The coolies knew it at once, and they also knew that their officers weren't much good anyway.

So they just slacked and chiselled and when they found that they could get away with it, they slacked and chiselled some more till they were doing darned little work at all. Matters came to a head when there was a rush job on hand to build a narrow gauge line for one of those twelve-inch naval guns, so that it could reach some special target a long way behind the German lines. An S.O.S. went out for anybody who knew the Chinese and thought he could handle them. Colonel Cornwall put my name up and I found myself back amongst the Sons of Han.

These weren't the folk I'd known in Canada. There I met (besides the prosperous merchants) cooks, laundrymen, small shopkeepers and so on—men who had either some craft, or some trade, or a tiny bit of cash behind them. These were just plain coolies—illiterate, unskilled, and completely ignorant. Still, I knew what I had to do and that was to appeal to their personal interest. A Chinese doesn't like work any more than we do, but if he is going to get something out of it, and if he can see what that something is, he'll work harder than anyone.

I talked to some of their overseers and I talked to the engineers in charge of the job, and I found out that they worked over-long hours, starting at dawn and going right on till seven or eight at night. I saw how much grading they did in a day's work, and it was darned little in spite of the hours.

Next morning I was out early with the field surveyors and we put in marking posts to cover twice the length of grading they'd averaged before. Then I lined up the laborers and told them that that was the work to be done that day and as soon as they'd finished they could knock off and cook their suppers. They worked like beavers and it was completed soon after four o'clock. They were pleased, the engineers were pleased; in fact, everyone was pleased.

A few days later there was a bit of bother. German aircraft came over and bombed us—they must have seen the lights earlier on when work was continuing into the evening —and some of the bombs fell in the coolies' compound and caused a few casualties. Next day they were working harder than ever and they finished their stint well before four.

"Good boys," I thought, "that's how they're getting their own back on the Huns."

But I didn't know my Chinese as well then as I do now, and neither did I know that there was a German prisoner-of-war camp not far away. As soon as they'd eaten their rice, a party sloped off, stole some Mills grenades from a near-by dump, and threw them into the prison camp. There was the hell of a row about it, but it was quite impossible to identify the culprits and no one could be punished.

I stayed on with the Labour Corps till the job was done and then rejoined my own unit just in time for the big break-through in March 1918. That was my liveliest spell. Our task was to wreck the rails behind our retreating troops so that the Germans couldn't use them. I was in charge of a light engine which towed a gadget something like a small plough. We slipped it between the sleeper and the rails and ripped them up from their bed.

Once we were nearly caught, and it was my own fault. We were going past a deserted Belgian farm, and there in a sty close by the tracks I saw three little pigs. They were just the right size for a barbecue and I hadn't tasted pork for a long long time. I put on the brakes and down we climbed. In a moment we were over the fence and into the farmyard. We grabbed the piglets, cut their throats, and took them aboard the engine.

Then we thought we'd explore the farmhouse. We found a phonograph and some records that our troops must have given the farmer's wife—the top one was "If You Were the Only Girl in the World." I also spotted a fine silk hat, polished and shining, just like the one my father wore to the Synagogue on the Sabbath. I put it on in the place of my tin helmet and we were just scrambling back aboard the engine as pleased as Punch with ourselves when—WHAM! —a bullet hit the engine.

The next volley smashed the phonograph records, and we scrammed. We lifted the wrecking gadget, opened the throttle, gave her all she'd take, and beat it for the tall timber. How she rattled and rocked! My only fear was that when we came to a bend she'd jump the rails.

It could only have been a leading German patrol, as the firing died down, and soon we saw our lads lining a ditch astride the line. They gave us a cheer, and then I realized that I was still wearing that top hat.

It wasn't long after this that I got my packet. Up till then I'd been pretty lucky with nothing worse than a scratch from a shell splinter down my thigh that I never even felt till I saw my trouser-leg was torn. This time I was hit in the head just below my right temple. It didn't seem much at first and, though I was sent down to the field dressing station for treatment, I persuaded them to let me rejoin my unit.

But presently the wound began to affect the working of my jaw. Now, jaws come in useful both for eating and talking and I like doing both. In the end it got pretty painful to do either, and come the middle of June I was invalided home and found myself in the Military Hospital at Franborough.

I was still there at the Armistice. Getting my jaws right proved to be a slow business. I was given electric treatment and my head was put in splints so that I couldn't chew and had to go on what they called a "liquid diet." It wasn't the right kind of liquid—not for me at any rate.

Even on November 11th they tried to keep the news from the patients in hospital. We had a good many cases of shell-shock and they thought it might be too much for them.

But when I was in bed that night my favorite nurse leaned over me and whispered:

"Morris, the war's finished! But promise you'll not tell the other boys."

"Sister," I said, "I'll promise you that and a whole lot more besides."

I hopped right out of my cot and threw my arms round her and gave her a good big kiss. She said that I was a bad lad and she would have to tell matron in the morning. Next morning I wasn't there.

As far as I was concerned, I'd enlisted for the duration of the war and, as soon as the shooting stopped, my contract expired. When the rest of the ward were asleep I got up and dressed and set out for the Big Cities and the Bright Lights. I had a little money on me and I could borrow more from my buddies. For the next few weeks, I stayed AWOL and made one big whoopee. As for the liquid diet, it just went down by the bucketful.

The Canadians were coming back pretty fast and I didn't want to miss my passage home, so I kept tab on the movements of my battalion, and when I heard that they were at Rhyl in North Wales and would stay there till they sailed, I blew the rest of my cash and gave myself up. I lost my stripes again, but that was all right by me.

We docked in Halifax on February 7th. There were all kinds of people on the wharf asking us if there was anyone we'd like to notify of our arrival. I'd set out a sergeant and I'd come back as a sapper, but that didn't worry me any and I was feeling good, so as soon as we'd disembarked I wired Joseph Andrew Clark, the Mayor of Edmonton.

I HAVE WON THE WAR. ARRIVING WITH MY HEROES.
Sergeant Morris Abraham Cohen.

When our train pulled into Edmonton and the flags were flying and the bands playing and the Mayor and Corporation and leading citizens were on the red-carpeted platform to welcome us, and the newsboys came running up to our carriage windows with the special edition, I saw my telegram under banner headlines on the front page. I felt a bit foolish. But who cared that day? And anyway, when I got my war medals just twenty-five years later, the inscription on the back said "*Sergeant* Cohen."

THE WHOOPEE OVER, I sat down like many another man and wondered what to do next. I didn't want to go back to the National Land Company. Why that was I just don't know. I'd been well treated and I'd done well for myself and—heaven knows—the prospects were good enough with trade expanding everywhere and a new boom in real estate on the way.

Somehow the war had unsettled me. I wanted to strike out a new line for myself, but what that new line was I'd no idea at all. I took stock of my assets. They came to more than I'd thought. I still had a little money in the bank from my pre-war savings, and I had my war gratuity. I sold that four-carat diamond ring I'd been so proud of. Diamonds had taken a jump in value and it fetched fifteen hundred dollars. So I decided to look around for a while.

I didn't have to look very far. As soon as I was demobilized they elected me to the Executive Committee of the Great War Veterans Association, and I found myself in a fight that—short of actual shooting—was as fierce as anything I'd seen in France.

Total Prohibition has always been a hot topic in Canada; maybe because they drink so much real hard liquor —not wine or beer, but neat spirits—and drinking does more harm than in other countries. While the boys were away at the war, the pussy-foot gang got going in a big way, and by the time we came home again Total Prohibition was almost an accomplished fact. We were only in at the end of the fight, but we faced the prospect of Alberta as a bone-dry province and we fought hard. We canvassed our pals and we held public meetings of protest, and whenever we heard of a pussy-foot meeting we went and heckled the speakers.

That was the part I enjoyed and, though I say it myself, I was pretty good. Once I even tangled with the Reverend John McQueen, the head of the Presbyterian Church in Edmonton and a famous preacher all through Western Canada. He got up and he gave us half an hour of the best; he told us of suicides due to drink and broken homes due to drink and he quoted the Bible to prove that all drink was evil and he finished up with the Book of Proverbs:

"Look not thou upon the wine when it is red."

"Is there anyone in this hall," he asked, "who would like to dispute this with me?"

"Yes, Your Reverence," I said, "I would!"

I got up and climbed over the knees of the people next to me (the hall was crowded out) and walked up the aisle and three steps up to the platform. Then I turned around and took a look at the audience. They were mostly women and middle-aged women, deadly serious and almost all dead against me. It was a tough proposition.

First, I sipped a glass of water, and then coughed and spluttered and pulled a face as if I wasn't used to it. That raised a laugh, but not much of one; I took a deep breath and began.

"Ladies and gentlemen, I agree with every statement that the Reverend McQueen has made."

That made them sit up and take notice and I went on:

"Drink has caused suicides and drink has broken up

homes and the Reverend Gentleman would like to prohibit drink. But how did these unfortunate people kill themselves? Some of them cut their throats—would the Reverend Gentleman prohibit the manufacture of knives? Some of them jumped into the river—would the Reverend Gentleman forbid the building of bridges? I guess not!"

I knew I had to keep it short and sweet, so I pulled out my other ace:

"The Reverend Gentleman has quoted the Scriptures. Now I am a Jew and so I only know what you call the Old Testament, but if he will lend me his Bible, I'd like to read you a verse."

"What would you like to read?" asked McQueen.

"Fourteenth chapter of *Deuteronomy*, twenty-sixth verse, but perhaps your reverence would like to read it aloud yourself."

There was no getting out of it for him now and he had to stand up and read:

"And thou shalt bestow that money for whatsoever thy soul lusteth after, for oxen, or for sheep, or for wine, or for strong drink, or for whatsoever thy soul desireth; and thou shalt eat there before the Lord thy God and thou shalt rejoice, thou and thy household."

By this time half the audience were laughing and the other half looking down their noses, so I finished quick:

"Ladies and gentlemen, don't think that I stand for drunkenness. If the Reverend McQueen would follow the teaching of the Bible and the lead of the other great churches, the Roman Catholic Church and the Episcopalian Church and my own Faith—and preach temperance and moderation in drink, then he'd have me and my own friends behind him. But Total Prohibition will do no good to anyone and a great deal of harm to some folks."

Prohibition came in just the same and all the trouble we'd foretold came in with it. The West was still pretty raw in those days and there were plenty of old-timers who didn't give a damn for anybody. One of them was called Leonard Baker, a prospector from the far north of the province. Now, Max Aitken had got his peerage in 1917 and, although he was well known to all of us, we knew him best under his old name. Not long after the war, when he came to Edmonton and put up at the leading hotel with his manservant, the reception clerk wrote in his register, "Lord Beaverbrook and valet."

The next guest was old Baker who walked in toting his camping equipment over his shoulder. He looked at the register and thought a bit; then he entered himself, "Len Baker and valise."

These characters had been a law unto themselves. When they were told that the townsfolk had decided that they couldn't have a drink any more, it just didn't make sense to them. They meant to have their drink and they set about getting it. In came the bootleggers with their bad bootleg liquor. Citizens would be found lying dead drunk all around the town. Some of them stayed dead too. They froze to death in the winter and in the summer they died of a mixture of hot sun and bad booze; and those that didn't meet in the morgue woke up in hospital or the hoosegow.

At last the veterans held an Executive Committee meeting at the Memorial Hall (that was our headquarters) and resolved—like all committees—that "something ought to be done." They turned and looked at me, and I realized that the next resolution would be that I was the guy to get busy. I couldn't deny that I knew most all the bootleggers in town and so I made the best of it and offered my services.

I went around to every bootlegger in turn and asked him to lay off selling booze to veterans and, above all, not to smuggle booze into the Memorial Hall. I asked them very nicely and politely. At the same time I made it plain that, if they did go on with their games, I'd make it tough for them. (How? Well, I wasn't quite sure of that myself; but we were all buddies and I hoped that they wouldn't call my bluff.)

The firewater merchants toed the line all right, but we went on finding drunks around the town and even in the Memorial Hall itself. I accused them of double-crossing me, but they denied it and I believed them. They were just as puzzled as I was; they reckoned some stranger was muscling in on their racket, and they even hired a private dick to find out what was up.

One evening I was in a poker game—yes, with my old bunch of rounders, just like before the war—when three of them came running in, all het up.

"Morris, you must come along with us; we've something to show you."

They took me to the Memorial Hall and down to the basement and into the lavatories. There were four veterans lying dead drunk and beside each vet. was an empty tin of "Canned Heat." You know those solid fuels made of fats and methylated spirits that people use for camping out. They'd been *eating* the stuff for the alcoholic kick in it.

"You just let them lie," I said. "I know where to find the Attorney General and I'm going to have him see what Prohibition is doing to Edmonton."

I brought him right down to the Hall and showed him the corpses.

"Say, look at this. These are good boys, but they can't even get a glass of beer and so they're eating poison. Why can't we have beer in here?"

"Okay," said he, "I'll fix it."

And he did. There was a brewery in Edmonton which

brewed for export to other provinces, and the Veterans got a special charter to buy their beer there. It had to be drunk inside the Memorial Hall, which thus became the only place in the whole of Alberta where you could buy drink legally. Later on when the Prince of Wales visited us and I was on the reception committee, we took him downstairs and gave him a glass of beer. I guess he was glad to get it.

My old pals in the Kuomintang hadn't forgotten me any more than had Dr. Sun. As soon as I was demobilized they came around asking me to go out on the stump and explain the situation in China to their lodges. Once again it was about as bad as it could be and once again it needed a whole lot of explaining.

Dr. Sun had been driven out of the country in 1913 and spent the next three years as an exile in Tokyo. He'd been head of a government in Canton for a short while in 1917-18, but now he was once more a refugee, this time in the French Concession in Shanghai. The country was in a state of chaos, with the North fighting the South as usual and the rest having a free-for-all amongst themselves.

The Manchus had gone and so no one could say any longer that China had to be liberated from a foreign tyranny. The Japanese had made their Twenty-one Demands and the Western Powers were being a bit old-fashioned about loans and treaties and concessions and the rest of it. But all this was a long way from a shooting war. No one could pretend that China was being attacked—or in danger of being attacked—by a foreign power. Equally no one could deny that the fighting that was always going on in China was between the Chinese themselves. Their cousins overseas couldn't see why they should hand out good money for either side. I did my best, but it wasn't easy.

Meanwhile trouble was blowing up from quite another quarter. The post-war boom had come to an end as booms have a way of doing. Money became tight and there was a certain amount of unemployment, a rare thing in Canada. Naturally the veterans felt that they should have the first pick of any jobs that were going, and presently one of them stood up at a meeting of our Executive Committee and complained that the one big meat-packing plant in Edmonton was employing Chinese labor while there were veterans outside in the street looking for work.

I saw this was political dynamite and might start something serious, so I acted quickly. That same evening I called a meeting of the Chinese community, told them what had been said and warned them where it might lead. I asked all the Chinese employed in the stockyard and packing plant to resign their jobs. That was a lot to ask and I didn't know whether I could carry them with me or not. They talked it over amongst themselves and took a vote. It was unanimous —they would take my advice and quit work.

The next day they drew their pay and handed in the notices. I called on the manager, told him the reason for this, and suggested that he call up the Great War Veterans Association and offer his vacancies to their unemployed vets. I left him doing it.

I sat back for four or five days, and then it was the manager of the packing plant who wanted to see me, please. The returned soldiers wouldn't look at the jobs the Chinese had been doing, the place was at a standstill: would I please get the Chinese back again p.d.q.?

That finished the "ruined by cheap Chinese labor" cry in Alberta. It was never raised again. The situation stayed tricky for some time, largely because Chinese weren't allowed to join the official labor union. I kept an eye on things, and whenever the Cooks' and Waiters' Union went on strike (which was often) I saw that the Chinese chefs came out in sympathy; and whenever a Chinese was taken on as a chef I took care that his pay was no less than the union man who'd had the job before him. Soon enough the feeling died down altogether.

Dr. Sun heard what I'd done and wrote me a nice letter about it. He suggested again that I might like to join him and he sent me a copy of his new book, *The International Development of China*, and asked me to find out what the Canadian railway experts thought of his plans. That wasn't difficult; I took it around to half a dozen of them and they all said the same thing. The writer was a dreamer and visionary who knew nothing of the practical side of railway development, and anyway he'd never be able to raise the money.

I hadn't the heart to write back and tell him this, so I answered vaguely and encouragingly. By return mail came a letter specifically asking me to try to interest some Canadian railway construction company in his projects and bring their representative to Shanghai to negotiate a contract.

All this sounds pretty silly with Dr. Sun sitting in a foreign concession and unable to stir out of it. The experts were quite right about one thing: he was a visionary and a dreamer, true enough—but sometimes his dreams came true. He already knew that things were running his way in Canton once more and that he could count on getting back there in the course of time. Anyway, he was a man who always lived more in the future than in the present, and it was just as well for China that he did.

I started out with his book under my arm and his letters in my breast pocket, and an uphill job it was. One thing helped me and that was that in July 1913, when he was head of the Central Railway Corporation (and a very few days before he had to fly to Japan for safety), he had signed a contract with the Pauling Construction Company of London for the construction of a line from Canton to Chungking.

The line was never built—in fact, it never has been built—but he had included a copy of that contract in an appendix to his book, and he remarked in his letter that it was the fairest agreement that China had ever made with any foreign company. The hard-boiled experts I approached were often inclined to laugh at me, but when they read that contract it seemed to make sense to them and they took me more seriously.

Eventually I reached Vancouver, the headquarters of the Northern Construction Company, the biggest railway builders in the Dominion. I had a pull there because General Stewart of Foley, Stewart & Welsh was connected with them. He'd been in charge of light railway construction in France during the war and known me there.

I saw the president of the company and he was interested from the start. I think that just because they were the biggest company of the lot and had correspondingly big ideas, they weren't scared of the size of a country like China. They'd driven the Canadian Northern Railway through from the Atlantic to the Pacific, and even China didn't seem as big as all that.

Anyway the preliminary negotiations were dead easy. It was arranged that I'd go to Shanghai, contact Dr. Sun and keep things warm till the arrival of Mr. C. V. Cummings, the vice-president. I sailed on July 28th, 1922, in the *Empress of Australia*. She had come up from Panama on her maiden voyage to the Far East. Like most liners on their maiden voyage, she developed engine trouble and we had to come back to Vancouver. We didn't reach Shanghai till the latter part of August.

Ostensibly my trip was just to help negotiate this railway construction contract, but, as always happens when you're working with Chinese, I had more than one mission, and the second was the more important—to me at any rate.

I'd already made up my mind to throw in my lot with Dr. Sun, and I knew why it was that he wanted me. He needed someone he could trust absolutely—a foreigner who'd keep right outside Chinese internal politics and who'd look after his personal safety as I'd done on his North American trips.

Call it a "bodyguard" if you like. I knew that the job would be what I made of it. I hadn't yet picked up the title of "Two-Gun," but if I was to look after the life of Dr. Sun, I meant to take the right tools with me. I set out on that voyage with eight guns in my luggage, and, when I landed in Shanghai I was so top-heavy with artillery, if you'd given me a push I'd have fallen slap on my arse.

CHAPTER V

Colonel Cohen, A.D.C.

MORRIS LANDED IN CHINA a few weeks after his thirty-third birthday, at an age, therefore, when the physical and mental make-up of most men has been finally settled for life. In appearance he was not greatly changed from the handsome, tough young fellow of those vigorous, bustling days before the Great War. Perhaps the most noticeable difference was in his figure. The combination of good and plentiful Canadian food with an Homeric appetite had had its insidious effect. The always stocky, heavily built youth had developed into the positively corpulent man. The "Fat Moishe" of his boyhood had returned and was to remain into his declining years.

In the face he certainly looked a full ten years older. His glossy black hair had begun to retreat up the massive brow, but the widow's peak was still in evidence and, if anything, emphasized by the recession around it. His features had been harshly marked by harsh experiences—in France as well as Western Canada—and a year of pain from his head wound and discomfort from the damaged jaw had drawn deep lines from mouth to nostril, without in any way diminishing the cheerful good-nature of his normal expression.

For Morris was a man of singularly happy disposition; throughout the years of our friendship I have seldom seen him worried and never seriously angry. That this equanimity was largely due to a perfect digestion and almost complete freedom from all physical ills may make it less admirable but none the less enviable. Possessed of inexhaustible vitality, he was never bored or depressed; he genuinely and unaffectedly like his fellow men and could never have too much of their society. The end of a long night at the card-table or in a stuffy, smelly, smoky, and crowded conference room found him as cheerful and good-tempered as had the morning. He could be patient with the aggrieved, tactful with the quarrelsome and was ever ready to out-talk the most garrulous. "Nerves," that commonest complaint of all Europeans living among Orientals, was an affliction which meant nothing to him and he could never even pretend to sympathize with it.

Canada had taught him much. He had met the hard cases, ranging from the genial trapper off on a blind drunk after months of hardship and loneliness out in the North West, to the genuinely vicious and dangerous remittance man blowing his monthly dole—and he knew how to handle them. He had met the professional politicians and they are very much the same in all countries. Over a poker hand, over his trays of "hoops" and "supers," and over an office desk, he had met a slice of mankind clean across the social structure of the Dominion. To earn his bread and butter he had been forced to study all of them and he had applied his logical, orderly brain, his excellent memory, and his natural intuition to good effect.

His greatest asset was his personal prestige among the Chinese, of which such extraordinary proof had been given when he was chosen to guard Dr. Sun during his Canadian tour. Although, as matters turned out, the trip had proved uneventful, his post had been no sinecure. The Doctor's enemies were numerous, powerful, and unscrupulous; in London itself he had once been kidnapped and imprisoned in the Imperial Chinese Embassy, to be saved only by the fidelity of a friend and the firmness of the Foreign Office. That his safety could be entrusted to a man of alien race, not even Canadian by birth and with no blood relations to be held accountable for his conduct—this was a truly astonishing witness to the reputation for absolute integrity which Morris had acquired and which he was ever after to enjoy among the Sons of Han.

Morris was well known to the Chinese in Canada, and about the Chinese race he knew a great deal; of China itself he knew nothing.

MY FIRST SIGHT OF SHANGHAI—said he—was the usual one for foreigners—from a ship in the Whangpoo River; and my first impression was also the usual one—of the contrast between the dignified European-style buildings along the Bund (banks, clubs, consulates, hotels, and office blocks) and the yelling mob of brown-skinned, bare-headed, blue-clad coolies that swarmed over the wharves, jetties, and lighters around the ship. Coming from Canada, I'd never thought to see such flaunting prosperity and such abject poverty side by side.

One other impression I had and it was a big surprise to me. I knew many Chinese of all sorts and conditions and, arriving in their own country, I expected to feel myself at home right from the start. But I didn't. I felt that I was a stranger in a very, very strange land and I felt lonely.

There was no one to meet me, so I left my luggage at the Customs shed and took a taxi to the Astor House Hotel. I saw the rickshaws waiting, and, after a look at the tiny, skinny rickshaw coolies, I reckoned that it would have taken just about four of them to balance me on a scales and somehow I couldn't bring myself to sit back in comfort and have the poor little devil lug my weight along. It was a long time before I got rid of that feeling.

As for taking a chair, it was still longer before I did

that. I wasn't worried about the chair coolies—they're always heftier chaps than the rickshaw pullers and there were two of them anyway—but I saw those long, thin, supple shafts and I was just plumb scared that they'd break under me.

I took a room at the hotel and after lunch set out for No. 44 rue Vallon in the French Concession where Dr. Sun had his office. There at last I found a friend, Chen See-yen, who'd formerly been head of the Kuomintang in Canada and whom I'd often met in Vancouver, a tall slim man of about my own height who never talked much and had some reputation as an amateur artist.

He took me along to 29 rue Molière, which was Dr. Sun's home at that time. He had moved in there as far back as 1916 when he returned from exile in Japan. It had belonged to him ever since, and now that he had had to clear out of Canton he was back there once more. It was a small, unpretentious, two-storied brick house just like all the others in the road, with a little lawn in front where they had laid out a croquet court.

He received me in a European-style room where the only picture on the walls was a portrait of Abraham Lincoln. Many Chinese men change very little through their middle years—the thirties, forties, and fifties—and Dr. Sun was one of them. He was fifty-six now, but he might just as well have been forty-six—or sixty-six, for the matter of that. Maybe his mustache was a little grayer and he had gone a tiny bit bald in front; but there was the same friendly twinkle in his eye and he still had the same figure, not paunchy and not noticeably lean.

To tell the truth I didn't look at him for very long, because we'd hardly begun to talk when Mme. Sun walked in and after that I'd only got eyes for her. I'd heard a lot about her already. Everyone knew of the three famous Soong sisters from Wellesley College in Massachusetts. Ching-ling

Soong (who actually graduated from the Wesleyan College at Macon, Georgia) was the second and, some people said, the cleverest of the three.

In Canada I'd met some Chinese ladies but they were mostly elderly married women, and women too who had had to work hard all their lives to keep their homes going. I'd expected Mme. Sun to be charming and gracious and dignified and she was all that; I hadn't realized that she would be as pretty as a peach into the bargain. When she welcomed me to her home, I didn't know what to say and just stammered and blushed like a boy.

That first interview didn't last long. Mme. Sun had come in to remind the Doctor that he had a string of appointments all the afternoon and so he told me I'd better come back and discuss the contract the following day.

Back I went to the Astor House Hotel, and then I really was alone with the day to get through and not another soul I knew in the whole big city. I hung around the bar for a bit, but that didn't make me feel any better and so I went out for a walk. It turned into a longer walk than I'd meant to take. I got right away from the European Concessions and into the narrow, twisty, filthy little back streets and then I just wandered on and on. I heard that awful Chinese music— I've never got to like it even today—and the rattle of the mah jong pieces and learned after a bit to jump out of the way when I heard a shout of "*Ohé!*" and heavy breathing behind me, because that meant porters on the march and they might be carrying anything from a giant jar of oil to a dead man in a basket.

I smelt those queer Chinese smells that you can't begin to describe because they're such a mixture and they change every few yards as you pass a different sort of shop. I saw the signboards with that vertical writing on them with characters that just stop short of being an actual picture of something and leave you wondering what on earth they can mean. I ran into those funny little processions that seem to have started from nowhere and to be going nowhere. I wandered on and on—I forgot all about my dinner—and when I got back to my hotel it was after midnight. I'd only been twelve hours in China but already China was beginning to get under my skin.

When I saw Dr. Sun again the next day I had another surprise coming to me. The times I'd been touting "The International Development of China" around those hard-boiled Canadian railwaymen, I'd heard him called a dreamer and a visionary and the rest of it so often that I'd half begun to think it might be true. Believe me, when he got down to figures and business propositions, he knew what time of day it was all right. He took the contract away into his private room and when, ten minutes later, he sent for me, he knew all that there was to know about it. The questions he asked showed me that. He said that it was okay by him and I just had to sit back for a fortnight and wait for Mr. Cummings to arrive and clinch the deal.

In that fortnight I had time to do some thinking. The main outlines of the contract were simple enough. The Northern Construction Company were to build fifteen hundred miles of railway in South China at an estimated cost of a hundred million gold dollars and on a "cost plus" basis of seven and a half per cent, or, say, seven and a half million dollars profit for them. What didn't appear in the contract was that I was to get thirty-five per cent of their net profit when it came in. That was an absurdly big cut for me and the mere fact that it was so big shows that there was some doubt about the profit ever being made. Even so, being with the Doctor again had fired up my old enthusiasm for the Chinese Republic and one day—to my own surprise—I found myself walking into his office, telling him about my cut and offering to turn it in for the good of the Cause. I could hardly believe it was me talking, but the words came out and it was my own voice.

Dr. Sun himself seemed surprised—very surprised. He went off into his own room and when he came back he had these figures written on a slip of paper:

CONTRACT FOR $100,000,000 @ 7½%

7½% on $100,000,000 . . $7,500,000 . . Total profit for the Co.
65% on $7,500,000 . . $4,875,000 . . Company's share.
35% on $7,500,000 . . $2,625,000 . . Cohen's share.

CONTRACT FOR $100,000,000 @ 5%

5% on $100,000,000 . . $5,000,000 . . Total profit for the Co.
80% on $5,000,000 . . $4,000,000 . . Company's share.
20% on $5,000,000 . . $1,000,000 . . Cohen's share.

"Morris," he said, "the laborer is worthy of his hire. Now don't give up your whole commission, but do this instead. Ask the company to cut their profit from seven and a half per cent to five per cent and tell them that in return you'll cut your own commission from thirty-five per cent to twenty per cent. That will save two and a half million for China and leave you with something to get along on."

I met Cummings as soon as his ship came in. He was just as astonished as Dr. Sun had been, but he laughed and shrugged his shoulders and said it didn't make all that difference to the company and he'd agree without even consulting them. Off we went to the office and had the alterations made in the original contract; the attorneys came in and looked it over; and it was signed, sealed, and delivered a few days later.

My million dollars? There were local civil wars, and there were big, full-scale civil wars with everyone joining in. There were the Japanese wars (don't forget there were two of them). There was the Second World War. I never saw one dollar out of that million, but the contract is still alive and maybe I shall one day.

The day after the contract was signed Dr. Sun sent for me again and asked if I'd like to stay with him permanently as his third aide-de-camp. That was the real reason why I'd come to China and I said "Yes, please, sir" almost before the words were out of his mouth. Earlier in my life I'd often worried whether or not I could hold down a job. This time I knew the job was just hand-made for me and I had no doubts at all.

Also, I had one tremendous break that made a big difference from the start. Both the other A.D.C.'s who mightn't have liked my muscling in on them and could have made things awkward happened to be buddies of mine from Edmonton, men who had actually enlisted in my little private army there. Their names were Wong Wei-lung and Mah Sang. For the next few years right up to the Doctor's death it was very, very seldom that the three of us were far from his side. In China "A.D.C." and "bodyguard" mean much the same thing, and the first duty of an A.D.C. was to look after the safety of his boss.

Wong was a big, slow, silent man whom I never got to know very well—he died a long time ago. Mah Sang was a regular guy if you like, and he's still going strong. He was short, just about up to my shoulder, but chunky and barrel-chested and enormously strong. He was quite young, too, say a couple of years younger than me, but already he'd begun to put on weight, which is rare with Chinese at that age. All the same he was quick as lightning with his fists, whether he had a gun in them or not, and just as quick when it came to spotting a wrong 'un.

He was a jolly son-of-a-gun, always laughing, but his eyes, although they laughed too, didn't laugh with the rest of his face, if you know what I mean. His face might be convulsed with merriment, but his eyes stayed alert and watchful all the time. Another funny thing was this; he never knew more than a little pidgin-English and I never learned much Cantonese and yet he and I never had any trouble understanding each other. I think the reason was we only had one idea in our two heads—that was the comfort and safety of the Doctor; and, when two people think all that much alike, they don't have any need of words.

I was given the rank of Colonel like the other A.D.C.'s, though of course I didn't wear a uniform while we were living in the French Concession. I moved from the Astor House into Dr. Sun's home and got to know the other members of his personal staff. There was Chen See-yen, who represented the Kuomintang and did the political screening —in fact he screened me when I first arrived—and Li Luchao (I always called him "Li Look-out" or "Look See-li"). I'd first met him with Dr. Sun in San Francisco back in 1909 —he'd been his private secretary since 1915. He spoke perfect English and was well educated by both Chinese and European standards, and he must have known the Doctor better than any man alive, but he never gave much away of what he knew.

The most important member of the staff was Mme. Sun herself. She never interfered during his office hours, but it was she alone who made his life possible by keeping him cheerful and happy no matter what went on. Every evening they would sit together reading and chatting; in fact, that was his principal recreation, except that now and then she'd organize a private movie show.

One day she got him to play croquet with the rest of the staff—that was on the front lawn at 29 rue Molière— but they just made a joke of it and teased each other. Whenever his ball got in her way she'd belt it into the furthest cor-

Morris on his first return to England in 1911, age twenty-two

Left to right: Liao Chung-kai, General Chiang Kai-shek, Dr. Sun Yat-sen, Mme. Sun, Col. Cohen, A.D.C.

General Mah Sang and General Cohen in later years

ner of the court and whenever he got the chance he'd do the same for her and she'd shout, "Look out! He means to win somehow."

I didn't have much time for croquet or movies myself. I was busy learning my job and learning it the hard way, by trying to do it and making my own mistakes. Whenever a visitor was announced, and there were dozens a day sometimes, I'd study his face and his dress and his mannerisms so that I'd know him again. Then as soon as he'd been shown into the Doctor's private room and the door was shut I'd start asking questions.

"Who was that gentleman?

"What does he do? Is he a general, a politician, or a merchant?" (He was usually a mixture of two of those trades, if not all three, but it made a convenient classification to start with.)

"Where does he come in the line-up? Is he on Dr. Sun's side?"

If the answer to that was "Yes," I'd put the most important question of all:

"Is he really working for the Chinese Republic, or is he just out for what he can get?"

When he left I'd ask his name again, just to make sure that I'd got it right; then I'd tuck all that information away in my top story. I've a good memory for detail and when that same chap reappeared I'd tell the staff what I knew about him. Quite often they'd have forgotten the very things they'd told me themselves. The door would close behind him and I'd say:

"Ach! He's no good."

"How do you know that, Mr. Cohen?" they'd ask me.

At first I could see that they were thinking hard about me. They weren't actually suspicious but just puzzled as to what a foreigner could be doing in such a post. But I was careful not to throw my weight about. I was so meek and humble you'd have been surprised. They soon saw that my devotion to Dr. Sun was perfectly genuine and they began to trust me and let me screen visitors on my own.

Besides the visitors I studied Dr. Sun himself and got to know all his little ways. When he was in a good mood his eyes had a friendly sort of twinkle but he never laughed out loud like Mme. Sun used to do. If the news was bad he wouldn't get grumpy and grouchy like other great men I've known; he just became rather aloof and very serious. He was human all right, but you never forgot that he was dealing with problems that affected millions of lives and you never bothered him with your own affairs unless he gave you a lead.

He didn't smoke and—an extraordinary thing for a Chinese—he drank little tea but a lot of fruit juice. He loved fruit; there was always a bowl of oranges in his room, and he'd eat them off-and-on all the time. He always had Chinese food, but none of it was meat. I should say he was a full vegetarian. In the winter Shanghai is cold and wet, and all the months we were there he wore the ordinary long Chinese gown of some thick, warm, dark gray material. Yet there was always something about him that was different from other Chinese; it might have been his exceptionally good eyesight; he never wore glasses, even for the smallest and smudgiest Chinese script.

His speeches, like his everyday conversation, were plain, direct, and straightforward with few flowery phrases. He'd slip in an occasional joke, but not often and then it was a good one. To a Chinese audience he'd use either Cantonese or Mandarin—he spoke both equally well—but with Europeans it was always English.

I was happy all that winter. There was no discipline in his office in the ordinary sense of the word, but we just naturally treated him with respect and did what he said without asking questions. We were certainly working for a man rather than a cause—for Dr. Sun rather than for the Kuomintang or the Revolution—but we all felt that it was through Sun Yat-sen and through him alone that one could hope for a United China. By the New Year (I mean the Chinese New Year at the beginning of February) I'd begun to get on top of my job. Then everything changed and I had to start learning all over again.

What had happened was this. The three big, important provinces of South China are Kwangtung, Kwangsi, and Yunnan. They eat the same sort of food and they speak the same language (apart from local dialects) and have the same ideas and were always ready to gang up together and fight the rest of China. When they weren't doing that, they'd turn to and fight amongst themselves. The best—at least the ablest—leader amongst them was a Cantonese, General Chen Chiung-ming. He was far the cleverest military politician of the lot, but he hadn't much use for Dr. Sun with his idea of a unified, peaceful and prosperous Chinese Republic. What he wanted was power in his own province and plenty of it.

Dr. Sun had been driven out of Canton in 1918 by an alliance of Kwangsi and Yunnan. In 1920 General Chen Chiung-ming led the Kwangtung troops against the other two provinces, defeated them and then invited Dr. Sun to come back. But that line-up couldn't last; Sun Yat-sen wanted to unite and reform China while Chen Chiung-ming just wanted to strengthen his own little kingdom, and so in 1922 he turned on Dr. Sun and drove him out again.

Now, just eighteen months later, when Kwangsi and Yunnan had built up new armies and thrown General Chen out of Canton, they asked the Doctor to come back. It was one of those "stop-go-stop" affairs. On January 27th we were

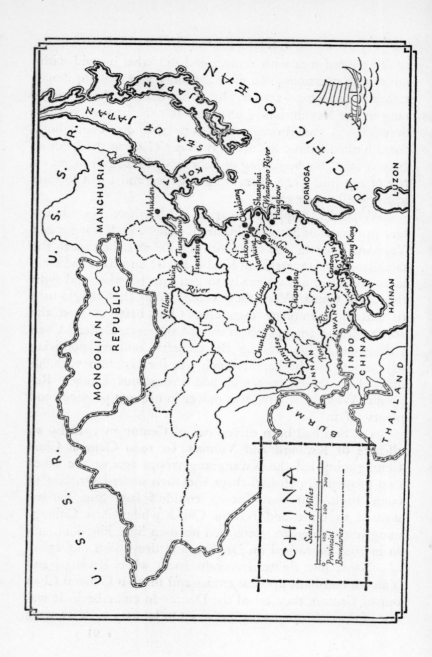

PACIFIC OCEAN

SEA OF JAPAN

JAPAN

U. S. S. R.

MANCHURIA

KOREA

Mukden

Tungchow

Peking

Tientsin

Yellow River

MONGOLIAN
REPUBLIC

U. S. S. R.

U. S. S. R.

Chungking

Yangtse Kiang

YUNNAN

BURMA

THAILAND

INDO CHINA

Pukow

Nanking

Chinkiang

Shanghai

Whangpoo River

Hangchow

Hankow

Kiangsu

Changsha

FORMOSA

LUZON

HAINAN

Macao

Hong Kong

Canton

KWANGTUNG

KWANGSI

Pearl River

CHINA

Scale of Miles

0   100   200   300

Provincial Boundaries

all set to sail the same day; then our departure was postponed; on February 10th the whole show was off for good; on the 15th we actually sailed for South China in a Dollar Line boat.

Of course she couldn't get up the Pearl River to Canton. We had to transship at Hong Kong and we weren't at all sure of our welcome there; Dr. Sun hadn't always been too friendly with the British. However, in Hong Kong there was an American lawyer called Norman who had been retained by the Kuomintang for some business or other and he had friends in the colony. He got busy on the wireless and the next thing we knew was a formal invitation from Sir Reginald Stubbs for Dr. Sun to stay at Government House and another message to say that Sir Robert Ho Tong, the famous comprador of Jardine Matheson & Co., had arranged for him to address the students of Hong Kong University.

We steamed under the big batteries that command the Lyemun Pass and into that lovely harbor and tied up at Kowloon. Deputations on the wharf welcomed us, and the Governor's big white barge with the A.D.C., all medals and epaulettes and aiguilettes, met us and took us across to Victoria where there were more deputations on the pier. A procession of cars with little flags on their bonnets took us up the hill and swept through the gates of Government House. While Dr. Sun was shaking hands with the Governor, I hopped out with my strong-arm men, who'd been following in the cars behind, and made one of the biggest boobs of my life.

I knew plenty by now about protecting Dr. Sun as a one-man job, but this was the first time I'd had the handling of a whole squad of bodyguards, and perhaps I'd not given sufficient consideration to the problem. Anyway it seemed simple enough to me; there were the Government House gates and they'd got to be guarded, so I posted my men around them, thinking what a fine tough lot they looked, and then went inside after the Doctor.

We'd finished lunch and he was walking up and down the lawn deep in conversation with Sir Reginald when a voice in my ear said, "Colonel Cohen, may I have a word with you?"

I turned around and there was the A.D.C. towering up in the air, straight and stiff. He must have been a full foot taller than I was and in his white uniform and glittering trimmings he made me think of one of those lighthouses you see along the China coast. He saluted me very correctly and went on:

"With regard to your dispositions for Dr. Sun's safety, may I make a suggestion?"

"Why of course, chum, but he's all right; the gates are guarded, aren't they?"

"Well, yes, the front gates are; but of course we have two back gates as well and then there are three wicket gates into the gardens. The main gates are only used by official callers and if anyone comes to assassinate your Chief this afternoon, I don't suppose they'll be wanting to write their names in the Governor's book."

I grabbed him by the sleeve.

"Be a sport and show me what to do!"

He was and he did and we just had those men of mine rearranged when the cars came round to take Dr. Sun and Sir Reginald to the University.

There the Doctor made one of the finest speeches I ever heard. He'd been a student at Queen's College himself and he began by talking about that. Next he told us how he went back to his native village in the Pearl River delta behind Macao and found the village elders made a pretty poor job of running it. He had a look at the district magistrate's administration, which was worse, the Provincial Government in Canton, which was worse still, and then the Imperial Government in Peking, which was the rottenest and most corrupt of all. Then he asked why the British governed Hong Kong so much better than the Chinese ran their own show just across the border and he pulled no punches about that.

He ended up: "We must carry this English example of good government to every part of China." That brought the house down.

Maybe he got carried away a bit by his own eloquence and said more than he really meant, but coming back in the car he remarked:

"Cohen, this visit has been a pleasant surprise. I like the British and I understand them. In the past it is they who have misunderstood me. If we could get together, we could do a lot."

That night at dinner he asked the Governor straight out if he'd be prepared to send half a dozen of his best cadets (i.e. civil servants) to Canton to help him reorganize South China. The scheme never came off; if it had there might have been one more free nation in the world today.

Next morning the cars came round to take us down to the river steamer for Canton. It was all very formal and ceremonious. Dr. Sun said goodbye to the Governor, his senior staff did the same, and then it was my turn. Sir Reginald was a short, square, heavily built man who had been a middleweight boxer in his day; he had a long straight nose and a prim, pursed-up mouth and a real poker face—you never knew what he was thinking. He held my hand a long time and he said:

"Colonel Cohen, I am particularly grateful to you for the dispositions which you made for the safety of Dr. Sun. The fact that you and your men were on the alert removed a great weight of anxiety from my mind."

The A.D.C. was standing behind him and he looked down at me and winked. If the Statue of Liberty in New York harbor had looked down at me and winked, I couldn't have been more surprised and I just winked back—a sort of reflex action—but the Governor never moved a muscle of his face.

We had a good send-off from crowds carrying banners on the Bund and plenty of fire-crackers from the sampan folk in the harbor. Dr. Sun told me they were born in their sampans, lived their whole lives in their sampans, and only came ashore to shop. We steamed through the narrow passage behind Ma Wan Island and under Castle Peak out into the Pearl River estuary and turned north for the Bocca Tigris. The forts there were a lot more imposing than the British ones at Lyemun, but I was to find out later that they weren't much good when it came to gunnery.

Once through the Bocca Tigris we were in a real Chinese river. I've done that Hong Kong-Canton run more times than I can remember, but that first trip I'll never forget. There was every kind of queer craft to be seen—junks with broadsides of sham cannon to frighten off pirates; stern-wheel junks driven by the crew working a kind of treadmill; junks loaded with coffins; flat junks carrying large loads of wood with cabins for the crew contrived inside the cargo; small junks shaped just like bedroom slippers; junks with two huge eyes painted on the bows—most of them had those, and they all had a little thin, decorated sham mast stuck at the top of the mainmast so the devils would break that in mistake and let the junk go free.

On the bank you'd see a big black water-buffalo with horns as long as my arm, and on its back a little nipper with a round pointed hat slung on the back of his neck, steering the great beast with a bit of string threaded through one nostril.

When we came into the last reach leading up to the Bund the excitement began again with swarms of sampans to welcome us, and when we tied up beyond the Custom House the whole place went raving mad. There's just one skyscraper in Canton. It's called the Sun Building. At every window on every story of it there was a Chinese throwing down fire-crackers. It was like a continuous cascade of fire from on high.

We got Dr. Sun through the mob and into his motor boat and made our way over to Honam Island, where his headquarters had been fixed up in the house belonging to the manager of the Cement Works. It was a handsome building, square in plan and three stories high with deep verandas on each floor and on all four sides. Dr. Sun was to live on the top story, the secretaries and personal staff on the second; the ground floor had been laid out as offices. Another similar building close by became barracks for the guard. Everything was very plain and utilitarian, but that was how he liked things to be.

We'd scarcely started to settle in when the visitors began to queue up, and the queue got longer and longer as the days passed. The very first man I admitted was an emissary from General Chen Chiung-ming, come to see if he could make terms. He was a fine old fellow called Dr. Chen Tso-bak. He'd been a good friend of Dr. Sun in the early days of the Revolution. The Doctor received him in the kindliest fashion, but was quite firm.

"General Chen," he said, "must present himself in person and ask my forgiveness."

He knew darned well that he'd never do that; and he knew, too, that, whatever Chen Chiung-ming promised, he'd only doublecross him again as soon as he saw his chance.

Right now I had to start in and learn my job anew. We were no longer in Shanghai where the utmost we had to fear was an attempted assassination, or maybe a kidnap. Canton was full of troops—Yunnanese, Cantonese, and Kwangsi— and a lot of them were unreliable. They'd fought on both sides already and they were as likely as not to switch over again at the spin of a dollar. Even if they didn't change sides, they might stage a mutiny any morning. (I can't altogether blame them; a mutiny usually meant that they'd not been paid for months.) So Dr. Sun's headquarters had to be guarded against a *coup de main* that might be delivered by a whole battalion.

The big trouble was the Doctor himself. He was by far the bravest man I've ever met, yet it wasn't ordinary conscious bravery but rather a complete indifference to his own safety. He just wasn't interested in personal danger.

To make matters worse, he had the old-fashioned Chinese attitude to the military. He hated to have a lot of troops around him. At first all he'd allow at his headquarters were thirty men on guard and another hundred or so in reserve. I got him to agree to the formation of a proper permanent household unit without telling him exactly how strong it was going to be. As soon as we opened recruitment thousands of names rolled in, and it was easy to pick around about six hundred good ones. They were put through a stiff training with plenty of time on the range, so that they really could handle their rifles, and drafted to Honam Island as soon as they'd finished the course. We were darned glad of them later on.

The next headache was looking after Dr. Sun when he drove out around Canton. Most high officials have a whole lot of guards with Mauser pistols standing on the running boards of their cars. They couldn't do much in the way of shooting; they were too busy clinging on for their lives; but their just being there discouraged assassins, and anyway their actual bodies gave some sort of protection to the occupants. Dr. Sun wouldn't have that. On top of everything else he wouldn't even wear uniform, which made him more conspicuous still.

The uniform argument went on and on. Before we left for the front we even asked Mme. Sun to persuade him, but it was no good. Out of doors he wore a *tung shun*, a plain jacket buttoned up to the neck with two breast and two side pockets and he never wore anything else.

Only once, when he was formally appointed Commander-in-Chief of the Southern Forces, did he put on a general's uniform. There were dozens of photographs taken of him on that occasion. A little later, when he was asked to decide on a picture of himself to go on the new banknotes of the Central Bank of China, those were the ones they put on top of the pile. He just passed the whole lot over to Mme. Sun saying, "Choose which you like, my dear, so long as I'm NOT in uniform."

Most of 1923 was spent in the field. As soon as Chen Chiung-ming realized that there was no hope of coming to terms, he attacked and at first we had a pretty bad time. He was a good soldier and had some good troops, and his headquarters, at Waiyeung on the East River, not much over sixty miles from Canton, were a lot too close to be pleasant.

That was the first time I ever saw the Doctor in action. One morning the office was in a proper panic. I asked what the matter was and they told me:

"Very bad news from the East River front; our troops are in full retreat."

"Yes, but just how bad is it? Where's our front line now? Anyway, what does the general say?"

"That's the trouble; we can't contact him."

"You can't contact him? Can't you reach his headquarters? Are the wires cut? Isn't the field radio working?"

They all began to look embarrassed and I realized what had happened. It wasn't the first time I'd heard of a Chinese general deserting his troops when things were going badly. I tried another tack.

"What does Dr. Sun say?"

There was another silence and more long faces and sideways looks. I saw that no one wanted to tell him the bad news. Something had to be done quick, so I knocked on his door, marched in, stood to attention and blurted out, "Sir, the East River Army's retreating and the general's run away."

Mme. Sun was sitting with him—which was unusual in his office hours—and they seemed a typical, quiet, middle-aged Chinese couple, as peaceful and placid as you could imagine. She looked quickly at him and you could see she was worried, but he didn't bat an eyelid.

"My dear," he said, "I think I'll visit the front for a few days. I'll take my 'Three Musketeers' and they'll look after me."

He thought a minute and turned to me:

"Colonel Cohen, you and Colonel Mah Sang and Colonel Wong Wei-lung will accompany me, and one secretary only. We'll leave by train at once. Find out where our railhead is now and arrange for a car to meet us there."

I passed out the orders and went off to change. The uppermost thought in my mind was that I was taking my Chinese colonel's uniform into action for the first time. The last time I'd been under fire I was a Canadian sapper corporal.

We hadn't got very far when we stopped in a little station somewhere near Sheklung. Mah Sang went off to find out what was wrong. While he was gone, in steamed another train coming the other way and it pulled up too. It was full of Chinese officers and we guessed at once who'd be amongst them. We were walking up and down the platform behind Dr. Sun. He didn't say a word; he just crossed the line by the foot-bridge, walked up to the train and asked, "May I speak to the officer in charge?"

He knew very well that it was the missing general. Presently they produced him. The poor devil was shaking in his shoes. He half expected to be shot on the spot—that often happens in civil wars in China—and anyway he thought he'd get a public slanging in front of his staff and lose so much "face" that his military career would be finished.

He saluted, and the Doctor touched his toupee and pointed up the line with his walking stick.

"There's some mistake, General," he said, "the enemy are in THAT direction."

The general's train pulled out of the station the same way it had pulled in, with the general on board and our train followed. That's how we reached the front.

After that, most of my time was spent arguing with the Doctor about keeping under cover, which was something he would not do. He wandered about talking to the troops in the front line—as far as there was any front line—and asking them what they were fighting for? As if they knew! And it was then, when he discovered that most of them had no idea what the score was—or any ideas at all beyond getting their next bowl of rice—that he first thought of a real systematic political indoctrination of the whole army.

Why he wasn't killed, I don't know. Luckily the other side hadn't much in the way of artillery—mostly machine guns, rifles, hand grenades, and maybe a few trench mortars. With the rifles they couldn't shoot straight enough to matter, and with the hand grenades they as often as not blew themselves up; but for the machine guns and trench mortars we had to watch out.

It was a machine gun that pipped me the very day after we got to the front. The Doctor was talking to some troops and I didn't like the way they were all bunched together on the skyline and was trying to pull him down under cover of the slope. There was a sudden burst of long-range machine-gun fire, and there was I hopping about holding my left arm and cursing as I hadn't cursed for years.

Luckily for me there was a surgeon handy. (You don't see many surgeons with a Chinese army.)

"I have a medical degree," he said, "from the University of Edinburgh and that is only a flesh wound."

What I said would have surprised him if he'd understood it properly. However, he wasn't a bad egg. He laid me on the ground and probed around and found the bullet. It must have been a very long-range one and nearly spent. He took it out and that made me curse some more, because they'd not got around to any anaesthetics in his little field hospital. When he'd bandaged me up I didn't feel too bad and wouldn't let them send me down.

In one way it was a lucky break. Dr. Sun was terribly concerned at having—as he put it—"exposed the staff to unnecessary risks," and after that took a bit more care of himself.

The next time he went to the front, he left me behind. I felt bad about it, but he was quite firm.

"I must have someone in Canton," he said, "to look after my wife and that man's got to be able to make a quick decision if it comes to taking flight and getting her right away to somewhere safe."

That was that. I just saluted and said, "Very good, sir"; and off he went with Mah Sang and Wong Wei-lung and General Chiang Kai-shek, who was his Chief of Staff by this time.

Mme. Sun saw that my feelings were hurt. That evening she sent for me and flattered me nicely, saying how safe she felt now that I was looking after her. She told me, too, what it had been like for her when, barely a year before, they had had to make their escape to Hong Kong in a British gunboat.

"It all blew up overnight," she said. "I went to bed as usual. We knew that things were going badly and that Chen Chiung-ming was wavering, but he seemed to be a safe distance from Canton and there was nothing much to worry about. At two o'clock in the morning Dr. Sun was standing by my bed fully dressed and shaking my shoulder.

" 'Chen's men have seized the city; I'm going on board our flagship to organize resistance; get dressed and come with me.'

" 'No, I'd only be a hindrance to you and I'll be safe enough here.'

"So he went away leaving about fifty soldiers around the house and within half an hour I heard rifle shots and that horrible cry, 'Kill Sun Wen! Kill Sun Wen!'

"Our boys fought well, but they were badly outnumbered and Chen's troops brought up field guns to shell the house. By eight o'clock our ammunition began to give out. Colonel Bow told the guard to hold out for another ten minutes so as to give us a chance to escape and then stop shooting and ask for terms.

"Four of us—Colonel Bow, Mah Sang, one soldier, and myself—tried to get over the little bridge across the canal behind the house, but that was under heavy fire. After lying there for what seemed hours we gave it up and returned to our garden. The firing had stopped while they were discussing terms of surrender and nobody was in a hurry to get matters settled, so we might have been all right, but at four in the afternoon General Wei Pang-ping, who had been sitting on the fence up to that moment, came down on Chen Chiung-ming's side and sent his Chief of Staff to take charge.

"Colonel Bow asked for a guarantee of my safety, but

they refused it, giving as an excuse that their troops were out of hand and they could make no promises of any kind. Of course what they wanted was to hold me as a hostage.

"So I took Colonel Bow's cap and Dr. Sun's raincoat and Mah Sang put on coolie clothes and we slipped away unnoticed to a cottage belonging to the family of my old amah. There they fixed us up with proper disguises, Mah Sang as a peddler and myself as an old peasant woman, and we got across the Honam bridge to a friend who lived not far from the Shameen. His house had been searched already and so we were safe for the night.

"The next day our flotilla bombarded the city and under cover of the panic they caused we managed to join Dr. Sun on board his flagship; but Canton was lost and the Bocca Tigris forts blocked the river and in the end we went down to Hong Kong in H.M.S. *Moorhen*."

Mme. Sun's tale gave me plenty to think about, especially the suddenness of it all, and I made up my mind not to be caught napping. I saw that the guards were properly mounted, knew their orders, carried fifty rounds apiece, and stayed awake *all* night and not only till they saw the light in my room go out.

It was just as well that I kept my wits about me. Some days later a couple of hundred wounded soldiers appeared at our gates and the guards let them into the compound before I could get there. They'd been quite right to do that; deputations from this, that, and the other were always turning up and Dr. Sun always saw them, whoever they were. In fact the humbler and more bedraggled and down-and-out they seemed, the more time he'd give them. So that was nothing out of the ordinary.

Still I wasn't happy and, while the clerks went to look for some suitable official to hear their troubles, I strolled amongst them with my eyes skinned. I couldn't see much to be suspicious about till the second-in-command of our guard—a smart boy that I'd picked out and promoted myself—edged up alongside me and whispered, "Colonel, these men are not wounded. Look closely and you'll see that those bloodstained bandages are fakes!"

I couldn't line up the whole lot and hold an inspection, so I took a chance. There was one fellow from whom the rest were obviously taking their line, a big scraggy guy with a pock-marked face and his right arm in a sling. I walked up to him with a friendly smile, took hold of his sling and jerked it over his head.

Out came a perfectly good fist and made contact with my poor, battered old nose. Out came my guns; he took the butt of one on the side of his head and down he went for the count.

That was the end of it. I let off a few rounds into the air and the guards came running and surrounded the whole mob. We picked on five or six who looked like the ringleaders, put them in the guard-room and booted the rest out of the compound.

Then came the third-degreeing. That's a part I always hate, so I went off to my room where I couldn't hear it going on and waited for the results. They were garrison troops who said they'd not been paid for months—and I don't suppose they had. So they'd collected a score of genuine wounded, put them in front and all the rest of the mob had faked their wounds and crowded in behind them. They'd meant to raid the Treasury and collect their pay for themselves!

It was a silly sort of show all through. In one way it affected the rest of my life—it was the first time I ever actually used a gun in each hand. The bullet that caught me in the left arm had made me think. Supposing it had been my right arm and I carried my gun that side, I'd not have been able to use it. As soon as we got back to Canton I got me a second gun, another Smith and Wesson revolver, and I packed it handy in my left hand. I practiced drawing and soon found that I was pretty well ambidextrous—one gun came out about as quick as the other.

So when this guy socked me, I pulled both my guns and fired them—not aimed shots, mind you. Now Hu Han-min, who was Dr. Sun's righthand man at that time, was watching the schemozzle from his office window. He was delighted at the way my two pistols appeared. When Dr. Sun came back he told him about it and so the tale got around. Soon afterwards I wanted to slip down to Hong Kong for a couple of nights, and there I, of course, had to have a firearms license. You know what officials are like all the world over. I got a polite note reminding me that I needed licenses for both my guns, so I took two licenses out. After that it was a matter of public record for any cub reporter who wanted a story. "Two-Gun" Cohen I became and the name's stuck ever since.

The next episode was more serious—nothing less than a full-scale attempt to capture Headquarters by some groups of guerrillas that Chen Chiung-ming had organized behind our lines. It was an original plan, too.

One evening I was strolling on the river banks, scratching my prickly-heat patches and thanking heaven for the cool dusk. This was my first tropical summer; I was a big fat fellow, heavy-eating and heavy-sweating, and it hit me hard. Presently I saw that three large junks had pulled out of the main flow of river traffic, lowered their big lateen mainsails, manned their sweeps, and were pulling in to our jetty. There was nothing very strange in that except that there were three of them and we weren't expecting any supplies that I knew of.

I turned and strolled towards the jetty myself, more out

of sheer curiosity than anything else. Then I noticed that faces kept on bobbing up over the gunwales, taking a dekko around and bobbing down again. Now that was queer, because there shouldn't have been more than half a dozen men in the crew and maybe a few coolies to help unload; and anyway those junk crews are about the most incurious people in the world and couldn't care less where they're going as long as they get their rice and their pay.

Suddenly I realized that something was wrong and ran towards our guard-house blowing my whistle. Just as the first junk came alongside and armed men began to jump ashore, my boys lined the compound wall and opened fire.

It was pretty hot for five minutes, but our lads had done their training on the range and it paid dividends that day. Besides, they were shooting from behind cover and knew they were on top from the first. Soon the junks ceased fire and tried to cast off again, but our lads charged down and rounded up the lot. This time there was no question of kicking them out. There was one mass drumhead court-martial, followed by a nasty messy business on the execution ground outside the city walls.

Still, I was pleased with myself. I felt I'd come a long way since that big blob at Government House in Hong Kong. From now on I'd the confidence to tackle any sort of assignment. When Dr. Sun got back from the front he evidently felt the same. Anyway, he took me with him on his next trip, and this time I really did save his life.

One of our troubles throughout 1923 was that we were fighting on two fronts. To the east there was Chen Chiung-ming with his headquarters at Waiyeung and directly threatening Canton itself, but away to the north astride the unfinished Canton-Hankow railway was a composite force led by various Northern generals which occasionally pushed south towards Shiukwan and had to be watched all the time. If they and Chen Chiung-ming had synchronized their attacks, we'd have been driven out of South China, but fortunately they mistrusted each other far too much for that.

This time Dr. Sun was visiting the Northern front and he took with him a larger staff than was usual. The train was made up of three coaches, the first carrying guards, the second staff officers, and the third the Doctor and his personal retinue. We all travelled in the same carriage, an old-fashioned one with the passage down the center. Dr. Sun and General Chiang Kai-shek sat side by side facing the engine, myself opposite them, while Mah Sang and Wong Wei-lung were across the aisle.

Presently the train pulled up at a little wayside station. It was a boiling hot day and I'd been dozing, but I half woke up—the way one does when a train stops—and looked out of the windows. There was nothing to see. On the platform side, a dozen scruffy lines-of-communication troops standing at what they thought was "attention" and looking as if they might fall down if anyone pushed them. On the other, a sea of emerald-green paddy stretching away to a four-square, gray-walled town with one white pawnbroker's tower standing up in the middle.

I was just pulling my head in again when I happened to look down at the track—and straight into the eyes of two characters who were crawling out from under the train itself.

For a split second I didn't react. Then they scrambled to their feet and I saw that they each held a heavy Mauser pistol.

"Duck down, sir!" I yelled at Dr. Sun, and pulled my guns and let fly.

We got action and plenty. Mah Sang and Wong Wei-lung jumped across the carriage and blazed away over my head—and too damn close to my ear, I was deaf for days afterwards. The railway troops woke up and jumped down off the platform, our guards piled out of their carriage next to the engine and the thugs were rounded up in no time.

There were four of them, all armed with Mausers and two with handy little bombs as well. We took them on with us to Shiukwan where they were "interrogated"—and the whole plot came out. This was no amateur attempt by locals. All four were professional killers hired for the job by a Northern general, properly trained, armed, and briefed, given good photographs of Dr. Sun so there'd be no mistakes, and promised payment strictly by results.

It was well planned and it ought to have succeeded. They could hardly miss with their pistols at point-blank range and, if they did, they could just pop their bombs through the carriage window. I doubt if the Doctor was ever in greater danger—not even that time he was held prisoner in the Imperial Chinese Embassy in London.

Mme. Sun thought so too. When we got back, she produced a Chinese-style apple pie, which she knew was Mah Sang's favorite dish, and she put it on the table in front of him.

"I cooked that myself," she said, "and now I want to hear what Morris really did. My husband's told me part of the tale, but he's too busy right now to worry for all the details and I know I'll never get them from Morris. So here's this pie and Colonel Mah Sang won't get a bite of it till he's told me the whole story."

As the summer went on the military situation grew worse and worse. Chen Chiung-ming had been building up his strength for a long time; now he staged another offensive and put in everything he had. He took Sheklung, he took

Suntang and came on around the north of the Pearl River delta right up to the city walls. And I mean the city walls; our men were lining the parapet (where it existed) and firing down into the paddy fields. They had lost heart too. Only the Yunnanese divisions were really reliable. They were strangers from up-country—you might even call them mercenaries—speaking a different dialect and so were less affected by local feeling. Things could hardly have looked blacker.

At dawn Chen's troops attacked the Five Storied Pagoda, which stood on a bastion where the city walls ran up to the brow of a hill. If they could break through there, Canton was in their hands. The Staff was frankly panicky. As usual when there was bad news to be broken to the Doctor, I was the one who had to do it. So I walked into his room.

"Dr. Sun, sir. The attack's begun and if they take the Pagoda, we'll have to move quick. Could you tell me, please, which of your valuables you'll take with you?"

He was bending over a map, but he looked up and studied my face for a moment.

"All I have of value here, Morris my friend, are a few books, but don't bother about them just now."

He went back to his map again and, without taking his eyes off it, said, "I must go now; order my car."

When he came out of the front door, there was his car and there were most of the Headquarters Staff waiting to see him leave and to take that as a signal for them to get out while the going was good. He climbed in, sat back and turned to me: "Morris, tell the driver to take us—to the Five Storied Pagoda!" I wish you could have seen their faces.

We were met by Yung Heh-ming, the Yunnanese general and a pretty tough nut, who was just as calm as the

Doctor. He said the position was a bit tricky and he was expecting another attack any minute, but he thought he could hold them and—what was more—he had one fresh battalion in hand for a counter-attack.

While they were talking the attack began. It was a noisy affair like all Chinese attacks—drums, bugles, and lots of yelling—but they came on in earnest and their covering fire was knocking chips off the Pagoda. I begged the Doctor to take cover but he wouldn't budge.

Our shooting was awful. I grabbed a tommy gun from one of the guards and pumped away myself. They came right up the slope of the hill and it looked as if nothing could stop them. Then Yung Heh-ming put in his counter-attack, the whole battalion at once through a breach in the walls just beneath the Pagoda. They rushed right past us and I had to stop firing for fear of hitting our own boys.

But the enemy had had enough. They weren't expecting a counter-attack, especially when it had looked like being a walk-over, and down the hill they ran with our lads yelling after them.

That one charge changed the whole course of the campaign. Chen Chiung-ming had shot his bolt. He stayed a little longer looking at our walls, but he never attacked again. A week later he started to withdraw the way he'd come. Dr. Sun sent for General Yung and thanked him publicly at a formal ceremony with the whole of Headquarters Staff drawn up to hear what he said.

As we walked off the parade ground, he beckoned me to follow him.

"Morris, we had a narrow squeak last week."

"Yes, sir."

"Now, General Chen's cleared off, but we don't know if he's on his way back to Waiyeung or just building up for another advance."

"No, sir."

"What we need are some airplanes to watch the fellow."

"Yes, sir."

"But the Western Powers have laid this embargo on the supply of arms to China."

"Yes, sir."

"So we'll have to build them here. I'm sending you to Canada to recruit the personnel and buy the materials. Ring up Hong Kong and book your passage."

This was my first independent mission for Dr. Sun and I was determined to make it a success, but it began badly enough. My one clue in Canada was an airman called Wop May, or something of the sort—an ace of the 1914-1918 war. I hadn't even got his name right for certain, but I ran him to earth in time. He was willing and anxious to work for the Cantonese Government, but it turned out that he needed a passport and, for China, an exit visa.

We applied for the passport, and a few days later I found a familiar uniform in the hotel lobby—the Royal Canadian Mounted Police had called to make "a few routine inquiries." A fat lot they needed to "inquire" about. They had my record in Winnipeg, they had my record in Saskatoon, they had my record in Edmonton, they had all the details of my war service, and when it came to China they knew more about me than I knew myself.

They greeted me as an old friend and a distinguished citizen. They took me to the bar and gave me a drink—and then they gave me the works. As far as they were concerned, the embargo on war materials for China applied to fighting men as well; there'd be no passport for my friend if he was sailing east, and what about me trying my luck south of the border?

I can take a hint as well as the next man and so south I went and started from scratch all over again. In San Francisco I struck a man called Abbott, one of those guys who are air-crazy and would sooner starve flying than prosper in any other line of business. He was a parachute expert as well and had been earning a hard livelihood barnstorming around the fair grounds with one rickety machine, giving displays of aerobatics and parachute drops. He just jumped at the idea of a regular job, and in turn he picked up for me an aircraft designer and a couple of aeronautical engineers. I triumphantly took all four of them back to Canton.

There they set to work and turned out a little two-seater job we christened *Rosamonde* after Mme. Sun, that being the name by which she went at College. It was a good little ship and, in the final campaign against Chen Chiung-ming, it did some useful reconnaissance work for our troops.

Presently we picked up some more pilots, and one day Abbott gave an exhibition of parachute jumping. Now there was a young joiner called Ah Sin who had helped to build the wings and fuselage of the *Rosamonde* and he was just another one like Abbott. He was descended from generations and generations of Cantonese carpenters and yet flying was in his blood. The first time he saw inside the cockpit of the completed craft, he knelt down and did a kow-tow the same as he'd have done before the ancestral tablets in his home.

When Abbott made his first jump, Ah Sin thought it just about the most wonderful thing he had ever seen and he stood there in a sort of dream, with his mouth open, his eyes shining, and his whole body twitching with excitement. (Never you believe that a Chinese can't show emotion —when he really feels something.)

I was standing near him and said:

"Ah Sin, you likee make jump all same Abbott?"

He grabbed my sleeve.

"Yes, master—please!"

I regretted my little joke, but there was nothing to do now but go through with it. Abbott put the parachute on Ah Sin and explained how he was to get himself out of the cockpit, slip over the side, count three, and then pull the ripcord. He piloted the plane himself and we watched, though not one of us believed that Ah Sin would actually jump when the moment came.

But jump he did—you could have heard the crowd gasp when they saw it—pulled the cord all right, and drifted down to make a perfect landing. The only trouble was that the aviation ground lay alongside the main night-soil depot of the city; the wind drifted him over and he landed plump on a great pile of human manure.

Later on Ah Sin became a fighter pilot and, in the big scrap at Lokchong in 1938, he helped to account for three Japanese medium bombers.

CHAPTER VI

"Save China!"

ONE BIG CHANGE I found on my return and that was that the Russians had moved in. It hadn't really happened so very suddenly; it only seemed sudden to me. One of the visitors I'd been accustomed to admitting into the Doctor's room in Shanghai had been Adolf Abraham Joffe, the Soviet Envoy who was then dickering with the Peking Government about Outer Mongolia. I knew before I left for Canada that General Chiang Kai-shek, who had gone to Moscow, was sending back enthusiastic reports about all he saw there. But I was new to the high political game in those days and hadn't noticed the build-up.

Things really began to move when Michael Borodin arrived in Canton. What a man! Born in Russia but educated in the States, he was still quite young and yet he had done "party work" in Mexico, Scotland, and Turkey and had already acquired two aliases—Berg and Grusenberg. He had great personal charm and at first the Cantonese leaders liked him. Later on they respected him and later still they were scared stiff of him, but by that time he'd got himself appointed official "adviser" to the Kuomintang. On top of everything else he'd secured the admittance of the Chinese Communists to full party membership. When it comes to political intrigue, you've got to hand it to the Russians; they're clever, they're disciplined, and they never stop working.

I've often heard Dr. Sun criticized for calling in the

Russians, but, after all, he was fighting for the future of China and he had to have help from somewhere. His entente with the Governor of Hong Kong had looked promising at first, but negotiations were held up all along the line; I've been told that it was Lord Curzon himself who vetoed them. The Western Powers had clamped down their Arms Embargo and washed their hands of Chinese internal affairs. That left Germany, who had scarcely begun to recover from the war; Japan, who always made impossible demands in return for any help she promised—and Russia. Russia was the best bet out of a bad field and I still think that Dr. Sun was right.

From the military angle there were two results, one immediate and one long-term. Chiang Kai-shek brought back with him from Moscow a soldier who went under the name of Galin but who, we all knew, was the famous General Blücher. He took charge.

Up till then our rifles had been made by a local arsenal at a cost of one hundred and twenty-five Mexican dollars apiece [for a long time the most widely accepted currency in China]—and they didn't shoot too well either. Galin brought rifles from Russian factories (via Vladivostok and the Trans-Siberian Railway) and sold them to Dr. Sun at sixty-five dollars each, and a much better weapon into the bargain. He brought in Russian instructors to teach our troops how to use their new rifles, and it went without saying that they were all good Communist Party members. Finally, the money we paid for the rifles didn't go back to Russia; it stayed right there in Canton, in the coffers of the Chinese Communist party, earmarked for propaganda purposes.

Our field forces were improved out of all knowledge; the troops were better fed, better armed, better organized, and better led. Within a few months Chen Chiung-ming had been chased back to Waiyeung and, though he managed to hang on there, he ceased to be an active menace; in fact, we almost forgot about him.

What was of even greater importance in the long run was the foundation of the Whampoa Military Academy, with Chiang Kai-shek as president and a corps of Russian instructors led by Galin himself. They took on five hundred young cadets, put them through it properly, beginning with the goosestep, and turned them out as real regimental officers. They also gave them an intensive course of political indoctrination on Kuomintang lines and maybe a bit of Communism as well.

Now, there's one thing I've learned in all these Chinese wars, and that is that troops only fight well when they've had some political indoctrination. It doesn't much matter whether their cause is right or wrong (anyway, who knows which is which?) so long as they believe in it. If they've really got the idea into their heads that they've something worth fighting for and the enemy haven't, then there's no limit to what they can do.

Of course results took some time to show; but these young men with some sound military training and a burning belief in their cause gradually percolated through the Kwangtung Army, down into the small formations and up into the large ones, and presently things began to happen. I'll give you an example.

One of the standard exercises at the Academy was called the "Storming Party." The cadets were lined up in teams of six or seven, each carrying a light scaling-ladder, about a hundred and fifty yards from the old city walls. The instructor gave the "Go!" and they ran forward with the ladders and planted them against the wall. Then over the top they went and the first men up held out their thumbs—just our own old "Thumbs up!" sign.

A little later we did actually take Waiyeung and settled up with Chen Chiung-ming for good and all. The walls were intact, we had practically no artillery, and the town had to be stormed. Some fresh troops were brought in that were trained and officered all through by Whampoa cadets. They were launched on a direct assault. They marched out with their scaling-ladders, rifles, and home-made Mills bombs, and deployed as if they were on parade. Then they ran in, threw up their ladders, and, believe it or not, the first man up each ladder turned as he sat astride the parapet and stuck up his thumb just as he'd been taught to do at the Academy.

The casualties were heavy, but Waiyeung fell and the following year when Chiang led his armies against the North, it was just Waiyeung over and over again. But all that was in the future. For the moment, the first thing the Russians succeeded in doing was to embroil Dr. Sun with the foreign powers over the Canton Customs Surplus.

To the inhabitants of Canton, the "Customs Crisis of 1923," as the Far Eastern press subsequently described it, appeared in various guises. For the general public, whether Chinese or foreigners, it all just happened. One day every sheet in the city carried banner headlines, and the river filled up with foreign warships—British sloops, French gunboats, American and Japanese destroyers, a tiny Italian torpedo-boat, and even a Portuguese man-of-war from Macao. Marines landed and drilled on the Anglo-French Concession, called the Shameen; they put up barbed wire and sandbag defenses on the landward side and of course demoralized the children by giving them more copper cash than they would have expected to find in the whole of China.

The visitors settled down to make the best of it. The officers went snipe-shooting and the sailors played football. The Canton Club and the Victoria Hotel did such business as they had never known before—especially the bars. The Americans gave a dance and the British a children's Christmas party, and the Scots of both countries held a sinister ceremony on New Year's Eve which involved drinking stuff that tasted like a mixture of whisky and honey, and eating minced sheep's guts.

Presently a few adventurous naval wives arrived in pursuit of their husbands and, as invariably happens when naval wives appear on the scene, the ships of their spouses promptly went elsewhere. One by one they unmoored and vanished down the river to Hong Kong, Saigon, Manila, Formosa, Macao, or Shanghai.

Children, both Chinese and European, found themselves deplorably short of pocket-money. Bar-tenders could rest their feet, and the snipe could rest their wings. Club secretaries and hotel managers hastened to replenish their stocks. The newspapers found other topics to pursue and life returned to normal.

From the point of view of consuls, customs officials, heads of European firms, gunboat captains, and other unfortunates who were forced to study the subject, this particular "Crisis" was merely another episode in a dispute that had begun with the fall of the Dragon Throne and was only to end—by *force majeure*—some eighteen years later with the Japanese Occupation.

The Imperial Maritime Customs, founded half a century before and developed by the genius of an Irishman, Sir Robert Hart, was the only dependable security possessed by China for the negotiation of foreign loans. Manned by Europeans of many nationalities, but with the British heavily predominating, it effectively controlled the coasts and navigable rivers of the whole of China, maintained buoys, lighthouses, and up-to-date charts (the full functions, in fact, of Trinity House), and returned to the Central Government in Peking an annual revenue sufficient not only to meet the interest on their external loans but also to provide a surplus.

This worked admirably so long as the writ of this government ran throughout the country, but, since the Revolution of 1911, this had seldom been the case. Insurgent or semi-independent provinces naturally objected to seeing their most reliable source of revenue paid over to a power with whom they were—or might any moment be—at open war; and by negotiation or by threat of force they attempted to seize these revenues for themselves. In this prolonged and ever-recurring controversy the Crisis of 1923 is peculiar only because, for reasons which seemed totally obscure at the time, it developed so suddenly and in so extraordinarily menacing a manner.

To Morris and his friends, however, these reasons were perfectly apparent. For the first time, the Comintern was making its influence felt in the Far East, and Dr. Sun's straightforward attempt to obtain funds for carrying on his campaigns was being bedevilled by envoys, open or secret, of the U.S.S.R.

THAT WAS THE FIRST TIME—he said—I saw Russian Communists in action and, believe me, I learned a lot. We had started out on some straightforward oriental bargaining, or so we thought. On our side there was a perfectly sound common-sense claim to the cash—at any rate to some of it. On the other, the Western Powers had their treaties and agreements and protocols and so on.

The argument begun, Eugene Chen fired off notes and manifestoes, our papers produced editorials, we gave the green light to a little mild agitation against the "unequal treaties," and everything went according to plan. Then one fine day we woke up to find that we were committed to seizing the Customs House by force, which would have meant certainly a blockade and quite probably a war with the West. Borodin was up to mischief, and all this was a gift to him.

I had my own little surprise, too, when the Doctor sent for me in his office.

"I've been studying the original Maritime Customs Agreements and I see that the post of Commissioner in Canton can only be held by a Foreigner."

"Yes, sir."

"So if we seize the Customs I've got you down for the post. Will you take it?"

He didn't want an immediate reply but asked me to think the matter over. It wasn't easy for me to raise any objections, because, besides being my boss and the father of his country, he was by far the strongest personality I've ever met. He was always kind and gentle and scrupulously polite, and yet his colleagues and subordinates often shirked their plain duty of putting their own points of view to him, simply because they hadn't the moral courage to do so. But I blurted out:

"No, sir. I'm not the right man for that job."

He looked at me—not angrily but just a bit surprised.

I pointed out my lack of qualifications—my ignorance of the Chinese Customs Service, and so on. The obvious man for the job, I suggested, was Dr. Norman, the American who was Dr. Sun's legal adviser, a man of great experience in many directions.

He appeared to be convinced by my arguments, and there the matter rested.

I went off from that interview and drove down to the Shameen on some business or other. At tiffin time I wandered into the Victoria Hotel and found the bar full of American naval officers drinking highballs. They were all very bored, most of them wondering what the hell they were doing in Canton. I tried to explain the position and to put the Chinese side of the case. Presently one of them said:

"Say, why don't we meet your Sun Yat-sen and settle the matter between us?"

"Why not?" I went to the telephone and rang up Headquarters. Sure enough, the Doctor was willing, and so the following day I picked them up on the Bund, all in their best clothes, piled them into a couple of cars, and drove them out to the Cement Works.

Dr. Sun treated them as he treated any other callers, high or low. He put his side of the question fully and fairly just as if they had been envoys and ambassadors. He never "talked down" to anybody. When they left one of them said:

"Doctor, I'm right glad we know where you live. If we have to bombard Canton City, we'll take care nothing comes in your direction."

"Gentlemen," said the Doctor with his eyes twinkling, "I must remind you that it is your duty to obey orders, however contrary they may be to your personal feelings."

Then he became serious and went on.

"I realize that this little province can never win by force of arms against your mighty fleets, but whatever happens I believe that right is on my side and that the verdict of history will one day acknowledge this."

Luckily it never came to a show-down. There were level heads on both sides. On ours Wu Teh-chen was always a moderating influence, and on the other there was Dr. Schurman, the American Ambassador, who turned up in Canton a little later. He called right away on Dr. Sun and extracted a promise from him to take no precipitate action till he (Schurman) had had a chance to bring his case before the diplomatic body in Peking, who had hitherto only heard the Peking Government's point of view. He left for the North again at once and wired back:

WOULD YOU AGREE SOUTHERN SHARE CUSTOMS
SURPLUS RIVER CONSERVANCY WORK?

I was there when the telegram was laid on Dr. Sun's desk. He chuckled and dictated his reply on the spot:

YES, PROVIDED NORTHERN SHARE CUSTOMS SUR-
PLUS DEVOTED SIMILAR RECONSTRUCTIONAL WORK.

He pushed the papers on one side and went on to some other question, but from that moment he abandoned any idea of seizing the Customs by force (if indeed he'd ever seriously thought of it). He'd made his point clear that he wasn't going to have Kwangtung revenue used to finance an expedition by the Northerners against Kwangtung itself and he was content. The controversy went into slow gear and dragged on and on; in fact, it still wasn't settled at the time of his death.

Borodin and his pals had lost out that time, but they didn't lose heart. They had another card up their sleeve; they simply set to work to jockey Dr. Sun into undertaking another expedition against the North. It wasn't very difficult. Having overthrown the Manchus and founded the Chinese Republic, he cherished as the dearest wish of his heart the desire to see China united under one government. Within three years of his death that was actually achieved by Chiang Kai-shek. But at this time, in 1924, we hadn't a chance. The Northern War Lords disposed of enormous armies and armaments; they had arsenals all over Manchuria and agents everywhere buying arms for them as well. Whereas Dr. Sun controlled the forces of one province and had a rather sketchy alliance with two others; and you've some idea from my story what our weapons were like in those days.

His army was already improving under the direction of Galin, and the first Whampoa-trained cadets were just coming into service. As long as his troops were kept concentrated in the South, they could deal with his local enemies, but the moment they'd been committed to a campaign elsewhere, we'd have had Chen Chiung-ming up to his old games—and the Doctor in exile again, too.

That was just what Borodin and his boys wanted. They knew that Dr. Sun was too honest a man and too great a man to be their stooge. They wanted him out of the way. They plugged the idea of a Northern Expedition *now*, and they very nearly succeeded. I'm no scholar and I picked up most of my history from the newspapers, but one thing I do know to be true and that is that "History repeats itself." Borodin in 1924 was playing just the same game as Joe Stalin in 1942 and 1943, with his "Second Front *now*" agitation, and with just the same object—chaos and a Communist dictatorship.

Anyway, the first result of their plots was that I was sent off on my second mission for the Doctor—and a tricky one it was. A general in Peking was secretly collaborating with him and had promised to change sides at the right moment and bring his troops over as well. Obviously, timing was of the first importance, so he had to know Dr. Sun's detailed plans, and equally, if these plans got into the hands of the Peking Government, it would be disastrous.

The papers couldn't be entrusted to an ordinary courier who might lose his nerve—or lose the package itself. Furthermore, they couldn't be carried by any of his known adherents because that might give the whole game away. So in the end it was put on my plate.

Although I wasn't so well known in those days, I had to be careful. I looked around for some suitable cover for my trip and decided that I'd better be an arms dealer. I'd never actually "sold sewing-machines in China," but I was just the sort of guy who might be in that business, and my recent mission to America fitted nicely into the picture. Dr. Sun knew, too, that the general whom I had to contact was in the market for foreign-manufactured small arms.

I sat around the Victoria Hotel, where the arms dealers used to congregate, till I picked up a salesman who knew Peking well. He gave me the name of a man there who worked for a German firm and was said to be pretty smart. Down the river I went to Hong Kong, up the coast to Shanghai, and up the Tientsin-Pukow Railway to Peking. What a city! Somehow it makes all the dirt and squalor and misery of the rest of China seem worth while—just to have produced over the centuries those lakes and gardens and temples and palaces.

I hadn't much time for sight-seeing. I telephoned the German, took a rickshaw to his hotel, and came straight to the point—at least to what he thought was the point—of my visit.

"I've fifty machine guns, five thousand rifles, and a million rounds of ammo for sale. Delivery in one month."

"What's the price?"

I hedged and haggled a bit about this for form's sake, but deliberately put it as low as I dared. I wanted him to be interested.

"What's there in it for me?"

"Fifteen per cent—if you find me a buyer."

"Terms of payment?"

"Fifty per cent on delivery and the rest—oh, easy, say, spread over two years. But there's just one thing: I like to form my own judgment of a customer's character and I must see him myself first."

The German called on me late the same evening and said he'd made an appointment for both of us at eleven the next day. He gave me the name of the prospective purchaser. Sure enough, it was Dr. Sun's general.

When I dressed that morning I put the papers in my right-hand breast pocket—where I sometimes carried my second gun. They were in a long narrow envelope with the names of both Dr. Sun and the general on the outside, so it was a sufficiently compromising packet even without being opened. The German picked me up in a car and we drove to the general's Yamen. His A.D.C. looked us over—just as I did with Dr. Sun's callers in Canton—and ushered us into a big conference room where the general was sitting alone at the head of a long table.

I sat down on his right and the German on his left so that we were directly facing each other. I was introduced, and the general—he was a cheerful, chubby little fellow—chatted a bit with my friend, in German. That didn't worry me at first, but when I ventured a remark in English, the German translated it into his own tongue, and I realized to my horror that that was the only European language the general spoke!

This was a bit of a poser. I knew no Mandarin—nor much Cantonese, for that matter. How on earth was I going to get the idea across to the general that I wanted to see him alone?

They argued and bargained away, with the German turning to me every now and then and politely explaining what was being said, while I racked my brains to think of some way out of the jam. Then my chance came. The general started on a lengthy harangue about something or other and the German half turned in his chair to look directly at him, which meant that he was no longer gazing straight at me.

I quickly unbuttoned my coat and pulled up the envelope so that one corner stuck out. The general didn't seem to notice anything, so I put my finger to my lips and gave him a knowing look. At least I thought it was a knowing look; the general told me afterwards that he thought I'd just gone crazy. I looked down at the packet sticking out of my breast pocket, and at that the general, thoroughly mystified, stopped talking and stared. The German turned and looked at me, too. I managed to hide the envelope just in time.

The general had realized that I was up to some funny business and that, mad though I might be, he had better see me alone. He said something to the German, who got up and left the room; then he turned to me, held out his hand, and said:

"Dein nummer is Mah Kun?"

I was so surprised I nearly fell off my chair, but I grinned and answered him in the same tongue.

It turned out that in his student days in Germany the general had lodged with a Jewish family and, being a natural linguist, like most Chinese, he'd picked up more Yiddish than I'd ever known myself.

I gave him the package and a message from Dr. Sun, and by the time the German came back, we were sitting staring silently at each other once more. It didn't take the general long to find a pretext for calling off the deal; the German drove me back to my hotel, while I bemoaned the time and money I'd "wasted" on my journey. I caught the night train for Shanghai.

When I got back to Canton we settled down to our regular daily routine. Dr. Sun still rose very early and got through most of his paper work before nine o'clock. He received visitors during the forenoon and in the afternoon he either lectured or went for walks in the city, or made little expeditions into the surrounding country.

The visitors were my pigeon, especially the foreigners. My best customer was Sir James "Monkey" Jamieson, the Consul General, who was always breezing in to discuss some difficulty or—occasionally—to deliver an official protest against something the Doctor had done. He was a man I could understand—stiff and dignified and pretty peppery too when things happened to go wrong, but absolutely straight, which didn't go for all the foreigners by any means. He stood strictly on his country's rights as defined by the old treaties. At the same time he was a great Chinese scholar with a real understanding of the Chinese people and more genuine sympathy for their aspirations than had some of those smarmy kow-towing types who came with protestations of friendship on their lips and some dirty double-crossing deal at the back of their minds.

We had one real set-to when he turned up early in the afternoon without having made an appointment and just when the Doctor was taking one of his rare after-tiffin cat-naps. They were both very punctilious men; Dr. Sun was always ready on time for an interview and "Monkey" would never have called without notice unless it was a matter of real urgency.

All the same, his hurry was none of my business.

"I'm sorry, Sir James, Dr. Sun is asleep. He hasn't been very well and he mustn't be disturbed."

"But, my good man, tell him that His Britannic Majesty's Consul General wishes to see him."

"I'm sorry, sir, but Mme. Sun said that he must *not* be disturbed. He only has a short doze and he'll be awake any minute now."

He glared at me and I thought, "Now for it!" but he

just said, "Hrumph! Well, you're right to do your duty; find me somewhere to wait."

So we sat and chatted in the A.D.C.'s room till Mah Sang came in to say that Dr. Sun was ready.

We tangled again once or twice after that, but with a man like "Monkey" one never minded, because there was none of that damned condescension that some of the other diplomats served out. With him it was just a case of one angry man bawling out another, all on level terms.

In the end we became buddies; he even called me "Morris" or "Two-Gun" when we met. Much later on when he was in Tientsin he told me: "I used to think you were a plaguey pest hanging round Dr. Sun when I wanted to talk confidentially, but at all events there was only one of you. Your boss was the only great man in China whom one could see even in semi-privacy. With all the rest there was a mob of secretaries and bodyguards and bottlewashers crawling round one's feet and getting in one's hair. I've found myself longing for an empty room and just your great ugly face in the background!"

There were so many foreign visitors at this time that, looking back, they seem to merge into each other and lose all individuality. Their car drove up and I found out who they were, told the Doctor they'd arrived, showed them in for ten minutes' talk, showed them out, saw them into their car; the car drove off and the next car drove up.

Only three of them stand out in my memory. The first was an American named Julius B. Woods, well-known correspondent of a Chicago newspaper. He didn't mind arguing with the Doctor and telling him that some of his ideas might be perfectly justified morally and ethically, but didn't make much sense from the point of view of practical politics.

The second was Mr. N. E. B. Ezra, founder and owner of the *Israel's Messenger* of Shanghai. He managed to persuade Dr. Sun (who was always rather cagey about putting his views on paper unless he thoroughly understood the question) to write him a personal letter for publication in his paper, supporting Zionism and the Jewish National Home in Palestine.

The third was Manuel Quezon, who became the first president of the Philippine Republic, but at that time was only president of their Senate and in the middle of his struggle for independence. He was a small fellow. Once, when we travelled together in the *President Coolidge* and got playing poker, he trimmed me properly. He and the Doctor compared notes about the Americans in Manila and the British in China. They agreed on two things. One was that neither the British nor the Americans were as bad as they might be; the other that, even if they were a whole lot better than they were, the Chinese and the Filipinos would rather run their own countries in their own way, and maybe make a mess of it in their own manner, than have help—and interference—from outsiders. Dr. Sun summed the whole thing up when he said to Quezon:

"In one way your country is more fortunate than mine."

"Why?"

"You have only one master, the United States of America. In a crisis she is bound both morally and by treaty to come to your help. China, on the other hand, has many foreign masters, but none of them are under any obligation to us. And with their extra-territorial rights, any foreigner could shoot a member of my own cabinet, and my government would have no jurisdiction over him. That's what we've got to change before we can hold up our heads."

When it came to Chinese visitors, the position was a little different, because then the question of security was much more serious. I was pretty sure that no foreigner would try to bump off Dr. Sun, but I couldn't be sure of any

Chinese, except his own personal followers, and I was taking no chances. I screened all of them, and if they were carrying guns they gave those guns to me before they got into his room—and that went for everyone, generals included. We had a few arguments and once or twice something like a rough-house, but I had my way in the end and presently it became known that everyone was treated alike, so people didn't mind so much.

The people I watched the closest were emissaries from the different factions in the North, who were always turning up on one pretext or another. This sounds odd, since we were at open war with them; and it seemed odd to me at first, till I came to realize that every civil war in China proceeds simultaneously on two fronts, military and political, and of these the political is the more important. While two groups of armies were fighting—not very hard—the two sets of leaders were constantly trying to come to terms with some faction on the other side. If they succeeded they'd join forces and turn on the ones who'd been left out of the deal.

Dr. Sun encouraged these overtures because they offered some prospect of bringing hostilities to an end and because he had a deep and genuine horror of fighting. He often said, "I am a man of peace—not of war," and that was true. He hated war, he hated violence, and he hated the whole military way of life, although—tragically—the whole of his own life was lived against a background of war and revolution.

"Well-organized nations," he said one evening, "count votes out of ballot boxes; badly organized nations count bodies—dead ones on battlefields."

So he received these gentry and listened patiently to their propositions, which were usually pretty crooked, put up his own counter-proposals, and never seemed discouraged when negotiations came to nothing. For myself I hated the sight of these agents and go-betweens from the North and never felt happy till they were clear of the compound. Still Dr. Sun was right (as he usually was) and late that same autumn all these endless and apparently useless talks really came to something.

Another class of visitor I hadn't much use for were the compradores, merchants, big business men, and concession hunters who came hoping to swing a deal of some sort. I don't think the Doctor liked them much either. Their interviews never lasted more than a matter of five minutes or so.

On the other hand, with poor people and little men he'd spread himself, especially if they came from overseas. In the old days Chinese who lived abroad had been rather despised. "The disinherited who had wandered away" was how they were described by strict old-style folk. The overthrow of the Manchus had changed all that, because it would never have been possible without the open purses of the foreign-dwelling communities. In fact the current saying was, "The parents of the Chinese Revolution are the overseas Chinese."

When some humble little San Francisco laundryman came to pay his respects, you saw the Doctor really relaxed and happy. He had a good memory for names, faces, and incidents, and he'd plunge into stories of the early poverty-stricken days of the Revolution, when he was handing around the hat to scrape together sufficient funds to keep going at all. He'd tie his yarns up with the time he'd last met the little man, and send him away as happy as a king.

The strangest of the humble folk I ushered into Dr. Sun's office was a spy who'd been caught by our counter-espionage and sentenced to death. By all the rules his life was over except for a walk to the execution ground. Then he would kneel down and the executioner would put the muzzle of a Mauser pistol against the base of his skull and blow out his brains.

We usually managed to keep that sort of event from the Doctor's knowledge, but someone slipped up this time and he got to hear of it and insisted on talking to the man himself. He saw him quite alone. Everybody was turned out of the room, including me, so no one knows what passed between them. Presently his bell rang and he sent Mah Sang for the head of the Intelligence and told him, "This man will work for me in the future!"

From then on till his death that chap worked loyally for the Doctor. He gradually became more and more trusted and learned more and more of our secrets; but when the other lot caught him, he died without telling them a thing.

There was another unlikely recruit that the Doctor picked up about the same time. Late one night Mah Sang said, "You come meet velly funny fellow—big piecee bandit!"

I walked into the A.D.C.'s room, and there, slouched down in a big armchair with a cigarette hanging from his lower lip, was a small, slim, smooth-skinned boy who might have been twenty and looked like an overseas student come home with his degree from a California college. In these days we're used to "pretty-boy" gangsters and "baby-face" thugs. At that time they hadn't been heard of, and he gave me a shock.

He spoke fairly good English too and didn't mind talking about his early life. He'd emigrated to Honolulu as a boy and wandered on to the Pacific Coast, where he'd lived some time and joined the old Tsing Chung-hui. After the fall of the Manchu Dynasty, he came back to China, collected a couple of thousand followers, and set up on his own, controlling and levying tribute from a big district in a remote part of Kweichow Province. Presently things got too hot for him there. He brought his band south into the Kwangtung mountains. What he was up to now, he didn't say and I didn't inquire.

When he left I asked Mah Sang, "How come that fellow can walk around city? Why don't the police nab him?"

"Ah," said Mah Sang, "now Sun Wen come back Canton, him want join Sun Wen army. Tomollow him come back and Sun Wen say yes, say no."

Sure enough, he turned up in broad daylight at ten next morning (he came in a closed chair though, so that no one outside saw his face), and had a long, long private talk with the Doctor. Then he went away in his closed chair again. A few days later there was a panic in the city. A strange army was streaming through the streets. They were heavily armed, carrying huge quantities of hand grenades and rifle ammunition in cloth bandoliers wrapped around and around their bodies, they spoke no known language, and they looked like bandits. Taking no notice of the townsfolk, they marched straight on to the central parade ground where General Gee Poy-duk (Chiang Kai-shek's adjutant-general) was waiting. There they halted and out of a group of horsemen in the middle of the mob rode the young brigand boy I'd met in the A.D.C.'s room!

Another bandit chief who must have been Dr. Sun's most frequent visitor of all was old Li Fuk-lum, whose Yamen stood at the far end of Honam, the same island where we lived. (It was twenty miles broad and forty miles long, so that didn't mean that he was right on top of us.) He'd been one of the Doctor's loyalest followers from the first and he stuck to him all through, whichever way the game went. His own private army varied in strength, but he could usually mobilize around about seven thousand men, and when Sun Yat-sen was in power in the South he usually commanded the local Cantonese levies as well, which made him a pretty important factor in our defenses. We saw a lot of each other.

His nickname was "Tang Tung," which means "lamp chimney," because once, when a hatchet-man caught him unarmed in his bedroom and it looked as if his number was up, he kicked over the table where his old-fashioned oil lamp stood, snatched up its polished metal funnel, pretended it was a pistol barrel, and held up the killer until his own guard arrived with real guns and shot him dead.

He was a shrivelled-up little shrimp of a man with a reputation for ruthlessness and very rough-tongued to his followers—which is unusual with that type. He didn't speak much—just sat puffing a long Chinese pipe and only took it out of his mouth to tick off somebody who'd annoyed him. One day I brought him a message from Dr. Sun and happened to see him in action.

A whole lot of minor gangsters owed him a loose sort of allegiance and occasionally touched him for some ready cash. I was just saying goodbye when, without any warning, in walked one of these gentry and demanded a hefty handout on the spot. I'd heard of him before—a real nasty character with a mean disposition and a violent temper.

Tang Tung didn't even offer him tea, which is a hell of an insult by itself. He just gave him the biggest bawling out I've every heard one Chinese give another. And this was in public, which meant that the fellow was "losing face" every second he stood there. At the end of it, old Li pulled out his own gat, pushed it into the man's hand, and pointed through his window to a pawnbroker's tower across the street.

The man went out and he turned to me grinning:

"I tell him go pop damn t'ing, but bling me back pawn-ticket!"

That was all very Chinese. It put over three ideas in one. First, that the bank was broke and he had to pawn his most precious possession to meet the other's demands. Second, that he was indifferent to his own personal safety. Third, that, though he'd insulted him in public, he still had faith in the chap and would trust him with his own life.

He had a sense of humor all right, but his jokes were broad and simple—like a schoolboy's. All orthodox Jews are a trifle fussy about what they eat and I was no exception, even if I did break the rules when it came to pork, so it took me some time to get used to Chinese food. I don't mean the plain coolie-chow—that was always excellent—but some of the odd dishes like sea-slugs and so on that you ate at a rich man's table took a bit of swallowing.

He knew about this. One day he asked Mah Sang and me to a big banquet. I sat beside him and he pressed two special dishes on me. One tasted like minced partridge and was served with white flower petals. The other was something like sucking-pig but darker in hue and harder to chew. I saw the old chap had some private joke that he could hardly contain and so I played up, ate hearty, and asked no questions. At last he couldn't bear it any longer:

"You liking my chow?"

"Yes, Tang Tung—fine!"

"Come 'long me, look see kitchen."

I downed a bowl of strong samshui wine (they serve it hot out of a sort of small teapot) and followed him. There, laid out on the serving board, were the skeletons of several medium-sized snakes.

He was a good son-of-a-gun all the same. He got to like me too. At least, he let me teach his three little boys to box, and when a Chinese trusts you with his sons that means something.

When we'd disposed of the morning's visitors, we had tiffin and a short siesta (it was summer-time again). Then,

Dr. Sun would go off to give one of his lectures on the "Three Principles of the Kuomintang Party—*Min Tzu-chu I, Min Chuan-chu I* and *Min Sheng-chu I*," which can be roughly translated as National Freedom, Democratic Government, and Socialist Economy. Since his death they've been endlessly discussed, praised, attacked, and defended. They've been made into a sort of religious code which is above argument, and they've been abused as being just a veiled form of Communism. To him the three principles seemed perfectly plain.

He only marked them up in their final form towards the very end of his life. He must have realized he hadn't long to live and was determined that as many people as possible should hear them from his own mouth. He lectured day after day to students, soldiers, shopkeepers, coolies, anyone who had enough intelligence to grasp his ideas, and a whole lot who hadn't. He knew his people and he kept his lectures simple, speaking in a language that ordinary people could understand.

Once I was sitting beside him and, while the audience—a mixed lot of students and soldiers—filed in and took their seats, he picked up a brush and started doodling on his blotter. Then he had an idea and drew a big circle with several smaller ones inside it. In the smaller circles he wrote "Conservatism," "Liberalism," "Socialism," and "Communism" and over the large one he wrote "Kuomintang Party." He pinned the blotter on the front of his desk where everyone could see it and explained that all these "-isms" had some good and some bad in them, but that China was wise enough to pick out the good bits of each and discard the rest. His lectures were as simple as that.

I couldn't follow all he said as it was in Cantonese, but sometimes he'd talk to me while we were driving out and back and I know that his own ideas weren't subtle at all, but as clear as they could be—just about as straightforward as "Liberty, Equality, Fraternity."

"I want," he said to me, "a China where there is no need to shut one's outer gate at night."

On afternoons when he wasn't lecturing, Mme. Sun would make him go out—just like any worried English housewife with an aging, overworked husband. He'd say he was far too busy, but he always did what she said in the end and those little expeditions were some of the happiest times we had. He'd stroll through the city, look into a rice go-down or a little fire-cracker factory, start talking to the coolies and get them to tell him their troubles; or else he'd stop some *chi'sais* who were walking with their parents, ask them how they were doing at school, and, if—as usually happened—they weren't attending school at all, he'd fix up somewhere for them to go and likely pay a year's fees as well. And, of course, if he saw a beggar he just sent me to give the poor bum a handout, whatever Mme. Sun might say.

One day he took me to the Temple of the Five Hundred Genii and walked me down those lines of grinning gilt Buddhas till we came to one image complete with beard and whiskers that was obviously meant to be a European. It was Marco Polo. You'll find statues of him all over China, but I'd never heard of him in those days. All the way home, Dr. Sun explained the difference between Buddhism, Confucianism, and Taoism (he was a Christian himself, by the way), and told me of the universal respect which the Chinese have for knowledge and learning, and how Marco Polo was venerated because he came from so far away and knew so much of the outside world.

Another time we revisited the Five Storied Pagoda, where we'd had such a narrow squeak the year before. It was a beautiful building and unique of its kind, but in a rotten state of disrepair, and the battle and bombardment hadn't done it any good either. Dr. Sun decided that it ought to be restored and, in his enthusiastic way, plunged into plans on the spot.

Nothing was done at the time, and his last illness and death shelved the matter; but years later, in a brief peaceful period when Lin Sen was Chairman of the National Government, I reminded him of the Doctor's wishes. "The Doctor's wishes" were law at that time, and Lin Sen obtained a big appropriation and not only had the Pagoda repaired but a museum assembled and housed in it and a carriage road built up along the old city walls, which made it into a point of pilgrimage for all South China.

Once in a while we'd drive out into the surrounding country, and those were the days he liked the best. He'd trudge over the hill with his walking stick and sun helmet, stopping to read inscriptions on the graves (in China you have no graveyards but bury your parents in "favorable spots" that may be pretty well anywhere) and to pick some wild berries that he'd recognized.

"Come here, Morris," he'd call, "do you know what these things are? They're plentiful where I was born. Try them; they quench your thirst."

One Sunday when Mme. Sun's brother, T. V. Soong, and her sister, Mei-ling Soong, who afterwards married Chiang Kai-shek, were visiting her, we went up White Cloud Mountain for a picnic. Dr. Sun found a four-leaved clover and Fu Pin-chang, who was later Ambassador to Moscow, took a snap of him holding it and looking so happy he mightn't have had a care in the world.

It was coming back from these little expeditions, when his legs were tired and his mind relaxed, that he'd sometimes talk about his early years as a revolutionary. He wasn't a man who went in for reminiscence as a rule. He lived so much in the present that his past seldom came into the picture. Towards the end of his life he began to look back and would sometimes talk about things that he might have done differently.

"The biggest mistake of my life," he said once, "was in February 1912 when, after forty-five days as President, I resigned in favor of Yuan Shih-kai. At the time it seemed the only thing to do. My life had been devoted to freeing China from the Manchu Dynasty—the Emperor had abdicated, and my great task was done.

"Yuan Shih-kai had spent his life in the Emperor's service and knew all that there was to be known about the government, the politics, and the people of China. He had his own political following and a great army under his own command; and he was well known in person to all the other generals and armies of China, whereas I was only a name to them. Also, he was desperately ambitious, far more so than I realized at the time; he wanted to be President and I did not. I realized that the future of China lay with her internal communications, her railways, her rivers, her canals, and her ports; and I wanted to get clear of politics and devote my days to their development.

"So I handed over to Yuan; he betrayed me from the start and two years later I was in exile again. I've made many mistakes in my life and, if I live much longer, I'll probably make many more—but that was about the worst one!"

One of the stories he told us had a fairy-tale sequel. It was about his visit to London in 1896, when he was kidnapped by the staff of the Imperial Chinese Legation and held prisoner while they arranged to ship him back to China as a lunatic in a specially chartered steamer. If they'd been successful, his fate would not have been just beheading but death by those appalling tortures reserved for the leaders of plots against the Dragon Throne.

Euguene Chen was with us. He was always a stimulating listener—when he wasn't talking himself—and the Doctor made us live through every minute of it. In that little locked room on the top floor of the premises between Portland Place and Weymouth Street he was wrapping messages around half-crowns, throwing them through the barred window, and wondering if by any chance one of them would fall into friendly hands, while all the time one had been picked up by a negro porter and the machinery of English justice was slowly stirring into action—Marylebone Police Station, Scotland Yard, *The Times*, the Old Bailey, the Foreign Office, and, finally, Lord Salisbury himself.

He described how on the Friday afternoon he was at last released and Dr. Cantlie took him back to their house in Devonshire Street, where Mrs. Cantlie gave him tea. On the Sunday they all three went to the morning service at St. Martin's-in-the-Fields and gave thanks. Then he turned to me and said:

"Morris, I know you think I'm a brave man and I suppose I am; but the reason I'm never frightened in battle now is just that those five days I spent in that little room with a revolting death coming nearer and nearer frightened me so much that I've never been able to take any danger seriously since."

He was silent a long time. Suddenly he said:

"Eugene! That colored porter who found my message and took it to Cantlie—we've not heard from him for a long time. I wonder if he's well. Why don't you write to Scotland Yard?"

Eugene Chen did so and the Metropolitan Police tracked him down and found that he'd died in the meantime but that his widow was still alive. The news reached Dr. Sun just before he left for North China on his last journey, and one of the last orders he ever issued in Canton was for the payment of a pension to the old lady for the rest of her life.

We passed the evenings in a variety of ways. Sometimes I showed them card tricks. I never played poker while I was with the Doctor, but I still liked the feel of a pack of cards and it kept my fingers supple. I liked my audience too. All Chinese have a streak of childishness in them and they all—even the worldliest of them—half believe in magic. I've done conjuring tricks for children all over the world and I love their yells of laughter and surprise at some simple little trick; but never in my life have I seen anything like the open-mouthed astonishment of Dr. Sun and Madam when I made the ace of spades vanish into thin air and then produced it from the pocket where Mah Sang carried his gun.

Sometimes the Doctor played chess, but not very often; there were only a few of his friends good enough to give him a game and most of those didn't like to beat him. Sooner or later he'd bowl them out making a false move on purpose to let him win and, when that happened, he never played with them again. I've been told that all great men like flattery. That may have been true of the Doctor but, if so, the flattery had to be very well disguised; whenever he saw through it there was trouble.

If the day had been easy and he still felt energetic, he'd sit down with his brush and stone ink jar and write out Chinese proverbs. Calligraphy is one of the highest forms of art in China; the principal ornament in a room is often one of those long narrow scrolls with a few characters written by some famous man.

The Doctor received countless requests for an inscription by himself. He kept a list of these and on a good evening he'd send for it and knock off forty or fifty at one go. His favorite maxim was "*Tien Woi Gung*" ("Within the four seas all men are brothers"), or else "*Bo ai*," which means love in its broadest sense—perhaps something like magnanimity is the best translation.

He worked fast, in a free, dashing style quite different from the careful correctness of other scholars. When he was in practice, he'd clear off the whole list before stopping to look through his work; even then he'd only destroy two or three out of the lot.

I used to try my own hand at Chinese characters and once that got me into trouble. It was a hot steamy afternoon and I was sitting on the veranda trying to write "Sun Yat-sen" in Chinese. Mah Sang was lounging against the wall keeping an eye cocked on the compound, when I noticed that he was grinning at someone standing behind me. The next thing I knew was a smart box on my ear and the Doctor's voice, "Caught you forging my signature, have I?"

I jumped out of my chair and stood to attention while he picked up the sheet of paper, had a good look at it: "Not at all bad!" he said.

He took it away and a few minutes later Mme. Sun came out of their room with a big plate of li-chi nuts and said, "You can have these if you'll write my husband's name again."

That wasn't real trouble of course, but once I nearly had a row with her sister, Mei-ling Soong. I used to slip down to Hong Kong about once a month for a little fun and games, and one evening when I was off by the boat next day she said:

"Morris, while you're in Hong Kong, go to that French place near the Gloucester and get me some of my special lip-salve. I'll write down the name of the shade."

"No," I answered, "that's a sissy thing to ask me to do and I'm not a sissy!"

She looked so cross and hurt that I quickly changed my mind and said I'd buy it for her after all.

Mme. Sun never much approved of my Hong Kong holidays. She must have guessed their main purpose. Like all happily married women, she was an inveterate match-maker, and she set about finding a wife for me. All the staff heard of her plans; it became one of those jokes that are known to everyone except the person most concerned. At a big dinner party I found myself sitting next to Tan Yen-kai, who was then Chief Secretary of the Kuomintang. He asked me straight out, "Cohen, why don't you choose a nice Chinese girl and get married?"

Although he was talking partly in fun, I knew that everyone was listening and I must pick my words. I thought it over a while and the table fell silent.

"No, Ah Tan," I said, "it's no use. A good Chinese girl would never marry a foreigner and a bad Chinese girl I don't want!"

"Quite right," said Tan, and the whole table stood up and toasted me.

We went to few feasts that summer. The Doctor's health was deteriorating; he ate practically nothing and sitting through banquets bored him. For the last twenty years he'd been a vegetarian, not from any religious reason or fanciful fad, but simply because meat made him ill. He suffered from some stomach complaint, contracted he would say—when he wanted to pull my leg—from living on dough-nuts and ice cream in Canada. This got rapidly worse till even boiled rice gave him horrible pain.

Fruit was almost his entire diet and visitors vied with each other to bring him the best from their orchards and gardens. It fascinated me to see the different kinds piled on plates around the table—persimmons and passion fruit and pawpaws and every kind of mango and lots of others I couldn't put a name to. My ignorance of Chinese ways let me in for some teasing.

One morning Mme. Sun put a dish on our table and said, "Here are some *lung nagan* for the A.D.C.'s. That means 'Dragon's Eyes' in your language, Morris."

They were about the size and shape of filberts and they certainly looked more like nuts than fruit, so I tried nut-crackers on one and the beastly thing squelched flat. I saw Mah Sang and Wong Wei-lung look at each other as they quietly took a handful apiece and left the room. I wasn't going to be beaten and so I tried to peel one with a knife or cut one in half. All I got was a pulpy mess that stuck to my fingers.

Back came the other two laughing and with their hands full of empty shells.

"We've eaten our fill," they said, "and now we'll show you how to do it."

It was quite simple; you just held the fruit up to your lips and squeezed it in exactly the right place; the shell split in half and the inside popped straight into your mouth. But by the time I'd learned the trick, those greedy devils had left me hardly any to eat.

Those were happy peaceful months. I enjoyed a kind of family life that I'd not known since my boyhood. Dr. Sun, as I've said before, was always rather formal and polite. When I first became a regular member of his staff he would address me as "Colonel," but since that time he'd returned to using first my surname and then my given name; now he took to the familiar nickname of "Mah Kun," which was what the houseboys and coolies called me. It was the nearest they could get to "Morris Cohen."

Yes, it was a good time and, like so many good times,

it ended badly. There were always hot local politics in Canton, and when, in the early autumn, the Doctor went to the Northern front at Shinkwan, taking most of his best troops with him, the cauldron boiled over.

In mid-October fierce fighting suddenly broke out between the Merchant Volunteers—a force commanded by Chan Ling-puk—and some of the government troops left in the city. It was a nasty business.

The fighting was severe, with both sides using artillery in the middle of the city, so the civilian casualties were heavy. It ended with the defeat of the Volunteers, a destructive fire, and an ugly massacre. The Doctor took it very badly indeed; in fact, some people said it broke his heart and that was why, when he set out for Peking, he was already a dying man.

Right on top of this disaster came an invitation from the three Northern War Lords, Chang Tso-lin, Tuan Chi-ji, and Feng Yu-hsiang, for Dr. Sun to join them in Peking at a conference which was to make a permanent peace between North and South, reorganize the Kuomintang on a truly national basis, and settle the future government of China.

This looked like being his last and greatest triumph, but it came too late. He left Canton on November 13th and one of his little cruisers took us down to Hong Kong. From there we sailed in a Japanese liner bound for Shanghai. There I said goodbye, for I was off on another mission to Canada, this time to buy Ross rifles for the army. I knew he was a very sick man, but I never dreamed he was actually dying.

My mission proved longer and more difficult than I'd expected. It needed patience and I'm not the most patient of men; besides, although the true state of Dr. Sun's health was a carefully guarded secret, I couldn't help knowing that things were pretty bad and that made me all the more anxious to finish my task and get back to him.

It was the middle of March and I was still kicking my heels in a Vancouver hotel when I heard of his death. I took the next ship for China and on that passage I played no poker, I spent no time in the bar, and, in fact, I scarcely spoke to a soul on board. I slept badly too and that's something that has never happened to me before or since. At Shanghai I jumped into the Peking express. I was hurrying all I knew because I couldn't tell how long the lying-in-state would last and I wanted to see his face again.

When I met Mme. Sun I just burst into tears. I may be a sentimental, emotional softy, but I've only cried twice since I became a man, and the second time was twelve years later when my own father died.

Dr. Sun lay for three weeks in the Central Park while people from all the provinces of China streamed past the bier. He was taken to the Azure Cloud Temple in the Western Hills. His Christian funeral had been held on March 19th, a week after his death; this was a Chinese funeral and his body was borne in a Chinese coffin. I don't remember a great deal about that day. The bottom had dropped out of my world and I still felt lost.

That evening I talked with Mah Sang till late. He told me about the mausoleum that was to be built on a site near the tombs of the Ming Emperors at Nanking for the final resting-place. He told me about Dr. Sun's will and how he had left practically nothing in the way of personal possessions except his library. Even his house in the rue Molière was heavily mortgaged and the Doctor must have died a poorer man than any other national leader of his day. He told me, too, about his three Testaments to the Nation and then he asked, "Any more you'd like to know, Mah Kun?"

"Yes, what were the last words he spoke?"

Mah Sang thought awhile and then answered:

"Doctor half unconscious long time before he die. Sometimes he mutter and I no hear proper what he say. But his last word I hear well. He say, 'Peace . . . struggle . . . save China.' "

While Mah Sang was telling me that, Sun's followers were already starting to argue about those Testaments—who had drafted them, what they meant, and all the rest of it; but when a man's dying, it's not what he signs but what he says that matters. For myself, I know that as he lay there, he had one clear thought in his mind, the same thought he'd had throughout his life. That was—"Save China!"

CHAPTER VII

General Cohen

WHILE MORRIS LOAFED AND FRETTED around the lobby of that Canadian hotel, far away in Peking the pattern of his future had been settled. Not long before his death the Great Doctor, his mind still unclouded, had taken leave of his staff and had specially named the absent A.D.C. as his loyal and trustworthy servant and faithful friend.

Up to this moment his position had been more than a little uncertain. Those Chinese who were closest to Dr. Sun reposed complete confidence in Morris and indeed said frankly that, so long as his face was to be seen in the background, they felt that their leader was safe and all was well; but in more distant circles where he was not personally known, the presence of a foreigner in the Doctor's immediate entourage had been questioned and not infrequently resented.

With Europeans his standing was even more equivocal, and few, if any, who had not met him in the flesh and discovered for themselves what manner of man he was could understand how he had attained so privileged a position, or for that matter, what sort of position he actually occupied. It was inevitable that anecdotes should begin to gather about him and equally inevitable that some of them should be not only malicious but also totally untrue.

Even his prowess with the pistol had been called in question, and the tale was told that one night, when he had dined with some young bloods on board a British river gunboat and performed his standard feat of tossing electric light globes into the air, to be shattered ere they touched the deck, his second gun was surreptitiously removed and unloaded, when it was discovered that the cartridges contained, not the conventional nickel-coated bullet but a charge of "No. 7" shot, which would certainly have gone far to account for his almost miraculous marksmanship.

But now he could afford to laugh at such silly stories. Dr. Sun had in effect bequeathed him to China and China honored her obligations in full. He was awarded a small state pension, which he could thenceforward be sure of drawing from whatever government might happen to be in power, and he was promoted to the rank of general by an act of the Legislative Yuan, his commission being countersigned—as a mark of special favor—by the presidents of the other four great departments, the Executive, Judicial, Examination, and Censorship Yuans.

Of infinitely greater importance than these honors and rewards was the fact that his close personal association with China's dead hero, already in the process of something approaching deification, had been thus publicly proclaimed and could never again be disputed.

To this must be added his universal reputation for absolute personal integrity. "Honesty," he once confided to me, "can be a kind of racket in itself—and a darned good racket too."

It is easy to understand why, for the rest of his career, he could approach any prominent personage of any political party and ask for employment with the certainty of being given forth-with a position of trust, but less easy to estimate his ability to fill such positions and maintain so unique a personal prestige. Many a European has risen to great heights under the patronage of some Oriental potentate, but when that potentate has met with death or disaster, the fall of his protégé has been equally swift and final. Why should Morris escape a similar fate and with what weapons was he equipped to face his future?

In the last few years he had learned the intricacies of modern Chinese politics in a way which was open to no other foreigner. He had accompanied Dr. Sun everywhere and had heard him talk freely and pungently on every topic and not least frequently on the moral qualities and personal traits of the last visitor to leave his presence. Morris was almost uneducated; he knew nothing of history, economics, or strategy; but he had an insight into and judgment of character, a recollection of detail, and a mind of true orderliness, in which a mass of information could be neatly and methodically stored for ready reference. In the course of time the Doctor himself had come to rely on Morris to supply some item which had escaped even his prodigious memory.

Fortunately for him, his great opportunity had not come till he was of an age to derive from it the fullest benefit. To be a "student of human nature" is a much misused expression, generally employed to explain and excuse a taste for gossip and the lower levels of conviviality coupled with a considerable degree of sheer mental laziness. But Morris might fairly claim to have studied his subject from the slums of East End London to the prairies of Western Canada, on ranches and on board liners, in camps and offices and gambling joints from San Francisco to Flanders. And his studies had been pursued with an added urgency, since it was by his knowledge of his fellow men that he had earned his daily bread.

The experience thus gained formed an ideal background for his newly acquired, specialized, and particular knowledge. About Chinese affairs he might be mistaken, but about the character, the actions, and the reactions in any given circumstances of an individual figure, he was seldom wrong; and in a country where personalities are of paramount importance his advice would be invaluable.

He was in a position to choose his new chief and a more ambitious man might have hesitated for long; but Morris had little ambition for himself. His old leader was dead and he naturally transferred his allegiance to his old leader's only son and heir.

WE LEFT DR. SUN in the Western Hills—he said—and for a while I felt that I'd left the best part of myself there too. I just mooned about and thought how empty my life was now and how little I'd realized my luck when he was still alive. It was old Gau Lim-pai, one of his closest friends, who put it best when he said:

"Working under Sun Yat-sen was like climbing a great mountain. While you were actually climbing, you were too close to the mountain to see it; the winding paths and the cliffs, and the boulders and the trees confused you and it seemed nothing more than a good big hill. It was only when you got to the top and looked back that you realized that it was no hill but a mighty mountain."

I needed something to make me snap out of it and come back to earth and that something was—as it usually is with most of us—the need for hard cash. For the last three years I'd never thought of money. I hadn't even bothered to draw my A.D.C.'s pay. I'd lived free in Dr. Sun's household and I drew pretty handsome expenses when I went on missions. But apart from that, if I needed more money, I just spent the savings I'd accumulated in Canada.

One fine day I realized that the till was empty and there was nothing coming in and I'd better do something about it. I put on my best suit and called on Sun Fo. The doctor was twice married and all his children, a son and two daughters, were by his first wife, whom he'd wed as a boy back in his native village near Macao.

Now it's not so easy to be a great man's heir. Long after this a guy thought he'd give my culture a boost and took me to see a French play about Napoleon's son, who was called the "King of Rome" and who reckoned he could do as well as his dad. All he did was bring about the death of an old sergeant who'd stood by him. The audience liked it a lot and at the end they stood up and sang the "Marseillaise," but while they were singing I thought about Sun Fo and how he'd never tried to be as big as his father, but had just stuck to his own level and done the things he'd known he was able to do.

He was a little chap, not much more than five foot five, but stood erect. You might have taken him for a banker or a teacher, or a member of any of the professions. He had his father's eyes all right, but not his father's phenomenal eyesight. He wore thick glasses that concealed their expression. Anyone less like the Great Doctor couldn't be imagined.

"I've come, sir," I said, "to ask if you can find a place for me on your staff. I want a job."

He blinked at me.

"Now, Morris, are you quite sure that any job I can offer is big enough for you? I'm not Sun Yat-sen. I'm the Mayor of Canton and what I've got to do is to keep the city streets clean and see that the police aren't too corrupt. If you join me, there'll be no more grand visitors for you to look after and no more exciting missions to America, but just a lot of hard work and perhaps unpleasant work too. Do you think you'd like it, Morris? Is it in your line?"

He took off his glasses and wiped them and, as he did so, he looked straight at me and for one second it was Dr. Sun himself sitting behind that desk. Then he put his glasses on again and began to doodle on his blotter.

I stood up straight and I let him have it.

"You're the heir of Sun Wen," I said. "I know how you cleaned up Canton and I can tell you plenty about it. I know how you drove those broad new highways through the fronts of all the shops and what the shopkeepers said they were going to do to you; and how you called their bluff and in the end you had them eating out of your hand and settling their own claims for compensation. And I was in the Nanti Club that night you told off the Military Governor for graft, and I know how he felt about it. Your head came just up to his row of medals and it'd have been funny if I hadn't been so frightened; but what I still don't understand is why you weren't bumped off that same night. I served your father and that's what I'll always be proudest of. If you'll have me, I'll be proud to serve you, too, in any way you like."

He blinked at me again.

"All right, Morris," he said, "you're hired. We leave for Canton on Friday."

So off to Canton we went and straight into trouble. You'll remember that Dr. Sun's most reliable troops were the divisions from Yunnan Province, partly because they were up-countrymen and a warlike breed and partly because they were foreigners and usually indifferent to Cantonese politics. The Doctor's death had played hell with their morale and, like all mercenaries, once their morale started to go, it went fast. One fine day they joined forces with some Kwangsi troops, and we had to clear out.

We got away just in time, crossed the river to Honam Island, and set up our headquarters at the Whampoa Military Academy where we had our best Russian-trained troops. The Yunnanese knew enough not to try an attack, so we just sat and sniped at each other from bank to bank.

I soon discovered that the most important duty of

my new post was to be unofficial liaison officer with the British Concession on the Shameen—that meant, of course, with the British Consul General. "Monkey" Jamieson was still in charge and he always seemed glad to see me.

One day I had to take T. V. Soong (Mme. Sun's younger brother) over to meet him. The interview lasted longer than expected so we made our return trip in the dark. We were just chugging along looking forward to supper. T. V. was saying that "the C. G. wasn't such a bad old basket after all," when the boat heeled over and I saw that we'd just missed ramming a seaplane that was moored in the stream.

The next thing was a flash and a crash and a volley of rifle-fire all around us—the Whampoa guard thought we were trying to pinch their seaplane!

Our crew weren't very worried at first; they just shouted "Soong" and waited to be recognized. When the next volley actually hit the boat, they lost interest and just lay as flat as they could. I made T. V. lie pretty flat, too, for that matter.

"Give 'em the password," said T. V. We hadn't bothered about any password when we left Whampoa and it was a bit late now.

Then I thought of something that didn't make me feel any happier.

"Jeez," I said, "that guard's under Russian command and they'll want a Russian password."

However, that did give me an idea. We had a red Communist flag in the boat and I ran it up on the ensign staff and shone a lantern on it and shouted for all I was worth.

"We are Roossians! We are Roossians!"

That did the trick all right. I heard a whistle blow twice and then the firing stopped and a voice shouted in English:

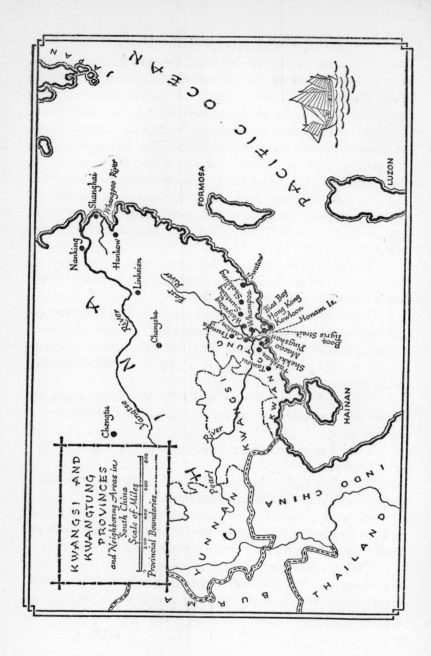

KWANGSI AND
KWANGTUNG
PROVINCES
and Neighboring Areas in
South China
Scale of Miles
200   400   600   800
Provincial Boundaries

"Stop your engines and we will board you."

Ten long minutes later a sampan full of soldiers—still rather trigger-happy—came alongside and we were recognized. I was darned glad to get my feet on dry land again.

While we were banging away across the Pearl River, the campaign was, as usual, being fought on two fronts. Chiang Kai-shek called in his most reliable garrisons from the rest of the province and concentrated them ready to mount an attack. At the same time under-cover negotiations were in progress.

You'll say all this is typically Chinese: to me it made perfectly good sense. It was a Southwestern Provinces quarrel and to be settled on Southwestern lines, and, if the lives of a few hundred soldiers can be saved by negotiation, then it seemed sound sense to negotiate. Later on, when the Japanese started in, we showed we could fight foreigners in quite another fashion, but this was a family squabble, and, if we could settle it in our own style, so much the better.

This time the negotiations didn't go too well. On June 1st we attacked. That didn't go too well either. It was a long day of confused fighting, but by nightfall we were back on Honam Island again. Our casualties were very slight; we soon reorganized and by the 6th were ready for another try. That night a higher-up sent for me.

"General Cohen," he began and I pricked up my ears because he'd never called me that before, "I am not a military man, but"—he took off his glasses and looked me in the eye—"I know our men. Last week they did not behave as they would have done had they been properly led. Their hearts were not in it and that is why we failed.

"Now, of all the Doctor's personal staff you were the most conspicuous and today you are the one most closely associated with him in the minds of the soldiers. Tomorrow I want you to take a battalion of Whampoa cadets, cross the river in the second wave and seize the Governor's Yamen!"

I'm not ashamed to say that, before I turned in that night, I sat down and wrote a letter to my old mother and another to the Hong Kong & Shanghai Bank, where I kept my overdraft. Next day I was going to be the only European in the battle (the Russian instructors from Whampoa weren't allowed near the firing line) and a pretty prominent feature of the landscape. The Yunnanese troops had seen me with the Doctor a dozen times; they knew me well and, if they chose to pick on me, they could hardly miss.

That morning I dressed in my general's uniform and I girded on my general's sword and both my pistol holsters, had a good breakfast, and went out to the parade ground to see my battalion. They were Russian-trained and Communist-indoctrinated and there they were drawn up, most of them, with little red flags tied to their fixed bayonets. Out in front was a standard-bearer almost buried in the folds of a red banner twice as big as himself. They gave me a cheer—Russian style—when I came on parade, but it wasn't much of a cheer and I didn't like the sound of it. I mightn't know much about tactics, but I'd learned the *feel* of troops and these didn't feel too good.

"If I've got to be a target," I thought, "I'll damn well give 'em something to shoot at!"

I inspected the ranks and then I stopped in front of the little standard-bearer, took his banner from him, held it high above my head, and sloped it over my shoulder. At this they gave me another cheer, but a real good one with some steam behind it, and we marched off to the Bund to embark for the crossing.

The first wave went over. The enemy's fire was wild— most of it passed over our heads, miles up in the air. Then came our turn to cross. I sat in the sternsheets, still clutching my banner and listening hard—you couldn't see much. It seemed to me the volume of fire was decreasing. The boat jarred alongside the Customs House jetty and I jumped out, unfurled my banner and yelled, "Come on boys!"

The firing died away and we went on almost unopposed. The Yunnanese had sold out overnight and were getting ready to bunk, but they'd left it a bit late and all we were doing was to chew up their rearguards.

I'd been expecting a real tough time and when it didn't materialize I almost felt cheated. I set off at the head of those Whampoa boys down the main street swinging my banner and shouting. I can remember passing a group of Europeans who looked dumbfounded to see a foreigner leading Chinese troops and I yelled at them, "We've got the bastards on the run!"

I can still see their puzzled faces following me around the next corner. We reached the Yamen to find it empty and looted and all the offices upside down. We set about putting it straight for the arrival of Sun Fo. That was the end of the day that I thought I'd finish up dead.

We had just one fortnight of peace, then we were up to our ears in trouble again. On May 30th, while we were still stuck on Honam Island, there'd been a nasty incident in the International Concession at Shanghai. It began with a strike in some Japanese cotton mills; a mob of students and coolies tried to rush the Louza Police Station, the Municipal Police were forced to fire, and there were a lot of casualties. China was just about ripe for another antiforeign outbreak, and disturbances spread up the Yangtse, down the coast to Hong Kong, where a general strike was called, and then up to Canton.

It ran to the usual pattern. The British and French packed the anchorage with gunboats and destroyers, landed troops on the Shameen, and put up barbed wire and sandbag defenses. The Chinese press printed inflammatory articles, the students held meetings and demonstrations. On June 23rd they organized a big "protest procession" routed down the Sharkee Road running along the far side of the canal that divided the Shameen from the rest of the city.

General Wu Teh-chen, Chief of Police, sent me to tell Jamieson he had taken all possible precautions to preserve order and there was no cause for alarm. At least that was the reason he gave for sending me, but I fancy he foresaw the danger and wanted to have a reliable, independent witness on the spot in case things went wrong.

They went wrong; there was no hope of anything else. The canal was just a narrow little creek. On the one side you had a sort of League of Nations under arms, a mixture of French and English Bluejackets, Royal Marines, Indian troops, Chinese police, and civilian volunteers of every nationality. Trailing along in front of them, madly excited and shouting anti-foreign slogans, was a mob of students, coolies, and riff-raff of all sorts, with some fanatical Whampoa cadets bringing up the rear. Things couldn't help going wrong.

The officer commanding the French force had an observation post with a clear view right down the canal. I stood beside him, but even so I couldn't really see what happened. A single shot was fired and, for myself, I felt pretty sure it came from the Shameen. The Whampoa cadets wheeled inwards and loosed off a volley at the old Consul General and the commissioner of Customs, a chap called Edwards, who were standing on the canal bridge; they hit Edwards in the leg, too.

The sailors on the Shameen saw Jamieson running for his life and they naturally fired back and the fight was on. It was a one-sided sort of fight. The Shameen garrison were behind sandbags while the Chinese were in the open. Buglers sounded the "Cease Fire" and officers ran up and down blowing whistles, but by the time the shooting stopped, there were fifty dead lying on the Sharkee Road and over a hundred wounded.

A heartbreaking business and nobody—or, if you like, everybody—was to blame. An old British business man, one of the most popular figures in Canton, who had helped endless poor Chinese families and was well known for his sympathy with China, thought he was responsible and killed himself in the Club that same day, but, whether or not it had been his finger on the trigger, no one will ever know.

There wasn't much time for post mortems either. Trouble flared up everywhere and the Russians rode the storm. Some people say it was a Russian who fired the fatal shot, but I doubt that. What they did was to seize their opportunity. Their policy was to ignore the international nature of the quarrel and concentrate all hostility against the British. They hoped by doing this to drive a wedge into the usual European solidarity and isolate the one nation. There was a good deal of trouble in India at that time, and they thought that the two in combination would break the power of Britain in the East. As to what would happen to China they couldn't care less. The strike and boycott that they helped to organize made a few British firms a little less prosperous for a time, but for millions of Chinese it meant grave hardship.

For me it meant the busiest and trickiest time of my life. My liaison job, that I hadn't thought much of at first, suddenly became important. I bustled to and fro between the different Yamens and the Shameen, carrying messages from Sun Fo and T. V. Soong and Wu Teh-chen, explaining and complaining and arguing and trying to keep matters on an even keel. I'd always fancied myself for a fast talker, and as a real-estate salesman in Edmonton I'd been the tops, but this was different. I began to realize how important mere words could be and I'd lie awake at night thinking out the best way to put a proposition and how to get the British to see the Chinese point of view and vice versa.

I had one lucky break that put up my stock with the British Navy. That counted for a lot because, in the last resort, they represented armed force and the Senior Naval Officer had the final say when it came to using it.

Early one morning I was driving up the Bund on my way to see the Consul General. A destroyer called the *Onslaught* was alongside landing some stores for an American named Banberry. (Owing to the boycott all kinds of services were performed by sailors; they even nursed the babies when the mothers were sick and their amahs on strike.) The usual crowd of longshore loafers were standing about shouting slogans and shaking their fists. That didn't worry me till I saw most of the mob suddenly scatter and run from one little group who were standing on the edge of the wharf close up to the ship. They weren't shouting or gesticulating like the rest; they were all facing inwards towards one man and watching something in his hands.

I smelled trouble, though as yet I hadn't the vaguest idea what it might be. I stopped my car, got out, and walked towards them. They were so intent on their business that they never noticed me till I was right up close and then somebody shouted, they all swung around, and I saw that they were up to. The man in the middle held a big, clumsily fashioned bomb; he'd just lit the fuse and it was spluttering away merrily.

There was no time to think. I jumped on him, pinned his arms to his sides, and got one hand under the bomb so that he couldn't drop it on the wharf and maybe blow the lot of us to bits.

Then I realized just where I'd landed myself. I always wore plain clothes for my visits to the Shameen and even my car carried no flag on the bonnet. Unless someone recognized me and quick, I'd find myself in the river between the jetty and the ship's side while the mob dropped brickbats on my head. I'd once seen that happen to a sneak-thief caught red-handed and he hadn't lasted long. Meanwhile the fuze was still fizzing and the man was struggling so that I could hardly hold on to him.

"*Hao p'eng yu!*" I yelled, "I am a good friend!" though I hadn't much hope.

My luck was certainly in that day.

"Mah Kun," said a voice, and I saw one of the old coolies from our compound pointing at me. Two others took up the cry, the man in my arms stopped struggling, and I grabbed the bomb and dumped it in the ditch.

It sent up a big splash as it sank. I thought, "That might have been me," and made tracks away from that wharf and towards my car. I had another worry too. The *Onslaught*'s sailors were watching the excitement on shore and, if they saw a European in the middle of a hostile mob, they'd likely decide to come to my rescue and we'd have had another Sharkee Road shooting match.

Into the car I piled with my coolie and as many of the bombing party as could cling on along the running boards. We drove off to the headquarters of the strike committee. When I got there I was among friends, and I just took time out to tell them not to be naughty boys any more and drove on to the Consulate General, arriving on the doorstep face to face with the captain of the *Onslaught*, who'd come to make his official report on the incident.

I let him talk while I marshalled my own thoughts. It was a nasty little business and a sensational story full of news value. If the press splashed it, there'd be no end to the harm it could do. The captain finished his tale and "Monkey" Jamieson turned to me.

"Well, General Cohen, what have you got to say?"

"Sir James," I answered, "if that bomb had landed on the *Onslaught*'s deck it might have killed twenty of your men. It went into the Pearl River instead and—I'll say it straight out—it was thanks to me that it did. Now I'm asking you just one thing in return. Let's forget all about it. No complaints, no protests, no fuss and bother and leading articles in the *South China Morning Post*. Just wash the whole thing right out."

"That," said the Consul General, "would be highly irregular."

He looked at the captain and they both began to grin and he pressed the bell on his desk.

"Boy, bring three pink gins!"

I've drunk a lot of naval-style gins since then but I've never had a glass that tasted quite as good as that one did.

After that my stock with the Navy stood high. The *Onslaught* presented me with a boat's badge with their crest—a bullrush dripping with gore—a "bloody rush," see? That autumn the captain of the *Tarantula*, flagship of the West River Flotilla, threw a birthday party and invited me.

"Look at my presents," he said, and showed me a child's shooting outfit with a toy pistol that fired rubber pellets at cardboard ducks.

"Ach," I said, "I can't shoot with one gun; you've got to give me two."

They had two ready for me. They set up the targets one side of the quarterdeck and I stood on the other, a toy gun in each hand, and let fly. When I hit both the birds, they were as pleased as Punch. So was I—surprised too. Anyway that killed the silly yarn about my guns being loaded with small shot.

The strike dragged on all that year and into the next. The British suffered, but the Chinese suffered a whole lot more. We had another reason for wanting to put a stop to it.

Right up to the end of his life Dr. Sun had striven to unify China and he'd failed. Now, at last, there seemed a reasonable prospect of success. The previous Northern Expeditions had collapsed because the troops weren't trained and the generals weren't trustworthy. Now things were different. The Russian instructors at Whampoa had turned out proper cadres of junior officers and N.C.O.'s and Chiang Kai-shek had knocked some sense of duty and discipline into the senior staff officers and commanders in the field.

His orders for battle discipline were short and simple, but they're worth quoting in full. In the local fighting with Chen Chiung-ming and the others, they had already been rigidly enforced:

(1) If a company of my troops goes into action and then retreats without orders, the company commander will be shot.

(2) This rule will also apply to battalions, regiments, divisions, and army corps.

(3) In the event of a general retreat, if the commander of the army corps personally stands his ground and is killed, all the divisional commanders will be shot.

(4) Similarly, if the divisional commanders stand their ground and are killed, the regimental and battalion commanders will be shot.

We had six divisions at full strength—say, about 90,000 men—well-fed, well-armed, well-organized, and well-led. We felt pretty confident, but we couldn't start out to conquer China, leaving Canton behind us in a state of continual turmoil and with the real danger that some local hothead might at any moment plunge us into open war with the Western Powers.

So negotiations continued. I flitted back and forth until one evening I arrived with a firm assurance for the Consul General that the strike would be called off the following day. "Monkey" Jamieson had been relieved by this time and had gone to Tientsin, but he must have left me a good chit; his successor, John Brenan, was always as friendly and helpful as could be. This time I was looking forward to our interview.

My news was hot and I was in a hurry. Instead of landing on the Bund and walking across the canal bridge, I made my motor boat land me straight on the Shameen. I ran up the steps, when suddenly a little civilian guard barred my way. I knew all the guards on the bridge and they knew me. This chap was a stranger, although somehow his face seemed faintly familiar.

"Are you carrying a gun?" he said.

"Yes," I replied, "I guess I am."

"My orders are to disarm all visitors. You must hand it over to me, if you want to come on to the Shameen."

I was in too much of a hurry to argue and anyway I liked the boy's nerve. I made a great parade of reaching behind me for my little hip-pocket pistol with a shiny barrel and mother-of-pearl stock, and called up the coxswain of my launch and handed it to him.

The Consul General was delighted with my news. He drafted a telegram for the Ambassador in Peking and another for the Governor of Hong Kong. Then he said, "That's enough of my damned desk; we'll go down to the Club and celebrate!"

We walked along the short, quiet, tree-shaded street. When we were still fifty yards from the Club we could hear the hell of a shindy going on.

"They must have had the news already," said Brenan, but that wasn't the cause of it.

We walked into the bar which was crowded out, but

nobody seemed to notice us. They were all listening to my little civilian guard friend, who was standing with his back to the window, a gin sling in his hand and talking away nineteen to the dozen. We just heard the end of his discourse: ". . . and six of the best my father gave him for that night's work!"

Then I realized why I'd felt sure I'd seen his face before. He was the elder son of Israel Ellis, the great headmaster of Hayes School, and he was just telling them how I'd been caned for stealing unripe apples and giving my dormitory the gripes.

There was a moment's silence when they saw the Consul General. The No. 1 boy brought us each a "gin and it" and the whole crowd started in on me.

"What's happened to your gun, Morris? Did he beat you to the draw? Don't you feel a bit naked without your artillery?"

I held the top cards but I didn't want to show my hand just yet. I let them have their laugh. When the British think they've got a good joke they don't like to leave go of it. They ribbed me and roasted me and just went on and on.

Then somebody pointed the stem of his pipe at me and said, "Stick 'em up, Two-Gun! What're you going to do about that?"

That was my cue. I turned to the Consul General and said, "You will excuse me, sir."

I put my drink down on the bar and put my hands inside my jacket and—very slowly—I pulled from my shoulder holsters the two heavy .45 automatics that had been there all the time.

There was a gasp and a silence. The Consul General stepped in. He raised his glass and said, "Gentlemen, it seems our guest is too smart for our guards. Let's drink good luck to THREE-GUN Cohen!"

CHAPTER VIII

High Finance

IN JULY 1926 Chiang Kai-shek set out on the expedition that was—for a time—to unite China. Seldom can any military commander have begun a campaign in the face of such universal hostility. The Cantonese have always been regarded by the rest of China with distrust, which is by no means unreasonable, since their quick wits, their energy, and their incurable clannishness have made them for centuries a focus of resistance against any central authority. The foreign communities feared, also with every justification, the Russian Communist influence that was known to dominate both their military organization and their political propaganda. With one accord, both foreign and vernacular press heaped abuse and ridicule on Chiang and his followers.

"He is advancing," wrote Charles Dailey, the Far Eastern correspondent of the *Chicago Tribune*, "with his right flank protected by the fountain-pen of Eugene Chen and his left by the pistols of Two-Gun Cohen."

The writer might have added that Chiang's rear was covered by an even more formidable military figure. For some months during this period Morris shared his room with a taciturn Russian who spoke—on rare occasions—excellent German. He was to reappear a few years later as the almost mythical Marshal Blücher, commander-in-chief of the Siberian armies of the U.S.S.R.

The story of Chiang's victories is an oft-told tale. Changsha fell in August and Hankow at the beginning of

September. During the autumn he fought his way eastward to the coast and occupied his own native province of Chekiang. Shanghai and Nanking were captured in the spring of 1927, and by early summer all China south of the Yangtse was in his hands. By this time Morris had been translated from the field of battle to the more rarefied realms of high finance.

IT WAS THE BIGGEST SURPRISE of my life—he said—when they told me that T. V. Soong had asked that I should be sent back to Canton and join his staff at the Central Bank of China. The bank had been one of Dr. Sun's pet babies. Two of the greatest evils in China were extortionate money-lenders and unsecured local currencies. Most of the peasant farmers borrowed on their rice crop and the usual rate of interest was fifty per cent per annum. Many provinces and private banks issued their own notes and nobody ever knew their real value.

The Central Bank had been founded to establish a uniform and stable paper currency that would be accepted throughout the whole of China, and to lend money, especially to the farmers, at reasonable rates of interest. It had got off to a good start. Now it was being called upon to do something it had never been intended for—that was, to finance the military expenditure of the Northern Expedition. The silver specie was being used to buy munitions of war, and when it came to paying the troops, the printing presses had to work overtime. The Cantonese knew as much about dud dollar notes as most people. If they started to suspect the Bank's paper, Chiang Kai-shek was going to find himself in a jam.

Naturally I'd heard all this discussed at G.H.Q., but it hadn't worried me much till now, when I was jolting along in the usual grubby railway-carriage south down the still un-

finished Hankow-Canton line towards yet another new job—
one that I didn't feel I knew too much about.

I reported to T. V. Soong in his finely furnished first-
floor office the following morning. He began by reminding
me that we'd already worked together when he was Finance
Commissioner for the province and had managed to get up
against the great foreign oil and tobacco interests. The tobacco people sometimes fought each other to the extent that
the poor Chinese consumer suffered severely. The oil companies went to war when it was proposed to tax their im-
ports.

They refused to sell their products in the South, and
T. V. hit back by forming a company to import oil from
Russia. Later on it appeared that they were discouraging the
production of oil in North China, for fear that it might com-
pete in their own market. That was where I came in. I set
about the formation of a Cantonese company to prospect
and bore for petroleum, and I took good care that the news
leaked out. The result was that pretty soon officials of the big
foreign companies were themselves coming to inquire for
concessions, and everything was well.

He asked after his brother-in-law and his friends at the
front and then:

"I'm looking for a man to take charge of our bullion
vaults and the new note issue. I don't mean the printing of
them—just their safe custody. He's got to be somebody I can
trust and somebody my colleagues can trust and somebody
our customers can trust. People say you're an honest sort of
man. Could you hold down the job?"

After that I could hardly refuse. The very next day I
found myself sitting behind a big, shiny-topped desk in a
fine airy room right next door to T. V. himself.

I picked up my work quickly enough. It was mostly a
matter of security precautions—sentries and safes and

strong-rooms and so on—combined with the supervision of
some simple accounting, such as checking the weights of
bullion boxes and the serial numbers of new note issues. It
all seemed a piece of cake till a time came when the news
from the North ceased to be all good and it began to look as
if the campaign might last a lot longer than we'd expected.
That meant a further drain on our silver reserves, and the
Cantonese knew that as well as we did.

The first thing we noticed was that there were no new
customers. Deposits dried up and one or two people came in
to change notes for silver or to close their accounts. Then,
without more warning, the stampede started.

Our banking hours were from nine-thirty to three.
That morning a queue began to form at eight and by nine-
fifteen it was a hundred yards long. As soon as the doors
were opened, the lobbies filled up with panic-stricken people
clamoring for cash. They brought coolies with sacks to
carry away the silver that was shovelled over the counters.
All the while the queue outside grew longer and longer.

T. V. had seen this sort of thing before and he wasn't
worried—at least not at first.

"Pay out as fast as you can," he said. "Presently they'll
see sense and bring it all back again."

It didn't work out that way. The clamor inside
increased and the queue outside got longer. The bullion
vaults were littered with opened crates and cases and began
to seem awful empty. I went down to have a look around and
it gave me an empty feeling too, just as if the inside had all
been taken out of my stomach. At half-past two the chief
cashier came to T. V. and said:

"We can't possibly pay off all these people today. Let's
switch over to small cash for the last half hour, that'll slow
things up and we'll keep as much as we can in hand for tomorrow."

"No," said T. V., "that's only putting off the evil hour. What we'll do is to give 'em something surprising to talk about. Put up a notice in the main hall and another outside: 'The Bank will remain open till six o'clock.'"

The cashier looked as if he thought T. V. was crazy, but he went away to write out the notices, and I put a confident smile on my face and a fat cigar in my mouth and went downstairs.

As soon as I entered the banking hall I was recognized. "Why, Mah Kun," said a voice, "you're smiling!"

"Well, why not?" says I.

When the notice went up the crowd gathered around it. I went back half-way up the first flight of stairs and stood where everyone in the hall could see me, smiling away till my face ached.

A fellow came sidling up the stairs and whispered in my ear, "Mah Kun, do you know something?"

"Maybe."

He went down and his friends gathered around him. Another guy came up.

"Say, Mah Kun, is it true that a Foreign Power is backing the Bank?"

"How should I know? Go upstairs and ask T. V."

Down he went to the hall, a crowd gathered around him too. When it broke up, each of them was the center of another little group. I could see the story spreading like the ripples on a pool. From that moment the rumor went around that some foreign power had come to our rescue. Withdrawals over the counter stopped, the lobby emptied, and, when I went out into the street, the queue had vanished. Believe it or not, before we closed at six, people were bringing their money back again, just as T. V. had said they would.

Which foreign power were they thinking of? Many of

the powers were backing the North. Russia came out very strongly at this particular time in favor of Canton. She did, in fact, give a great deal of financial assistance.

Life went quietly for a while after that run on the bank and my job became a bit of a sinecure. I began to feel restless and managed to get myself sent off on a mission to Manila to inspect Philippine prisons with a view to reorganizing the jails of Kwangtung Province on modern humanitarian lines.

We were always trying to secure the abolition of Extra-Territoriality, which meant, roughly speaking, that foreigners in China were amenable only to the laws of their own countries. One of the main arguments in favor of its retention was that Chinese jails were unfit for Europeans. We reckoned to cut some of the ground from under their feet by reforming and modernizing our own hoosegows.

Bilibid Prison is one of the show places of Manila, it is cool and clean and comfortable; the food is excellent and recreational arrangements are lavish. Even the execution chamber is all done up de luxe. You approach it through a garden with the flower beds laid out like a skull and cross-bones. The words "Death House" are painted in scarlet letters two feet high over the entrance, and the room itself is all chromium and white enamel like the operating theatre in a hospital. I sat down in the electric chair—as all visitors do— and felt it would be almost a pleasure to be bumped off in such surroundings.

The convicts seemed as cheerful as crickets, especially the women, who were allowed to talk as much as they liked. Before they were locked up for the night, they all marched round the yard singing the "Bilibid Song." The warders, I was told, were mostly ex-convicts themselves. The only thing that made me stop and think was when, while I was actually there, the printing presses of a gang of counterfeiters who had flooded the Philippines with bad paper notes were found in the prison laundry.

That didn't alter the fact that it was all very modern and humane and, as soon as my Dollar Line boat was clear of Manila Bay, I sat down to write my report. It finished, "To see Bilibid Prison would have warmed the heart of Dr. Sun himself!"

I began to wonder what he'd really have thought of it. I remembered an episode that grew out of one of those rambles we used to take around Canton. I was still fairly new to China in those days and I simply couldn't stand the sight of the miserable beggars, ragged and crippled and covered with sores, who infested the city streets. I was always pointing them out to the Doctor. In the end he agreed that I should try to do something about them.

I was as pleased as a dog with two tails. A committee of twenty was formed, mostly influential people who could oil the wheels, but including a couple of good medical men. We requisitioned a compound on the outskirts of the town, put up rows of matsheds, and filled them with three or four hundred cheap plank beds. Then Wu Teh-chen, the chief of police, pulled in every single beggar off the streets and brought them along.

First we cropped their heads to get the worst of the lice away, we cut their nails so they couldn't scratch their sores, and gave them a damn good bath reeking with Lysol. We gave them a good meal, and last of all a good suit of coolie clothes. We told them that their troubles were over, there'd be lots of chow for them and the best medical attention, and we were going to make them into good citizens.

In a week's time there wasn't a single beggar left in the compound; every man-jack of them had escaped. I went to Wu Teh-chen and asked him to pull them in again. There wasn't a beggar to be seen on the streets. The whole lot had gone into hiding.

"Never mind, Morris," said Dr. Sun, "the way of the reformer is hard. But take my advice. Never plan for what people *ought* to do; try to think instead of what they'll *want* to do."

It was dusk by now, the liner was lying over to the northeasterly swell, and Bataan Head was dipping down behind the horizon. I thought of those cool, spacious, airy cells in Bilibid and the filthy, stifling hovels where the Cantonese coolies live and I knew what would happen when my fine new jail was built.

I tore up my beautiful report and wrote: "If you build a prison that is at all like Bilibid, you will need a doubled staff of warders—not to keep the prisoners inside, but to keep the poor people of Canton out, because they'll all be trying to break in!"

Meanwhile, the Northern Expedition got a move on again and things went well. The Southern troops were partly directed and actively assisted by Russians all the way to Hankow. Once he'd reached Hankow, the Generalissimo got rid of them. After that the last thing in the world the Communists wanted was a united, a peaceful, and therefore a strong and stable China. With Chiang Kai-shek sweeping the board and emerging as a great military leader as well as a statesman, that was just what was coming to pass. The fact that the Russian Communists were themselves largely responsible for the Kuomintang victories didn't make them any happier.

Quite early in the year they started to intrigue against Chiang more or less openly. They found that he was a pretty tough nut to crack. Borodin was recalled in disgrace (poor devil, his only fault was that he'd been too successful) and relations grew more strained than ever. The Soviet Consulates throughout China became centers for sabotage and subversive propaganda. Chiang determined to close the lot.

December 14th was the day fixed for the coup, but there was the usual leakage and the Communists in Canton felt strong enough to jump the gun. Chan Fat-kwoi was in command of the garrison. He happened to be out in the west of the province suppressing a local general who'd got too uppish, and anyway the Communists thought that he was on their side. The troops remaining in the city were known to be disaffected and the stage was set for a successful insurrection.

The government got a little warning, but not much, and we had to work fast. For the moment the Communists had all the cards and there wasn't a hope of our holding Canton. On the 9th, I went down to Hong Kong with two suitcases full of vital documents and a whole lot of arrangements to make. I ran around all day and most of the night like a scalded cat; I'd forgotten to shave and I fetched a few frosty looks from some of the old taipans I called on. But I managed to get things moving and I caught the morning boat back.

I needed a drink as much as I've ever done, and the second the hawsers were cast off I was into the bar. But quick as I moved, one man was ahead of me, T. B. Wilson of the Dollar Steamship Line, a long, lean Pacific Coaster, born in Seattle and raised in Alaska, with a slow, lazy way of talking like a Yankee on the stage. He'd done me one or two good turns and I didn't like to see him shove his head into the shambles that was waiting for us. The Communists were out-and-out fanatics and the Cantonese hated them and whichever side won would give no quarter.

"What are you doing on this boat?" I asked.

"Waal," he drawled, "they do say there'll be some feuding in Canton City and I thought I might as well check up on my branch office. And seeing it's Friday, I guess I'll take the weekend off and shoot crap with the boys."

"It won't be crap they'll be shooting." I said. "The Communists are going to rise tonight—maybe they've risen already—and this time tomorrow they'll have Canton in their hands and be starting in to settle old scores. Take my advice and come back on this same boat tonight. And tell your agent and his staff not to stir out of the Shameen!"

He argued a bit, but he knew that I knew the form and he promised to do as I said. I dashed around all day, but I found—as I'd feared—that things had already gone too far. The best thing I could do was to get out again and try to join old Li Fuk-lum, who was bringing up his own men as fast as he could get them on the move and concentrating loyal troops in his own stronghold on Honam Island.

We met again in that same steamer's bar that evening. I still hadn't shaved and I hadn't even washed for forty-eight hours. He cocked an eye at my face and hands, but all he said was, "I've taken your tip, thanks."

He picked up the only taxi on the jetty at Hong Kong and offered me a lift.

"Where do you want to go, Morris?"

"West Point Wharf."

"Why on earth are you going there?"

"I've a wallah-wallah [power boat] waiting to pick me up."

"Where are you off to now?"

"Canton, I guess."

"What the hell? You've made me pull out and now you're going back yourself."

"Ah, but I'm taking a roundabout route—up the West River and then by the back channels to Honam Island; and

« 177 »

there'll be some scrapping before I set foot in Canton again."

He thought this over while we skidded along the crowded street, accelerating and honking and braking as the driver tried to push past the chairs and rickshaws. The launch was there all right. As soon as the engineer saw me, he started up the motor and I stepped aboard.

"Thanks for the buggy ride," I shouted as we headed off, but Wilson was still thinking hard.

"Say Morris, do you *like* fighting?"

"No!" I yelled back, "I'm just a poor, peaceable, bloody banker, but I've got to look after my ledgers!"

By the time I reached Li's headquarters, the Communists controlled Canton and the horrors they perpetrated hit an all-time high—even for that turbulent township. They slaughtered, they looted, and they burned; one tenth of the whole city went up in flames and among the buildings that I could see ablaze was the Central Bank itself.

For two days they enjoyed themselves while we watched from across the river. Through my binoculars I saw sights that made me sick. Meanwhile Li Fuk-lum deployed his men, and Chan Fat-kwoi declared against the Communists and brought his troops in on our side. On the 14th we attacked in overwhelming strength, but it wasn't like when we drove out the Yunnanese. These Communists had had the full dose of indoctrination and they fought to the last man —and the last woman too.

I was panting to get across and see what had happened to the Bank's bullion vaults. I kept close to old Li Fuk-lum, because he was never very far behind his own front line troops. Before the Bund had been cleared of Communists, he called for a motor launch and went aboard with Chan Fat-kwoi and myself.

"What about an escort?" asked General Chan, but old Li only laughed.

"We've got Mah Kun," he said, "what more do we want?"

Our men had the upper hand by now, and when we neared the Bund there were no more Communists to be seen, though a few were still sniping from windows.

Out of a side street came running ten girls in uniform. They weren't fifty yards away from us. None of them could have been more than twenty and their bobbed hair flapped out from under their peaked caps.

They lined up across the Bund, drew their Mauser pistols, and opened fire on our soldiers. For a moment our men were too surprised to shoot, but then they let them have it. Four were killed at once, then two, and the rest went down one by one. The last girl of the lot was still firing when she fell.

Li Fuk-lum and Chan Fat-kwoi were pretty tough hombres and you wouldn't call me exactly a softy-pie, but we landed very, very silently, even though our side were winning. The other two made for their advance H.Q., but I went up the Bund to get to the Bank. I had to step over one of those ten young bodies—lying still in line—and I've hated that damned word "indoctrination" ever since.

I hadn't much time to moralize over the fate of those poor children because the Bank, when I reached it, was still burning and the first thing to be done was to round up some soldiers, organize a bucket chain from the river, and put the fire out. Luckily it was a solidly constructed brick building. The strong-room section itself was of reinforced concrete three feet thick. The Communists had just set fire to piles of office furniture and, although the banking hall was gutted, the vaults were intact.

I made sure that the locks hadn't been tampered with, and went off to our headquarters to report. I found that they were more interested in what was happening at the Soviet

Consulate. Our troops had occupied the place, found machine guns in the upper story windows their barrels still warm, and, rather naturally, shot some of the Consulate staff they suspected of having manned them. Chan Fat-kwoi was worried.

"Take my own guard," he said, "get there as quick as you can and protect any Russians who are still alive."

As I left the room, he shouted after me, "While you're about it, just sweep up all the documents you can find."

I was in time to save the lives of the Consul General himself and the womenfolk. They were taken into custody by Chan Fat-kwoi's troops and were safe enough for the time being, but the rest had been paraded down the main streets to the execution ground and shot amid general enthusiasm.

I've never seen the Cantonese so savage. They were going through the town looking for Communists and lynching them. Most of them had worn a red scarf or necktie as a distinguishing mark and, when they sweated, the cheap dye had run on to their necks and shoulders. Every suspect had his collar ripped open and, if there happened to be a scarlet stain on his skin, it was just too bad for him.

Meanwhile, I was busy. The Consul General's office looked more like a divisional headquarters, with a powerful portable radio transmitter in one corner and the walls hung with maps of the city and surrounding country all marked out with troop dispositions, even an Order of Battle showing the location of Communist cells in the various Chinese units. Papers were scattered everywhere. I filled a trunk with them and took it off to my flat on the Shameen, where I started to sort some out. I was stuck because I can't read a word of Russian and everyone who could was either dead or in the cooler.

At last I remembered the Ferriers, a newly married couple who lived in what used to be the Imperial Russian

Consulate in the French Concession—a stuffy, old-fashioned, red brick building with black teak-wood floors and a general air of gloom. They rented a little three-room apartment; like most newly weds, they were hard up. Vivian Ferrier represented a French silk firm and, to help pay the bills, he also acted as unofficial correspondent for the *South China Morning Post*, which, incidentally, was opposed to Chiang Kai-shek—but he didn't know that I knew that.

I'd played bridge with them once or twice and Olga Ferrier had told me that she was the daughter of a Russian diplomat of the old regime who had managed to escape after the Revolution. She could surely do the translation and I could think of no one else. I grabbed a handful of the likeliest looking documents and set out for their end of the Shameen. It was past midnight, but I never thought of that.

I knocked on their front door. There was no answer. I shoved, the door opened, and I found myself in a tiny hall. Still no sign of life. I turned the handle of the nearest door, looked in—and saw Vivian in his pajamas. I was excited and, without any explanation, just blurted out, "Say, I want to see your wife!"

Only then did I realize that I was in their bedroom and that the mop of black hair and the huge dark blue eyes regarding me from behind a pillow belonged to Olga, who was already in bed.

Vivian was over six foot and all of two hundred pounds and I could hardly have grumbled if he'd thrown me out on my ear. But he had a sense of humor and could see the funny side of most situations.

"Well, there is my wife!" he said. I could tell that he was amused.

I still had only one idea in my head and that was to find out what the papers were about—and quick. I stuck the top one into her hands and said, "Please translate this into English."

She wrinkled her forehead, and presently began:

"These are instructions for someone in Canton to contact a Chinese general whose name is given in code and to collaborate with him in organizing Communist cells in Indo-China. He is to . . ."

"General Cohen," Vivian chipped in, "this looks like being a lengthy business. Perhaps it would be as well if my wife got out of bed and we continued under more conventional conditions."

We settled down to make a night of it. She brewed some Russian-style tea—she had a little samovar—and he opened a bottle of cognac; as she sipped and dictated Vivian and I sipped and scribbled till we both developed writer's cramp.

By morning we'd broken the back of the job. The papers I'd got hold of turned out to be most important—high-secret, of course—and a revelation to me, though I wasn't without ideas on the subject. We'd uncovered something that would give a lot of people a headache, not to mention myself.

I bore the translations off in triumph to Chan Fat-kwoi, who said, "I think maybe the Russians protest about this."

They never did. Three fourths of their whole Consular staff had been publicly executed and yet the U.S.S.R. never said a word. You might look on that as a confession of guilt —or else they just didn't care.

By that time I felt I could do with some sleep, so I went back to my flat, where I couldn't be got at too easily, had a bath and a shave and a good big breakfast, and went to bed. I slept till the middle of the afternoon and then sat up and thought, "Jeez! What about the Bank?" Out of bed I hopped, dressed, strapped on my guns, and took a rickshaw down the Bund. I was only just in time.

While I'd been asleep events had moved fast. The Canton paper currency was secured on the silver in the vaults of the Central Bank, but now anybody who cared to stroll along the Bund could see that the Bank building was burned out and most of the roof had caved in. Naturally they came back wondering what had happened to the silver. They decided to get rid of their paper money while the going was good and rushed out to buy rice and wine and rolls of silk and gold ornaments and anything else they could think of. Prices shot up and the value of our notes began to spiral down. All this happened in the space of two or three hours.

The Chamber of Commerce became alarmed and held a meeting around about noon. Kan Kum-shek, the chief of the Government Economic Department, heard of this and invited the whole lot of them to take tiffin with him and talk matters over. He brought into the party a young ex-overseas student called Frank Szto, who, though only twenty-eight and only recently returned from his studies abroad, was already head of the Finance Bureau of the Canton Municipality.

They ate and they drank and then they got down to business. What the Chamber of Commerce wanted to know was: "Is that silver still there?" What they most wanted to do was to get inside the strong-room and see it with their own eyes. Old Kan had done himself quite nicely over the lunch and was in an expansive mood. He saw no harm in the proposal and there and then he invited anyone who felt like it to come along with him while he opened up the vaults for their inspection.

Young Szto smelled danger. Order had scarcely been restored in the city, and it seemed more than likely that the populace, having finished with the Communists, might turn around and start looting their better-off neighbors. The streets were swarming with excited and disgruntled groups of soldiery ripe for any sort of mischief. He himself had already received—and refused—offers to provide a guard for the Bank from most of the least reliable military leaders. He could see that for the Chamber of Commerce to march down in a body and open up the strong-room would be asking for trouble in a big way.

Poor little Szto raised these objections but was brushed aside. The merchants had eaten well and drunk well and were in a fine, bold, optimistic mood. Thirty of them accepted Kan's offer on the spot and got up to go. Then Szto had a brain-wave. He pointed out that to admit strangers to the bullion vaults was a high-level decision. Valid permission could only be given by the Chairman of the Political Bureau—a chap called Chen Kung-po, and a cunning old devil who might be relied on to find some way out of the mess. Szto slipped out of the banquet chamber and telephoned his Yamen. The answer came back that the vaults could not be opened without a written authority which would be sent down by messenger if, after due consideration, Chen decided it was in the best interests of the Bank.

This was where I came into the picture. I'd hardly left the Shameen when I realized that I'd never known the streets look quite so nasty. I stopped my rickshaw, paid off the puller, and went on foot. I've always had a soft spot for those poor skinny devils between the shafts and I didn't want to involve him in the ructions I saw looming up for myself.

I was still a quarter of a mile from the Bank when I heard a yell behind me. I'll freely admit that I jumped out of my skin and reached for my gun. It was only little Szto, who had run on ahead of the delegation and now grabbed my arm and poured his troubles into my ear. He was one of those very youthful-looking Chinese and at twenty-eight he might have still been in his teens—a scraggy little fellow too, with sharp peaky features and thick glasses. Usually he was a pretty cool customer. This time events were too much for him.

While he talked, we were walking on towards the Bank with the Chamber of Commerce deputation tagging along behind. They were still pretty pot-valiant, talking loudly and puffing fat cheroots and collecting some ugly looks from the loitering soldiers and other riff-raff. Chen had promised his decision within half an hour. I reckoned we might just manage to hold up the proceedings that long. What was going to happen then?

If he said "Open up," that was the last we'd ever see of the Bank of China's silver reserve. We'd probably have our throats cut into the bargain. If he said "No," that would confirm the worst fears of the Chamber of Commerce, the delegation would rush off to unload their own notes, the news would spread, and we'd have—not just another run on the Bank—but the complete collapse of the Cantonese currency. I prayed that the old boy would think up something quick.

We stared gloomily at the gutted shell of the Bank. The deputation caught up with us and formed a semi-circle waiting for the keys to be produced. Behind them some tough-looking characters sauntered up and formed another semi-circle.

"We've got to stall them some way," said Szto.

"Yes, but how?"

"You make them a speech and I'll translate it."

"What'll I talk about?"

"Tell 'em it's impossible for the note issue to have been burned—don't mention the bullion—because the strong-room's so well constructed."

The portico of the main entrance had collapsed. The

stump of one of the sham marble pillars still stood about four feet high and a convenient pile of rubble lay against it. I climbed up cautiously, shifted my feet around till I felt pretty sure it would stand my weight, and began in my best pompous "Board of Directors" style:

"Gentlemen, I am delighted to be able to set your doubts at rest. It is quite impossible for the Central Bank's unissued notes to have been destroyed or even damaged in this regrettable fire. Access to the strong-room is through two gates . . ." I caught a warning look from Szto and hurriedly switched the subject.

"The interior is forty feet long, thirty feet wide, and six feet high, and is entirely enclosed by walls of reinforced concrete three feet thick."

I ran dry for a moment and whispered, "What'll I say next?"

"Tell them how it was built."

That was a useful lead and I followed it. I'd picked up a good deal of the Bank's history from talking with T. V. Soong. I went right back to Dr. Sun and his plans for the financial future of China. I've always liked an audience and this was an easy one. Szto took his time over the translating and, while he was at it, I had a peep at my wrist watch. Over half an hour had passed—but there was still no sign of Chen Kung-po's messenger.

I told them everything I could think of about the Bank, and whispered again, "What am I going to tell 'em next?"

"Talk about yourself!"

So I did. It went down quite well because I got around to Dr. Sun again and any Chinese would listen to tales about him. Only Kan Kum-shek began to get restless. He felt he was "losing face" by this long delay in showing the Chamber of Commerce what he'd promised them they could see without difficulty. He piped up and asked when we were going to open the strong-room doors?

"What shall I say now?"

"Just keep talking hard. Recite your schoolbooks—or anything."

That wasn't good enough for Kan. He began to interrupt in earnest.

"Shout him down!" whispered Szto.

I opened the throttle and made a good loud noise, but it's not so easy to go on at the top of your voice when you're not quite sure what to say next. Then I remembered my Shakespeare. It had been well hammered in by old Israel Ellis at Hayes and I'd never forgotten it. I took a deep breath and let them have the full blast.

> "Have I a tongue to doom my brother's death
> And shall that tongue give freedom to a slave?"

Once you start Shakespeare you find that you can't damn well stop. I gave them big chunks of *Richard III* and was just going on to the *Henry VIII* when Szto pulled my arm. There was a young officer in Municipal Police uniform getting out of a car with a big sealed envelope.

"Thank God!" I murmured, mopping my forehead—and those were the last words of my speech.

We weren't out of the wood by any means. I could only think of two alternatives for Chen Kung-po and either one spelt trouble. Szto suggested that the officer should himself break the seals of his envelope and read the contents aloud, which he proceeded to do. We listened and sweated with anxiety, but we'd vastly underrated that old gentleman's cunning. His *huchao*, the official order, began with the usual phrases about honesty and financial rectitude, and continued:

"Unofficial visitors cannot, under any circumstances, be admitted to the vaults of the Bank. However, the Government of Kwangtung, in their anxiety to restore full confidence in their currency, is prepared to transfer the Bank's strong-room, together with its contents, over to the sole custody of the Canton Chamber of Commerce—provided only that the members of the said Chamber of Commerce will assume *full personal, collective and individual responsibility* for the safekeeping of the said contents."

"Robbing the People's Government" was a capital crime—it always is in revolutionary regimes—and Chen's huchao meant that, if they accepted his offer and, when the inventory came to be taken, there was a single dollar adrift, the whole Chamber of Commerce would make a one-way trip to the execution ground.

The Chairman took a look around him. He might have noticed that the crowd of toughs and loafers had doubled in size and closed in a bit. He cleared his throat and said:

"After hearing General Cohen's admirable and exhaustive address and seeing that the strong-room doors are intact, I am in a position to announce that myself and my colleagues are satisfied that the contents are untouched and we shall have much pleasure in issuing a reassuring statement to the public."

Frank Szto said a few kind words of farewell and they took themselves off. I said nothing at all. My throat was sore and my mouth was dry. I couldn't have got out another sentence to save my life. I'd talked myself to a standstill and for the first time—and maybe the last time—in my career, I was literally speechless.

CHAPTER IX

Protocol and Pirate

FOR THE NEXT EIGHTEEN MONTHS everything went right. Chan Fat-kwoi led his victorious but troublesome troops out into the western districts again. I must put on record that his bill for their pay, which was duly presented at the Central Bank, worked out at the right figure, with no demand for a percentage squeeze on top—and that was so unusual for Canton that it hardly looked legal.

The city settled down again in no time. It was wonderful how much that township could take without seeming to suffer permanent harm. In April Oi Yang-chang became head of the Municipal Bureau of Public Safety. He was a buddy of mine and he even hauled me in for his inaugural group photograph. That was the first time I'd posed for my picture with a party of cops. It made me think back to those old day in Alberta—and in Stepney, too, for that matter. Oi was a first class policeman, and as long as he held the post, crime in Canton didn't pay.

My job became easy and I was able to give myself a holiday in Hong Kong and throw a party or two in the Peninsular Hotel. I didn't forget the Ferriers either. I fetched those two young lovebirds down the river and gave them a real whirl. I've known myself what it's like to be hard up. I took care that they had no expenses except the journey, and I left a bottle of champagne in an icebucket up in their hotel bedroom to remind them of that all-night battle with their bottle of brandy back in Canton.

Meanwhile, the Northern Expedition went ahead like a house on fire. Chiang Kai-shek crossed the Yangtse early in the New Year and advanced rapidly. At the end of May he forced the passage of the Yellow River. On June 3rd Chang Tso-lin, the great Northern War Lord, evacuated Peking and was himself assassinated en route to Mukden. On the 8th the capital fell and the campaign was over. Long before this I was on my way to England.

As soon as it was certain that the Kuomintang was going to control the whole of China, the question of the new regime's recognition by foreign powers became acute. Up to then they'd each maintained their embassies in Peking accredited to whatever government happened to function there—and with China in a permanent state of civil war you could hardly blame them. Now all that was changed. We knew too that one of Chiang Kai-shek's first acts would be to move the capital from Peking to Nanking, which was not going to be popular in ambassadorial circles. A strong mission was formed headed by Hu Han-min, who was one of the real old revolutionary fighters and at the same time a man of culture and dignity. Sun Fo was to handle any constitutional, commercial, or economic questions that might crop up. He asked me to tag along and be on hand when they got to London.

That suited me fine. It was nearly ten years since I'd been home. My father and mother were getting old and wanted to see me again before they died, and I wanted to see my brothers and sisters—my nephews and nieces too—and find out how they were doing up in Manchester, where the whole family had moved a few years back. The mission sailed in an American liner—the *President Wilson* I think it was—and we travelled together as far as Ceylon, where I parted company. I wanted to see my sister Rose, who'd settled in South Africa, so I went that way around while the others headed for Palestine.

When we met again it was early July in Paris. I found a lot of long faces looking at me. Up to that point the mission had been a success, especially in Palestine. There'd been an understanding between the Zionists and the Kuomintang ever since Mr. Ezra had persuaded Dr. Sun to write for *Israel's Messenger*. Now that they'd had a chance of showing their sympathy, they'd grabbed it and laid down the red carpet. Other countries had also been pretty forthcoming. They realized that, whatever the legal position might be, Hu Han-min's mission represented the *de facto* government of China and they treated them that way.

Now only London remained. The British were being noncommittal as usual, and it was essential that the mission's last and most important visit shouldn't be a flop. You can go to most of the main European capitals on the way to somewhere else, and if things go wrong you've got an alibi. To get to London involves crossing the Channel and it's the end of the line too. If we arrived there and the mission was not accorded official recognition, there'd be no way of camouflaging the rebuff.

Sun Fo told me all this while we sat in his apartments at the Meurice where the carpet pile was so thick you tangled your feet in it and the chairs were so deep and so overstuffed you could hardly get out of them. When he stopped and took off his glasses and looked at me, I knew what I had to say. The next afternoon I was heaving my guts up on that filthy Channel crossing.

That was about my toughest assignment up to date, and I couldn't afford to fall down on it. I could only think of two people who might be able to help and on them I had no sort of claim, apart from the good will they might bear to China.

One was Sir John Thornycroft. I'd had indirect dealings with him over the sale of motor torpedo-boats to the Kwang-tung Government. The other was Sir William Shenton (only plain "Mr." in those days and usually known as "Bud"), a member of the Hong Kong Legislative Council who'd played a big part behind the scenes in the negotiations that had led to the ending of the strike and boycott in Canton two years earlier.

I called on both of them the night I landed. I wouldn't have been surprised if they'd both shown me the door. But that's where you've got to hand it to the English. They're stiff and they're starchy and usually they're pretty slow on the move, but they've long memories, and, if they're once your friend, that stays for keeps. Both my interviews went much the same way.

"When is your mission arriving?"

"They won't come at all unless I cable Paris that they'll be received by what they call 'the Fountain Heads.'"

"I'll see what I can do. Go back to your hotel and I'll ring you there."

I went back and waited without any too much con-fidence. They were both better than their word. Sir John went to the Admiralty and Sir William to the Colonial Office. Those two departments got on to the Foreign Office, and the Foreign Office in turn got on to the Chinese Em-bassy, whose position in the matter was tricky to say the least of it. The following day I was able to telegraph: "You will be received by 'Fountain Heads' please wire time of arrival." Fu Ping-chang was so pleased that he forgot to reply. When the mission landed at Dover there was no one there to meet them.

After that, things went with a bang. They were received at the Foreign Office and the China Association, which had not always agreed with Kuomintang policy, gave them lunch at the Mayfair Hotel. I saw none of that because, as soon as I'd done my stuff, I was away up to Manchester to see my own folks.

I'd looked forward to this visit a lot. Now at last I was coming home as a successful man-of-affairs of whom my family could feel really proud. I'd left them a sergeant and I was coming back a general, and that's quick promotion in any army. True, I hadn't made a great deal of money, but I'd got plenty for my needs and, beyond that, I'd had a finger—but if only a small one—in great events. In China at all events I could claim to be a public figure. I'd not only met the great ones of the earth, but I'd lived and worked with them. I couldn't help knowing that my experiences had given me something that I'd lacked before.

The welcome I received was as warm as it could possibly have been. My mother said nothing, but just held my hand and cried a little to show how happy she was. My father took me to the Synagogue and to meet the new circle of friends he'd made in Manchester. My brothers and sisters brought their children to be introduced to me. Several of them I had not seen before. The family house on Bury New Road in the Strangeways district was well kept and comfortable and, in fact, everything was going well.

Yet, as I travelled south again, I realized that my trip had been a disappointment to me. Ten years is too long to be separated from one's family. In that time I'd grown away from them. That was not because I'd gone up in the world —very far from it—but just because you can't help growing your roots in the earth where you live and when you're uprooted, the earlier roots wither. "Old China Hands" had often warned me of the same thing. Gliding along in my first class carriage over those English railway lines so well laid that you could hardly believe you were moving at all, I made up my mind that, whatever happened, I'd never stay away so long in the future.

Back in London I found the mission packing up for their departure, and was just in time to drop into my old A.D.C. duties for the farewell calls being paid them in their Savoy Hotel suite. The visitors came and went in a constant stream. Except that I didn't have to frisk them for their guns, it was just like the old days with Dr. Sun. After lunch the rush began to tail off. I was just thinking how lucky this was, as callers from both the Admiralty and the Foreign Office were about due, when a visiting card was brought in and I read "Captain J. U. P. Fitzgerald, Royal Navy."

That was a well-known name in South China. He'd been Senior Naval Officer of the West River Flotilla and, in the course of a dispute arising out of the anti-British boycott, had enforced his demands by bombarding a West River town. That had got him into a lot of hot water and at one time it had looked as though he might be retired. I'm not going into all the details; it was a long and complicated story and it never directly concerned me.

The Kwangtung Government, though they naturally resented the shelling of their town, knew Captain Fitzgerald as an honorable man who'd always behaved reasonably and fairly and had done his best to understand the Chinese point of view. They were determined that he shouldn't be allowed to carry the can for an action that was probably quite unavoidable. They discussed the matter and it was decided to write him a letter expressing their sympathy and their continued confidence in his character and judgment.

At the time Eugene Chen was Foreign Minister and he wielded a fluent and fiery pen, especially when he disapproved of anyone or anything. Most of his letter was a vitriolic denunciation of the British Government's policy, but it concluded: ". . . and if these gentlemen see fit in their wisdom to place you on the retired list, I am authorized to inform you that you will immediately be offered the command of the Southern Chinese Navy."

Captain Fitzgerald hadn't been retired, and he'd come around to pay his respects to his old friends. That was just the sort of occasion that the Chinese love, and I left them to enjoy it. I heard roars of laughter, shouts of *"gambei"* and *"gamsing"* [bottoms up] and more laughter. I knew that my next job would be to stall off any other callers.

Presently the Admiralty representatives arrived and I explained, "Their Excellencies Mr. Hu Han-min and Dr. Sun Fo are in conference."

They took the wait good temperedly enough, sat down, and lit cigarettes. In walked the Foreign Office party and I had to say my piece again. They weren't any too pleased and they looked even more old-fashioned when they heard the cheerful shindy that was coming from the next room. I did my best to make polite conversation, but my efforts seemed a bit feeble, even to me, and I was relieved when at last the door opened and Fitzgerald appeared.

The effect on my charges had to be seen to be believed. They'd been expecting some big noises from the City of London, or at the least some heavyweight journalist from *The Times* or *Morning Post*. Instead of that, out walked—surrounded by a haze of good cheer—that very Captain Fitzgerald who was supposed to be in such bad odor with the Government of Kwangtung.

That incident shows the curious courtesy and chivalry in Chinese dealings with the British. The Sons of Han have often had good cause to hate the policy of the great foreign powers, and, since the British have always played the leading role in China, it follows that whenever things went wrong they bore the main brunt of the anti-foreign feeling that would then brew up. Yet you usually found this strange little link of sympathy and understanding that seemed to grow stronger just when it was most needed.

Back in China we found things still going well. At the end of December the "Young Marshal" (Chang Tso-lin's son, who controlled Manchuria) threw in his lot with Chiang Kai-shek. Our blue flag with the white star was hoisted over Mukden and for the first time in thirty years China was united and at peace.

There was a little squabbling between provincial governments and the usual "circular telegrams" were flying around, but that never meant much. In January 1929 Chiang convened a Disbandment Conference at Nanking to discuss how to deal with the two million troops that various generals had under arms with no more fighting to be done. Merchants and bankers saw the green light, and loans were forthcoming for railways, highways, canals, port extensions, and all kinds of constructional projects. Engineers and technicians, both foreigners and foreign-trained Chinese, flocked in and it began to look like peace and prosperity for everybody.

My own star was in the ascendant too. After the mission's success in London, my stock was high and I could almost take my choice of jobs. I started by getting out of the Central Bank. T. V. Soong had been relieved by his brother-in-law, Dr. H. H. Kung, and I thought it was time to make a move. I suppose I'm what they call "a one-man dog," either I give my loyalty wholeheartedly, or not at all. I'd nothing against Dr. Kung, but I didn't know him very well and I felt I'd be happier elsewhere.

Meanwhile, Sun Fo had become Minister of Railways and Communications and he appointed me his Adviser on Foreign Purchases. Maybe that was where my reputation for honesty came in useful. It promised to be an interesting job, but it was hardly a full-time one and my eyes began to turn southward, back to Canton, where I always felt myself most at home.

The new Governor of Kwangtung Province was a little chap called Li Chai-sum. I'd met him first when I was just beginning my A.D.C. duties with Dr. Sun. I grew to like seeing his face because he always left the old man in such a good temper. One day the Doctor followed him out into the ante-room and, as the door closed behind him, took me by the shoulder:

"You saw that man, Colonel Cohen? You watch him in the future. He's a very short man—in fact, he's a very small man physically—but he's a very fine soldier. He's won his battles for three reasons: he's got brains, he's got courage, and he really cares for China. I like him more than most of the generals you'll see here."

Coming from the Great Doctor, that had really meant something and I thought that this must be a man I could serve happily. I sat down and wrote him a letter. English composition isn't my strong point, but it did the trick. He took me on to his staff without even first summoning me to an interview. When I reached Canton and was handed my official appointment, I found that I wasn't just one of the A.D.C.'s, I was "First and Principal Aide-de-Camp and Liaison Officer with the Government of Hong Kong and all Foreign Powers in South China."

I soon found that that was no empty title. Everyone was busy beating his sword into a ploughshare, and Li Chai-sum threw into the development of his province the same energy he'd put into defeating rival generals in the field. He initiated projects for building additional textile factories, sugar refineries, and cement works. The last of these became my special baby. I cast around for a foreign firm to undertake the job and had a real stroke of luck in contacting a chap called Stig Nielsen, who represented some big Danish concern.

That was a man in a million. Right from the start he made it clear that he wasn't just out to sell us a large-scale undertaking but to build something that would really work. He began by telling Li Chai-sum that his ideas were altogether too grand. He cut down the size of the proposed plant to one third of the original plan. He refused to have it erected close to the city itself, which would have suited some of the interested parties, and insisted on a site near the sources of the necessary raw materials, like limestone, and nearly a hundred miles from Canton.

Li Chai-sum took it all like a lamb. I discovered an astonishing thing—that he was making a genuine effort to cut out corruption and "squeeze." Now "squeeze" originated, not because Chinese are more corrupt than the rest of us, but because, by tradition and custom, Chinese officials are paid much less than a living wage and are expected to make both ends meet by means of a rake-off at every stage of a transaction.

In fact it's impossible to imagine a sum of money passing from Mr. A to Mr. C via Mr. B, unless some of it adheres en route to Mr. B's fingers. Call it a "commission" if you like—that certainly sounds more respectable. The fact remains that it's part of the way of life out there. The only question is whether the figure's reasonable, or way up in the twenty-five and thirty per cents, or even higher. To try to abolish it altogether was probably a hopeless task, but all the same it gave me a good feeling to be working on such lines.

Soon after my arrival I found General Li studying a large-scale map of the Pearl River Delta.

"Cohen," he said, "a quarrel between Hong Kong and

Canton is like a quarrel between the mouth and the belly. If they fight, the whole body suffers."

"Yes, sir," I replied, "but there's been so much bad blood between them all these years that it's going to be difficult to improve matters now."

He was a pertinacious devil. He'd made up his mind to get relations on a friendly basis and he stuck to his policy. The foundations for better feelings had been laid back in 1926 by Lord Willingdon's Mission, which arranged that the British share of the Boxer Indemnity Fund, reparations paid by the Chinese Government for damage done to foreign interests during the Boxer Rebellion of 1900, should be devoted to "projects mutually beneficial to Britain and China." In the outcome, a very large proportion of the money went to completing the Canton-Hankow Railway. That did no end of good to South China, besides making it possible for the first time to travel by train all the way from Canton to Calais.

So once again I was constantly on the move. I found myself flitting up and down the river between Canton and Hong Kong just as, three or four years ago, I'd flitted backwards and forwards between Honam Island and the Shameen. Luckily for me I had two stalwart friends, one at each end. In Canton, Brenan—he became Sir John Brenan a few years later—was still Consul General and in Hong Kong Mr. "Bud" Shenton was by now on the Executive as well as the Legislative Council. Those two weighed in and helped in every possible way.

One sore point for many years had been what was called the "British Yamen," some beautiful buildings surrounded by a beautiful compound and situated bang in the middle of the city. How they had come into British possession was something I never found out. At this time they were used to accommodate British language students, cadets for the Consular Service, the Hong Kong Government, and the Hong Kong Police. A cheerful, jovial party of young men in the early twenties they were—quite as well-behaved as any boys of that age ought to be, but their presence there on what was legally British territory naturally irritated the Chinese. It was rather as if Apsley House in Piccadilly and the garden behind it was legally Chinese territory and was inhabited by a crowd of jolly, carefree young Chinese students.

Another problem was a British loan for the dredging of the Pearl River Delta and the development of the docks at Whampoa so that ocean-going steamers could unload right in Canton, instead of transshipping their cargoes to river craft in Hong Kong harbor. The Chinese had formerly mentioned this proposition without much hope of agreement. It would obviously result in the reduction of Hong Kong's entrepôt business and seemed directly against the interests of the colony. What they didn't realize was that a peaceful and stable South China could keep two or three Hong Kongs busy, and that anyway trade makes more trade and both sides would benefit equally from a freer flow of traffic.

Eventually I found myself escorting from Hong Kong a strong deputation which consisted of Sir Joseph Kemp, the Chief Justice, and Halifax, the Secretary for Chinese Affairs. In Canton they were joined by the Consul General and sat down with Eugene Chen, T. V. Soong, and another Chinese official. It was obvious from the start that they all meant business.

I was present in my capacity as liaison officer, and I watched my chance and brought up both these points. The rendition of the Yamen came first, and it went through with surprising ease. All the British asked was that the Chinese should pay the cost of some improvements they had recently made in the property, and that was agreed to straight away.

The British loan was trickier, and I handled it cautiously. One morning on the Shameen I mentioned it privately to Sir Joseph Kemp. He liked the idea, and so I told Eugene Chen at dinner that evening. Chen said, "We'll probably refuse, for reasons of 'face,' but it would be a splendid gesture." At the very next meeting the loan was offered and duly refused. From then on everything went with a bang.

The goodwill was consolidated when the Hong Kong Chamber of Commerce paid them an official visit and laid a wreath on the tomb of the Seventy-two Martyrs.

The final touch was given to Anglo-Chinese understanding when we arranged for official visits to be exchanged between General Li Chai-sum and the Governor of Hong Kong. There were long months of negotiations at all sorts of high levels before this could be fixed up, but the idea originated in a quiet chat between Shenton and myself one hot afternoon in his office. I'll always be proud of the part I played in putting it through.

The most difficult of all our enterprises, and one that nearly led to fresh ill-feeling between Canton and the colony, was the cleaning up of the Bias Bay pirates. The funny thing was that we only came to undertake the job by accident.

The story began when the Shanghai Defence Force was returning to England. [This was a British force sent out to defend the International Concession in Shanghai, which appeared for a time to be endangered by the startling success of Chiang Kai-shek's Northern Expedition.] They had a lot of military equipment which, it was reasonable to suppose, they wouldn't want to cart all the way home again. I had my eye on some splendid six-wheeler trucks which would have been just the thing for our army, which was as short of transport as it always used to be. In those days most of our ammunition followed the troops slung beneath a bamboo pole on the shoulders of two coolies. Food? Why they foraged for themselves and lived on the local farmers. If they didn't, they starved.

I popped down to Hong Kong and put the proposition to General Luard, the G.O.C., but I got nowhere. The trucks had to go right back to the U. K. I turned my attention to several hundred mules which they could hardly want to ship half-way around the world again. I was right about this. They were for disposal on the spot, but one difficulty remained. Even in the temporarily peaceful state of China, the British authorities were scared of an accusation that they were helping to arm the South against the North. They asked me why we needed the mules. I had to think up something quick and—half as a joke—I told them that we were planning an expedition to wipe out the Bias Bay pirates.

Nobody in their senses ever believed that it was possible to prevent piracy on the China coast and I never dreamed that my words would be taken seriously. Bias Bay is a whacking great inlet, mostly shoals and shallows, just outside the territorial waters of Hong Kong. The people who lived on its shores were farmers and fishermen part of the time and pirates just when it happened to suit them. They worked on unconventional lines and seldom with their own craft, though they had some fine big fast-sailing junks when they chose to take them to sea.

Their usual method was to board a coastal steamer—at Hong Kong or Macao or Swatow, sometimes even further afield—disguised as ordinary passengers. As soon as the ship was safely at sea, they'd draw their guns, hold up the white officers, and seize the bridge, the engine-room, and the wireless office. Then they'd run her into Bias Bay, loot her at their leisure, and land with their booty in their own sampans that put off to meet them. By the time a British or Chinese patrol boat came along—if one ever did—they'd be peacefully ploughing their paddy fields, or hauling their nets out in the bay.

Quite often they'd take two or three of the better-off passengers along with them to be held for ransom, just like their bandit brethren in the interior. The procedure was quite simple. Your family got a note asking for as much cash as they thought you could afford to pay. If it was forthcoming, you were released. They always kept their word. If it wasn't forthcoming, your sorrowing relations would receive the lobe of your right ear—just to show that the pirates meant business. If they still held out in spite of the pleading letters that you were, by this time, writing them, the pirates cut off and dispatched more painful portions of your anatomy.

Being "pirated" was just about as likely a misfortune on the China coast as being run over while crossing a street in London. Many wealthy merchants habitually travelled disguised as coolies so as to avoid the discomfort of being cut up for ransom notes.

But the pirates had their own little ways of finding out a man's financial status. For instance, they'd give their prisoners a big boiled fowl or a mandarin fish for supper and watch how each of them tackled it. The genuine poor man who'd probably never seen such food in his life before waded into the fat fleshy portions, the breast and the legs and wishbone of the chicken, or the shoulders and flanks of the fish. The rich man who was something of an epicure knew that the tastiest bits are the little finicky morsels close to the bones—the "pope's nose" of the fowl, or those tiny pockets of flesh just under the eyes of the mandarin fish. They'd fiddle about with their chopsticks to get those tit-bits out, and give themselves away like that.

In the nineteen twenties piracy grew and grew till it became a full-size permanent pain-in-the-neck to every shipping company operating on the coast. What made matters worse was that not one of the various efforts at prevention showed the slightest sign of success.

Searching the passengers as they came on board was tried but found quite impracticable. They streamed up the gangway in uncontrollable mobs carrying masses of miscellaneous luggage. To enforce a proper search would have meant a stay of days instead of hours in each of the little coastal ports. Enclosing the steerage passenger spaces with iron grilles was given up when a ship in collision sank, taking all the steerage passengers down with her. Small-craft patrols couldn't be everywhere, and the wireless operator in a pirated steamer knew that, if he tried to send an S.O.S., he'd just be shot and thrown to the sharks.

They tried armed guards of White Russians or Sikh Police, but the pirates always had the advantage of numbers. Being equally well armed, they could choose their own moment for attack. The element of surprise was on their side. After one or two of these guards had got the worst of it, the morale of the others wasn't so hot.

In the end detachments were provided by the Royal Navy. That certainly worked, but at the cost of almost immobilizing the China Squadron. Presently the Commander-in-Chief put his foot down and said that the provision of anti-piracy guards by the Navy must stop. They had other things to do.

Matters had just reached this impasse when I came along with my offer for the mules and my rather rash reason for wanting them. I got them at fifty Hong Kong dollars (say £3) a head, which was a knock-out rock-bottom price, and went back to Canton very pleased with myself.

My pleasure lasted just twenty-four hours. The following morning a telephone call summoned me to the Yamen of General Wu Teh-chen. I've mentioned him once or twice before as Chief of Police in Canton. By this date he'd risen to command the garrison troops of both the city and the whole province. Being responsible for all internal security, he still retained a supervisory control of the constabulary.

General Wu was well known as a trouble-shooter and in China the trouble-shooter usually ends by finding himself in trouble too. He'd played a big "back-room boy" part in Chiang Kai-shek's early rise to power. Several times he had restored order after local rebellions by methods which were drastic even for China. He was afraid neither of bloodshed nor of making enemies. Later on his enemies caught up with him and he spent six months in disfavor and, in fact, under some sort of arrest or detention. Later still the Japanese War gave him his great opportunity. He rose very high indeed. At this time he was just considered to be an exceptionally capable administrator and a strong man.

Foreigners liked to deal with him because he always came straight to the point and always did precisely what he'd said he'd do. He was tall for a Chinese, very dignified —remarkably so in a country where personal dignity is almost natural. He was the sort of man you naturally called "Sir" even before you knew who he was. On this particular morning, he dropped the dignity and was out to make me feel foolish.

"Good morning, Morris," he began, "I hear you've decided to exterminate the Bias Bay pirates . . . Splendid! . . . When do you plan to make a start?"

"How did you know, sir?" I asked, playing for time. He flipped across his desk a letter from the Governor of Hong Kong that must have come up-river in the same boat

« 205 »

as myself. It was beautifully phrased and quite obviously meant to pull our legs.

His Excellency had been informed by General Luard of our purchase of the military mules and, although he had entertained grave doubts as to the advisability of permitting this transaction, he was now delighted to learn that they were to be employed for so admirable a purpose. The best efforts of the British Navy had hitherto proved ineffective against the pirates of Bias Bay, and now it only remained to offer their fullest cooperation in this difficult and dangerous undertaking, cooperation which we would also receive in the fullest degree from the garrison and police force of Hong Kong.

In other words, "I'll believe in your expedition when I see the pirates' heads."

I read it to the end and then I looked at Wu Teh-chen. He was still enjoying his joke.

"Well, Morris, it only remains for me to offer you the cooperation of the Kwangtung garrison troops and police as well. Now you ought to be all right!"

"Aw, hell, sir, give me a break!"

He smiled and picked up a sealed envelope.

"You know as well as I do that the pirates'll hear about the expedition as soon as preparations start. That can't be helped, but they'll also be warned the day you leave Canton, they'll have a running commentary on your progress all the way. Long before you get anywhere near Bias Bay, the whole lot'll have vanished."

Of course I knew it, so I said nothing and he went on:

"However, I've put in a little work with dossiers from our own C.I.D. . . . You know, don't you, that their leaders live in Hong Kong?"

"Yes, sir, everyone knows that, but there's never been any proof."

"Perhaps not. Still in that envelope you'll find a list of Hong Kong residents who definitely draw dividends direct from the pirates, either by the sale of loot or by ransom payments into their own banking accounts. Open it and have a look."

I did and I gasped. The first name on the list was that of a prominent and highly respected citizen, the managing director of one of the biggest Chinese banks and well in the running for the Legislative Council!

Now Wu Teh-chen really got down to business.

"I'll tell you something more, Morris," he went on, "all the pirates' information—sailings of patrol boats and merchant ships, cargo manifests and rich men's names on passenger lists—comes through Hong Kong. If you want to catch them napping, you'll have to persuade the Hong Kong Police to arrest the people named on that paper.

"They can think up any charge they like and let 'em out again later on, but unless you can get those gentlemen behind bars for ten days while you're on the way to Bias Bay, you've not a chance of success. We'll have the whole Hong Kong Government shrugging their shoulders and saying 'just another Chinese promise!' "

Next day I was off down the river again, with that list in my pocket, my tail between my legs and my heart in my boots. The Inspector General of the Hong Kong Police was a big, genial, jovial sort of bloke. He didn't always see a joke, but when he did he liked to make the most of it. This one about myself and the Bias Bay pirates just suited his style of humor.

"Well, well, well, General Cohen," he greeted me, rubbing his hands and beaming all over his fat red face, "I was expecting to see you here. What can we do to help? His Excellency the Governor has said that you're to have all possible assistance and it's yours for the asking. Shall we empty the new Stanley Jail ready for your prisoners and captives?"

I let him run on because I wanted to get him in a good temper. Presently I slipped in my little oar. I went at it very, very carefully. I was respectful and deferential and quite unlike my usual self. I told him that, as he well knew, the pirates had an excellent intelligence service; that all their lines of communication up and down the coast obviously funnelled through Hong Kong; and that they were universally believed to have their headquarters in Hong Kong itself. Then I came to the point. If I gave him the names of their leaders, would he have them locked up for a week or two while my expedition was getting under way?

He hummed and hawed a bit at that.

"Remember, General, that British law and justice run in this colony. You can't just throw a man into chokey on suspicion. An arrest means there must be prima facie evidence of the commission of some crime—and a magistrate's warrant. Anyway, let me see your list!"

I laid it on the table and watched his face as he picked it up. You've heard of people "going purple with anger" and thought it was just a cliché, but I can tell you it really happens. His face was red anyway, but a wave of pure purple seemed to come from under his collar and mount up his neck around his chin and towards his ears. His mouth opened and shut but at first no words came out and when they did, it was in a funny squeaky little voice that he said,

"I dined at his house last night!"

At last he found his tongue again and let me have the rough side of it.

"What do you mean by giving me the name of one of the honorable and most respected men in Hong Kong and daring to accuse him of being the head of the Bias Bay pirates? Outrageous nonsense! I know why you make these disgusting accusations. It's because he happens to be opposed to the present regime in Canton and you hope to discredit him. I shall see the Governor and tell him what I think of such disgraceful tactics!"

I could still hear explosions of "Nonsense!" and "Disgusting!" as I went downstairs.

Wu Teh-chen was just as obstinate.

"Very well," he said, "no preliminary arrests, no expedition": and there matters stuck for some months.

The I.G.P. had practically thrown me out of his office, but I'd left a tiny seed of suspicion in his head about our banker friend. Presently he began to wonder if he was quite as fine a fellow as he'd thought. He put his own Hong Kong dicks on to him and they unearthed plenty. Right out of the blue one morning Wu Teh-chen received a telegram:

> MR. . . . — . . . — . . . ARRESTED ON SUSPICION COMPLICITY RECENT COASTAL PIRACY STOP GRATEFUL IF YOU COULD FURNISH CORROBORATIVE EVIDENCE.

Wu Teh-chen replied:

> COHEN LEAVES ON NEXT BOAT WITH ABSOLUTE PROOFS OF GUILT STOP STRONGLY ADVISE YOU NOT REPEAT NOT GRANT BAIL.

This time I drove into the Central Police Station compound and walked up the I.G.P.'s stairs feeling real good. I had a shock coming to me. I'd hardly sat down in my chair when he blurted out:

"I'm terribly sorry, Cohen; I don't know what General Wu will think of us, but the magistrate insisted on granting bail on ten thousand dollars' surety. We protested, but it was no good—British justice, you know. He put the money up himself and of course he promptly absconded and got out of the colony."

"Which way did he go, sir?"

"Macao—but he's had twelve hours' start and he'll be into the interior by now . . . Hie! Where're you off to?"

I'd heard all I needed. If he'd gone to Shanghai, or Manila or Singapore, he'd have been safe, but the poor boob had walked straight back into our territory. Now it was only a question of tailing him before he'd gone too far. I ran all the way down the hill to the G.P.O. and set the wires buzzing. I caught the afternoon boat back to Canton.

The Bias Bay expedition started two days later, but there wasn't much of a story in it. It became at the last minute a combined operation with the British Navy. We managed to corral most of the pirates either on land or sea. They put up surprisingly little fight. We took about seventy-five of them back to Canton where they were tried and condemned in batches of ten at a time.

In the court some of them seemed to recover their courage. They got a bit tough, but it didn't do them much good. I sat with the judge for the first day's trial and saw Chinese justice in action.

It all ended with one of those horrible shows on the execution ground. The only thing about that part which pleased me was that our Hong Kong banker was there too. Wu Teh-chen's sleuths had caught up with him before he'd gone a hundred miles, and he met his pirate friends in the dock.

They were good times with everything going well for China—and for Morris Abraham Cohen too. The climax came in June with the State Funeral of Sun Yat-sen.

Not long after his death I'd accompanied Mme. Sun and Sun Fo and a few of his intimate friends to choose a site for the Mausoleum. In China the position of a grave is a matter of great importance even for the humblest of men. The surroundings have got to be just right. For days we'd walked over the Purple Mountains, a famous historical burial ground—the great Ming Dynasty buried their Emperors there—till at last a site had been selected.

Ever since then the building of the Mausoleum had continued through wars and plagues and floods and famines. Now it was complete and magnificent—worthy of the Great Doctor himself—but almost impossible for me to describe. Most Chinese architecture is symbolic and therefore meaningless unless you happen to understand the symbols. It was approached by three hundred and sixty-five steps, and the main structure represented Dr. Sun's Three Great Principles. Even a foreigner like myself could appreciate its grandness.

I'd hoped for an invitation to the funeral, in spite of being tucked away out of sight, so to speak, down in Canton. I wasn't prepared for what actually happened. I was summoned, not to Nanking, but to go first to Peking and accompany Dr. Sun's body all the way from the Azure Cloud Temple. I was the only European present. I was used to being that, but there were very few Chinese either, just his immediate relatives and a few of the real old revolutionary warriors who'd served with him when he was a hunted exile and could only set foot on Chinese soil in disguise and risked his neck every time he did.

I realized the extraordinary honor that was done me, but somehow I couldn't feel pleased as I ought to have done. On that journey there was no room in my heart for anything but sadness.

When we reached Nanking I had to move fast. They'd put me in charge of all the foreign delegates attending the funeral. I was a sort of Marshal of the Diplomatic Corps.

The first thing I had to do was to arrange them in an order of march for the funeral procession. There I bumped up against something called "protocol." I'd met it before, when I was in Paris with Sun Fo and again when we were trying to fix up the reciprocal visits between the Governors of Canton and Hong Kong, but I'd never really tangled with it till now. I'd sized the delegates off for height so that they'd look all right walking through the Nanking streets; but that wouldn't do—it all had to be settled by seniority and precedence. The result was that the British Ambassador, Sir Miles Lampson, who was well over six foot tall and broad in proportion, had to walk with the Japanese Ambassador, who was something under five foot and weighed maybe ninety pounds. Side by side they looked like the giant and the midget out of a circus.

It was a completely Chinese funeral and on a scale I've never seen before or since. A hundred coolies carried the coffin on crossed bamboo poles, with drums beating, white-clad professional mourners walking, banners and lanterns in the traditional funeral colors of silver and blue. A whole people was mourning the man who'd made them into a nation.

I walked with the family, feeling very conspicuous in my top hat and black cut-away coat. It was a steamy, sweltering summer day—the sort you get in the lower Yangtse valley—with clouds that seemed to bear down on our heads, and stifling dust rising round our feet. I looked at Dr. Sun's coffin swaying in front of me and wondered what he'd have thought of it all.

The pomp and show and the glory, the almost religious adoration of his own people, the respect and admiration of the rest of the world would have meant less than nothing to him. But that China was free, China was united, and China was at peace—that would have made those long years of hardship and danger and discouragement and repeated failure seem worth while.

I knew he'd be happy wherever he was—but, oh, how I wished he was with us still.

CHAPTER X

The Triple Threat

SUN YAT-SEN'S FUNERAL was a climax in more ways than one. Up to that moment everything went right. From then onwards I had no luck at all—and neither did China.

The trouble began before I got back to Canton. It was the old one of Southern Separatism. In this particular case, a plot to secure the Southern domination of the middle Yangtse valley. My own chief was involved, though he was always a moderating influence who thought he could keep the peace between the two factions. As so often happens, it was just the moderate, well-meaning man who got the worst of both ends of the stick.

Chiang Kai-shek decided to get his blow in first and invited him to Nanking to attend a Party Conference. Li Chai-sum took this for an olive branch and determined to accept the invitation. He broke the news to me late one night. I saw at once that it was a dangerous move and begged him to take me along. I was his first and principal A.D.C. and responsible for his personal safety. I even stuck my neck out to the extent of pinching a staff car and calling on the leaders of the Kwangtung-Kwangsi clique to see if they couldn't somehow stop him.

I succeeded in getting one or two of the bolder spirits to see General Li and tell him that, if only for the sake of "face," he should ask for a guarantee of good treatment and an assurance that he would not be detained in the north.

This started the telegrams flying back and forth, which was all to the good because it stalled matters a little longer. Eventually two of the elder statesmen in Chiang's party (I forget their names, but they were both men with something to lose in the way of personal honor) pledged their *lives* that Li Chai-sum would be received with all due dignity and allowed to return south whenever he wished to do so.

I'd done all I could but I didn't like the look of things any more than before. Without telling my boss, I arranged for the two of us to travel by sea, which meant a journey of three days instead of thirty-six hours. What was even more important, we had to stop off in Shanghai, where we were still in touch with the outside world, before finally walking into the trap—because I knew damn well it was a trap.

It was just that stop-off that led to disaster. Li Chai-sum knew he was putting his head in the lion's mouth, and he didn't want to drag me in, too. He'd been planning to give me the slip and now was his chance. That night I threw a party—I always did when I landed in Shanghai—and it was a good one. I don't remember very much about that evening, but I woke up in my hotel next day with a head that hurt and a mouth that felt as if it was lined with sandpaper. My watch said twelve o'clock and our river steamer sailed at half past one.

I washed and shaved and dressed and packed without hurrying myself, downed a brace of bromo-seltzers, and strolled along the corridor to my boss's room. The door was open, his luggage was gone and the room-boy was making the bed. I panicked; I went down the main staircase three steps at a time and rushed to the reception desk. The clerk was a sardonic White Russian. He gave me that sideways look that you get from reception clerks when they know that someone's made a monkey of you.

"General Li caught the early morning train," he told

me. "The General particularly said that you were not to be disturbed."

He'd only got six hours' start of me, but his train was the only one and would reach Nanking the same evening, my boat would spend a night on the way. I cursed myself for a fool.

Usually I enjoyed a trip up the Yangtse, where everything is quaint and strange—the big "carpenter-flies," with their forelegs something between a lobster's claw and a hand-saw, the flocks of duck cruising downstream to market, herded by men in little round coracles, the "bird-fishers'" boats, with their small square sails and rows of big, black, long-necked cormorants sitting along the gunwales. Other times I'd delighted in those sights. Now I just stamped up and down the deck, looked at my watch, and growled at anyone who spoke to me.

Out of the Whangpoo and around the Woosung Forts; the dull, flat shores till we passed the Langshan Pagoda; Tungchow and Kiangyin, and then we anchored for the night off Beaver Island. Next morning we made good time as far as Chinkiang. There we ran into thick fog. The skipper tried to push on for a while and our siren echoed back from the Chusan Hills, starting on the port beam, coming from ahead and finally fading away on the starboard quarter. It was no good and we had to anchor again. I spent the next few hours listening to the damned fog bell clanging out every two minutes and wondering what had happened to my boss.

When at last we got in, it didn't take me long to find out. The first man I met told me that Li Chai-sum had been arrested outside the Customs shed and was imprisoned in a private house near the Drum Tower.

Then I really blew my top. I was mad with everyone concerned. Most of all, I was mad with myself for being

Generalissimo Chiang Kai-shek; the scroll by Dr. Sun Yat-sen, the painting by Mme. Chiang

Yu Yu-jen, President of the Control Yuan; General Cohen

Left to right: Dr. George K. C. Yeh, Minister of Foreign Affairs; General Wu Teh-chen; General Cohen; Dr. Wang Chung-hui, President of the Judicial Yuan; General Ho Ying-chin, former Prime Minister; and Dr. Wu Tseh-hsiang, Minister to Chile

made to look a sucker. The rest of that day I went about shooting off my mouth to everybody I met. It's a wonder I didn't land up in the hoosegow myself.

Next morning the whole situation seemed fouled up. I couldn't think what to do next. Suddenly I saw that my only hope was Sun Fo. He was still Minister of Communications, but was immensely more powerful than you'd guess from that. If anyone could help, he could. I got into a rickshaw and shot off for the Yamen.

I found him immersed in piles of papers, looking just as he always did. He doodled away on his blotter while I poured out my tale of woe. He put down his pen, blinked in his usual way, and started to take me to pieces.

"Things are seldom as bad as they appear, Morris. You must surely know that two of my venerable colleagues have guaranteed with their lives that General Li would be safe in Nanking. The senior of these has already honored his people. He made the customary preparations for the self-destruction and warned General Chiang that, unless he was allowed to share Li Chai-sum's imprisonment, he would commit suicide within the hour. He is now incarcerated with your chief."

That altered the whole set-up. With an elder statesman sitting in the same room and determined if necessary to die with him, my boss was safe for the time being at all events.

"I've also arranged," went on Sun Fo, "for you and me to visit General Li tomorrow afternoon, when we can discuss this regrettable situation and what course of action we can take."

I could have fallen through the floor. I began to stammer out thanks and apologies, but he cut me short. Off came those thick spectacles of his. For one instant it was the eyes of Sun Yat-sen that bored into mine.

"It was indeed fortunate that you called on me. If you were not already in my Yamen, you would now be in serious trouble yourself. Times have changed, Morris. Times have changed!"

He turned back to his papers.

I went to that interview with my eyes skinned. General Li's English wasn't any too good and neither was my Chinese, but we could understand each other on simple straightforward matters. On this occasion we thought it best to play up the language problem for the benefit of the guards and have Sun Fo formally interpret what we said, as if we couldn't understand each other at all.

While he was talking I had plenty of time to look around and make a few mental notes. Li's quarters were quite comfortable but rather cramped. The reason for that was, not only that the old statesman was there as well, but also that the house itself was small, which of course made it that much easier to guard. Well guarded it certainly was—with a patrol outside the compound walls, another patrol inside, and a couple of sentries on the roof. There were three control points—a sergeant on the gate, another on the front door, and an officer and four men in the room—and all three points checked our credentials. A rescue by force wasn't going to be too easy.

Li Chai-sum was surprised to see me. He nearly shook my hand off, but he couldn't say much with so many people present and Sun Fo took care to keep our conversation to generalities. I came away comforted at knowing that my chief was getting good treatment and was evidently in no immediate danger. I had time to lay my plans.

I was sick of my hotel. Sun Fo had warned me not to make myself conspicuous around Nanking any more. The next day I hired a gharry and drove out to Dr. Sun's Mausoleum in the Purple Mountains. It took me well away from the city and I somehow felt that, if I brought my troubles right to where the old man lay, he might be able to help me. It sounds silly enough now, but that was at the back of my mind.

The monument had weathered well. It looked superb and fitted into the landscape. I felt better for just being there. I was mooning along one of the terraces wishing that the Doctor was still with us and thinking how different things would be if only he were, when there was a shout of "Mah Kun!" Someone slapped me on the back and nearly knocked me off my feet.

I turned and looked into the honest, ugly, wholesome phiz of old Mah Sang, who'd been A.D.C. with me from when I'd first come to China right up to the Doctor's death. The last time I'd seen him was at the funeral. He'd been in tears. Now he was grinning like as if his face might come in half at the mouth. I hadn't seen many happy faces these last days and it did me good to look at him.

"Colonel Mah!" I said, "Well, well, well."

"No more colonel," he beamed at me. "Now I general all same you. I commanding permanent guard on Sun Wen tomb—two battalions full strength. They good boys; some of old personal bodyguard you and I pick up Whampoa side. Not much work, but I make 'um train—train damn hard. What you do here?"

I told him. As I did so, an idea came into my head. He listened with sympathetic grunts. I guess he was the loyalest guy I've ever known, and he could understand loyalty in another man. At the end he cleared his throat and spat.

"These days no damn good. Other time we all serving Sun Wen and Sun Wen serving China. Now each man fight for himself and for China no one fight. For me, I mind my own pidgin. No mix in politics." He paused and thought. "Allee same; Li Chai-sum damn fine fellow. Dr. Sun liking

him a lot. Damn shame put him in jug . . . Politics stink!"
He spat again.

I saw my chance.

"Say, General Mah, I wonder if you'd do me a favor?
Could you pick out some of the old gang who knew me in
Canton—not more than twenty or so, but good tough guys—
and give them forty-eight hours leave and no questions
asked?"

He grinned.

"No bloody fear! Me lose my head and then who guard
the tomb?"

We walked on in silence right round the terrace. I knew
my man and I wasn't worrying. At the main gateway he
stopped.

"All litee—can do. You damn fool, me bigger damn
fool. Come back tomollow night. Twenty men here; coolie
clothes, no rifles, Mauser pistol, and ten rounds each; two
carry hand grenade and two piecee tommy gun." I could
have kissed him.

Next morning I had a very different interview to face. I
put on my best suit and called on the captain of the British
gunboat anchored out in the river. We'd known each other
down in Shanghai, and I could come straight to the point.

"See here, captain, if I brought Li Chai-sum on board
your ship, would you give him sanctuary? Don't answer now,
I'll come back in two hours time for your decision."

When I did he received me very formally.

"General Cohen," he said, "I'm not concerned with Li
Chai-sum or Chiang Kai-shek or any of your military leaders.
If a public personage takes refuge in my ship and tells
me that his life is in danger ashore, I'd naturally refuse to de-
liver him up until proofs had been produced to our Consul
General that he had committed some serious crime. If, mean-

time, any pressure was put on me to hand him over, I'd up anchor and sail for Shanghai."

He rang the bell for his steward and dropped the official mask.

"Pink gin, General? Here's luck, and you look out for your own skin, too!"

Everything was going beautifully. After tiffin I went to tell Sun Fo about it—and that was the end of my plot. I'd never seen him really angry before. He glared and he pounded on his desk.

"Morris," he said, "I wish you'd get to hell out of Nanking and go back to Canton where maybe you know what the score is. You're a darned nuisance here and you make me tired. I've been negotiating for a week to protect Li Chaisum and I've risked a lot to do it. Now at last I've Chiang's promise that he's safe for the present and'll be released shortly. You come poking your big clumsy fingers into the works and wrecking everything. For God's sake go some other place and stay there!"

I was struck dumb with astonishment. I'd made mistakes before but I'd never seen Sun Fo like that. Afterwards I realized that he was feeling just like Mah Sang felt. The United China that his father had slaved to build and had given his life for was coming apart at the seams and he just couldn't bear to see it. He was doing his own best, but it wasn't enough. He was sick at heart and he took it out on me.

At the time I couldn't figure the thing out at all. I was angry and hurt. I went back to my horrible hotel room, wondering what I could do. After hanging on in Nanking for a day or two, I went down river to Shanghai. There I stayed while matters went from bad to worse. The Peking faction split off, the Hankow group of cities split off, the South was in semi-open rebellion over General Li's arrest. We were steering straight back to the old days of civil war while the outside enemies of China looked on and bided their time.

There was nothing for me in Shanghai. I headed for Canton and hung around there, sad about China and sad about myself. Look at it how you like, it was the first time I'd fallen down on a mission. On top of that I'd been cursed for a fool by the man I most admired in the whole country.

Presently a chap called Chen Chi-tong was appointed Governor of Kwangtung Province in General Li's place. As soon as he arrived he asked me to join him. I was still sore and I refused. At last came a bit of good news. Chiang Kai-shek had kept his promise. My boss was at liberty and in Hong Kong. I was off like a rocket to see him, and found him settling into a big house above West Point where a lot of rich Chinese exiles lived. We held our own inquest into the Nanking episode. Soon we were both laughing about it. When I left he said:

"Give my regards to Chen Chi-tong and tell him he's lucky to have your services."

"I don't understand, sir. I've nothing to do with General Chen."

"But I wrote him a long time ago telling him he'd better take you on to his staff."

"Look here, sir, you hired me and I'm your man till I'm sacked!"

"You're an obstinate devil, aren't you? Very well, I dismiss you from my service and recommend you to my successor."

That was how I became A.D.C. to Chen Chi-tong. A new and rather different part of my life began. It wasn't a very happy part either. Up till then I'd served my chief whoever he was—Sun Yat-sen, Sun Fo, T. V. Soong, or Li Chai-sum—with my whole heart and without thought of personal gain. With Chen Chi-tong it wasn't quite the same. I was with him for longer than anyone else, a matter of five or six years from first to last, but I never got very close to him.

Some of his followers squeezed immoderately. Their demands weren't reasonable. One of them made so much out of bribery and polite blackmail that he had to found a real estate company to take care of the proceeds. Another smuggled on a gigantic scale—he used to transport his contraband in the gunboats of the Cantonese Navy.

Later on, when the Japanese attacked, Chen Chi-tong made a great comeback and handed ten million Hong Kong dollars over for Chiang Kai-shek's war fund. But at this time his money was spent in silly ways, and ways, too, that gave offense to the people of Canton. He built a great new pagoda on a conspicuous site just outside the city, where it was a permanent eyesore to the wretched coolies living in mat-sheds and mud hovels all around.

He was a tremendous believer in fortune-tellers and gave huge sums to astrologers and necromancers. I got sick of the crowd of four-flushers you always found in his Yamen, busy examining the intestines of turtles, or watching the flight of gulls or listening to the barking of chow-dogs. In the end I kept away as much as possible and got myself sent off on detached duty whenever I could think up an excuse.

Much of my time was taken up with the troubles of the missionaries. We had a great number of them in South China. With civil war threatening and troops on the march, life was becoming harder again for the coolie and the peasant, and they wanted somebody to blame for it. The Chinese naturally blamed the foreigners rather than themselves. The one lot of foreigners they had always with them, not just on visits, but all the time and living in the remotest out-of-the-way spots, were the missionaries.

Military commanders at all levels spotted this development and cashed in on it. Whenever they wanted quarters or chow for their troops, they picked on the missionaries, billeted their men in the mission compounds, and commandeered the rice and livestock of the Christian converts. The missionaries complained to their consuls, the consuls complained to Chen Chi-tong, and he'd send me to put matters to rights.

It wasn't often a difficult assignment. General Chen was always reasonable over this particular question. Before I left I'd arm myself with a huchao to evict the troops by force if necessary, but usually all that was needed was tact and patience, which, by the way, not all the missionaries possessed.

On the whole, though, they were a splendid lot. They may not have made a great many converts and some of these converts may not have been the best of advertisements for Christianity, but the example of pious, unselfish living and ideals that were not of this world was something that all Chinese could appreciate. In general their respect and admiration for the "Jesus-men" was unlimited. Communism was to change all that and to change it almost overnight, but that was still in the future. At this date the Communists hadn't shown their full hand.

It happened to be a naval instead of a military dust-up that sent me off on my queerest trip. The head of the Cantonese Navy—I forget his exact rank but he was covered in gold braid and spent most of his time on the smuggling racket—came up to me one morning in the A.D.C.'s room:

"Hiya, General, pirates pinch'um John Lake wallah-wallah; Governor wanting you bring back chop-chop!"

"Pirates are your pigeon, Admiral; why don't you take a gunboat and go yourself?"

"Me no liking lepers!"

John Lake was a properly ordained clergyman, but he'd dropped the "reverend" and insisted on people using his name without a handle. Many years before in Dr. Sun's days he'd taken charge of a big leper colony on an island near Macao. It had been a pretty dreadful place before this, just a barren hump in the sea where the poor devils were marooned to die. The changes he'd made were miracles— decent living quarters for the early stages of the disease and a hospital for the end when they couldn't help themselves; vegetable gardens to provide occupation and fresh food; and first-rate doctors. There were even rumors, never quite believed, that some lepers had been cured.

Where the cash came from no one ever knew. The Kwangtung Government gave him a little, more was supposed to have been put up by his rich brother in America. Some of the lepers were themselves men of wealth, or had well-to-do families. But none of these sources could account for the money he poured out. His finances were just as much a miracle as everything else about his little kingdom.

He was a man I honored without exactly wanting to be his guest. I sailed for the island with rather mixed feelings. The first thing I saw as we approached the jetty was that launch of his, a familiar craft all up and down the delta, tied up alongside.

It was a temptation to turn around and beat it for home, but I landed and walked up the well-kept path. On both sides of me I saw those terrible "lion" features with the flattened, decaying nostrils—the earliest symptoms of the disease. I passed through the gates of Lake's compound and stopped in amazement. He was sitting surrounded by the leading lepers of his community and seemed to be holding some sort of court. Whether he had the proceedings in hand or not wasn't very clear.

He was talking to a party of four people standing in front of him. A small sharp-eyed Hokklo, or sea-gipsy, I recognized at once as one of the few pirate leaders to escape from our Bias Bay operations of the previous year. Two sheepish-looking individuals with their hands pinioned behind them and their shirt collars cut away to leave their necks bare. And a muscular character with a squint, a mouthful of gold teeth, and one of those horrible heavy-bladed executioners' swords.

Lake saw me and leapt to his feet.

"Cohen," he cried, "thank God you've come!"

I'd known he liked me all right, but I wasn't prepared for quite such a welcome. I wondered what was up. The explanation didn't take long.

"For heaven's sake," he said, "take these poor devils back to Canton and put them in the jug where they'll be safe. They stole my motor boat two days ago. They'd planned to give it a new coat of paint and sell it down the coast around Hainan Island. Now Ah Hop's brought it back and them along with it and he wants to behead them here in my compound!"

"But, Reverend, do you know who Ah Hop is?"

"I thought I did. He's taken me fishing every Saturday this summer. Now it seems he's their pirate king!"

I headed for home with the two boat thieves cautiously feeling the backs of their necks to make sure their heads were still there. Ah Hop and his executioner went back to their pirate lair, and John Lake was left to look after his lepers in peace.

One difficulty with the missionaries was that the best of them—those you really wanted to be friends with—were too proud to ask you for help. Not so long after John Lake's launch incident, I was walking down the Bund when I saw a crowd of loafers around a little white-haired foreigner. They were mocking him and making fun of him, but they were listening to him as well. When I came up and looked over his shoulder, I saw why.

He was dealing them out religious pamphlets, but with each tract he also gave them two or three copper pieces. The surest way to a beggar's heart is a hand-out. It was plain that he'd have an audience just as long as there was anything left in his pockets.

"Say, stranger," I began, "are you trying to succor the poor of China? Because if so, you've taken on a man's size job!"

He turned around. When I saw his face, I gasped. It was the Pete Robinson I'd known in Edmonton ten years earlier. In those days I met him quite often. He had a job in the Attorney General's department, looking after a Home for Delinquent Children. He also had a jolly little Irish wife and a fine baby boy. He had a big heart too—as big as his body was small. His delinquent children weren't enough for him. He'd founded a Sunday School for Chinese children to occupy his spare time.

"What the hell are you doing here?" I asked, and his face seemed to sadden.

"You remember that little nipper of mine, Morris, you used to play with? He grew up into a fine lad and he always came with me to my Chinese Sunday School. I suppose it was that that gave him the idea of being a missionary— anyway he set his heart on it.

"But that wasn't Our Lord's will. Two years ago there was a typhoid epidemic all over the Western Provinces and he caught it bad. He knew he was dying almost as soon as the doctors did and he took hold of my hand in his feeble little fingers.

" 'Dad,' he said, 'I'll never go to China as a minister now. Promise me you'll go in my place.'

"He died that night, and here I am."

"But, Pete, how're you making out? Where're you living? What are you living on? Where's Mrs. Robinson?"

"I manage all right. I've got a cubicle in the Oi Mei Hotel. I have *congee* [rice and vegetable gruel] for breakfast and *chow fan* [fried rice] for supper. The wife I left behind in Edmonton till I saw how things shaped here. Well, that isn't quite true. As a matter of fact we couldn't raise the passage money."

"I suppose the other missionaries are helping you."

"Not much, Morris. You see, I'm not an ordained priest. I never took Holy Orders. I'm afraid they say that I've no business to be here at all."

That made me mad. But Pete was such a saint, so happy in himself, and so unaffected by malice or misfortune that it was impossible to feel angry when you were with him. You just felt good and that was all. I went straight off and told his story to some of my Chinese friends.

I won't pretend that his troubles were over when he met me, but his fortunes did begin to mend. I hauled him out of his filthy hotel and found him decent quarters. I brought him along to official functions where he met the well-to-do Chinese Christians who could help him. We raised the money for his wife's passage, and she got a nice little home together for him—she learned to preach in Chinese nearly as well as he did. Last of all, I got a small grant from the Education Department and with it we built a little Mission School where he taught the poorest of the poor—and he was as happy as a king.

He made everyone else happy too. One day when he had a bout of malaria, I went to see him and he said:

"General Cohen, I'm going to pray for you."

"Why, Pete, am I that bad?"

"You're not so good, General, but that you could do with some saving. I've known you a long time, so you can't kid me!"

A year or two later I was passing through Edmonton

on my way to England when I ran into the Reverend John McQueen, the same Presbyterian parson I'd tangled with over Total Prohibition after the First World War and I'd outquoted from the Scriptures with *Deuteronomy* xiv, 26. He bore me no malice for that. I was puzzled by the amount he knew about me till he pulled out of his pocket some letters from Pete Robinson. It turned out that they corresponded regularly. He read me the last one and it was quite short.

> Dear Reverend,
>   I have discovered since I've lived in Canton that there are more Chinese in Heaven than there are Presbyterians. . . .

The next time McQueen read that letter it was from his own pulpit. He made it the text of his Sunday morning sermon.

Pete didn't last very long in China. People seldom do who come out to the Far East late in life, and he was a frail little fellow at the best of times. He had fever all one summer and then the cold spell at Christmas finished him. What a funeral that was! Everyone was represented, from the Governor of Kwangtung Province—by me—to the Canton Beggars Guild, by the Father of the Guild himself. The British Consul General came and most of the foreign community and most of the missionaries, who'd realized by now what a great guy Pete was. Whether he saved many souls I don't know, but we were all better men for having known him.

However, my main activity in those days had nothing at all to do with the missionaries. When Sun Fo became Minister of Communication, he made me his Adviser on Foreign Purchases, and I still held that appointment. When the rival provincial leaders began bickering again and the South started to re-arm and, particularly, to purchase munitions abroad, I was the obvious man for the job.

It was hard, complicated, exacting work and often meant a lot of running to and fro with nothing much to show for the trouble. First, I had to get in touch with the manufacturers or their Far Eastern representatives, then I had to check the latter's credentials and business reputation —and the sort of guys who sold "sewing machines" in China weren't all models of commercial rectitude. Then I had to arrange for expert examination and approval of their samples.

Once I decided that the goods were what I wanted and there was a fair chance of the bulk consignment being up to specification, the bargaining began. They'd stick on the price because they guessed we needed the arms bad. They were trying that game on an old hand. I'd learned my bargaining as a boy back in Alberta and I enjoyed a bit of it. If I couldn't beat their prices down by twenty or thirty per cent, I reckoned I was losing my grip.

It was when the price had been fixed that the real haggling started—over terms of payment. They wanted cash in advance. I stuck out for a token sum down and the rest only after delivery and as long after as possible. I wasn't just being obstinate either. The South was short of funds and we no longer had T. V. Soong, with his financial wizardry, to tide us over. The usual reason why I dug my toes in was that, if I'd signed a check, there wouldn't have been money in the bank to meet it.

Back and forth we used to argue. Inches of hotel bedroom carpet we wore through, stamping up and down between the window and the door; yards of cheroots we smoked and gallons of hooch we poured down our throats— or, in my case, if no one was looking, into the wash-basin.

The deals were nearly all put through in Hong Kong (though this was strictly against the laws of the colony), and I became a bit of a landmark around the hotel lobbies.

In the end the terms were usually much the same—one-third down on signing the contract, one-third on shipment, and the rest on delivery. On that basis we bought in any market we could reach—tommy guns from the U.S.A., Madsen machine guns from Denmark, "seventy-fives" from France, A.A. artillery from Britain, aircraft from Italy, and rifles with ammo from almost every country in Europe. My biggest single deal was twenty thousand factory-new Mauser rifles from Germany with five hundred rounds apiece. The price was a hundred gold dollars each, or a total of two million bucks, which made a nice little rake-off for Morris.

I must explain that I was now working on commission—usually two and a half per cent and always paid, of course, by the foreign seller. It was a new departure for me. At first I didn't like the idea at all; but times had changed, and I had to change with them. I was over forty, an age when a man's got to take a look at the future. I had my father and mother back in Manchester to think of, and as well as them, a whole raft of relations who, without being in any way dependent on me, would certainly look to me for help if they were in a jam. Our family ties were very strong and it was now my plain duty to make and put by whatever money I could.

My troubles weren't over by any means when the contract was signed. There was still some sort of ineffective international embargo on the supply of arms to the warring factions of China. The shipping of them at one end and landing of them at the other often presented problems which needed all my gift for negotiation to solve. Call it "finagling" if you like—I don't mind.

In any case the Nanking Government had more claim

to *de jure* recognition than we had, and they weren't slow to take advantage of it. Sometimes I found myself lined up against old friends, which wasn't pleasant.

Towards the end of 1930, or maybe the beginning of 1931, a German boat steamed into Hong Kong harbor with one of my largest loads aboard—five thousand rifles with half a million rounds of S.A.A., two hundred machine guns, a couple of airplanes, and tons of explosives for our own munition factories. The stuff was consigned to me personally. We'd have been in the clear but for one thing, the rest of the cargo was destined for Shanghai, and there the Central Government were in control.

It hadn't occurred to me to bother about that and I took a wallah-wallah off to the "Explosives Anchorage," where the ship was lying, without a worry in the world. Up the gangway I bounded to be met by the captain in a fine Teutonic fury.

"Vat am I to do with this?" and he thrust a wireless signal pad under my nose.

The message was short and quite clear.

YOU ARE WARNED BY THE GOVERNMENT OF CHINA THAT IF ARMS DESTINED CANTON ARE UNLOADED HONG KONG BOTH SHIP AND CARGO WILL BE SEIZED AND CONFISCATED ON ARRIVAL SHANGHAI.

T. V. Soong, Minister of Finance.

"Vell, vat am I to do?"

"That's easy—don't go to Shanghai."

"But vat about the rest of my cargo? The value of your consignment is only a leedle of vot I am carrying. I shall up anchor and sail for Shanghai at vunce!"

That was quite enough for me. I hopped ashore, went to my lawyer, and swore a deposition that goods consigned to me and which I'd paid for were about to be illegally removed. We carried this off to the Harbor Master's Court and had the Deputy Admiralty Marshal arrest the ship. He did it in style, too. He couldn't actually nail the Warrant to the mainmast like in the old tea-clipper days because the mast was steel and not wood; but he lashed it on with spunyarn, and the German captain tore his hair out in handfuls. He was on "time charter," and any delay meant money lost.

So far so good, but the Nanking boys weren't beaten yet by a long chalk. They put diplomatic pressure on the Hong Kong Government to forbid the transshipment of my arms for passage to Canton taking place within the territorial waters of the colony, on the grounds that it violated the old embargo on supplying arms to China. I had another fight on my hands, but I had a good lawyer, too, and he proved that by the Barcelona Convention a neutral nation could not interfere with the transshipment, provided the goods were consigned to a private individual—and that was me!

I mayn't have got the legal details quite right, but the essence of the thing was that, as long as I could prove that the arms were my personal property, everything was hunky-dory. I was able to do this. It was with a considerable kick that I signed my name on the Bill of Lading and other documents as the sole consignee.

My munitions of war were ferried up to Canton and the German skipper sailed for Shanghai, where he and his ship were promptly put under arrest by the Central Government, just as they'd threatened to do. He produced papers to prove that in Hong Kong he had only yielded to force, and they were obliged to release him. I had a friend in the Ministry of Finance and he told me what happened next.

T. V. Soong flew into a fine temper. He knew he was a smart guy and just hated anyone else to outsmart him. He sent for the papers, and his staff stood well clear of his desk while he read them. He went through each one carefully, muttering to himself meanwhile, till he came to my signature. He threw the whole file on the floor and burst out laughing.

"That damn Cohen—he's a loyal son of a gun. I wish I had him here!"

He meant it too. A few days later I got a wire:

COME TO SHANGHAI STOP NEED YOU IN MY WORK—T. V.

But I couldn't do it. I wasn't all that happy in the south, but still they were my people and I had to stick to them.

Not all my ventures turned out as well as that one. Sometimes no arms were forthcoming, sometimes they were blocked, and sometimes the bulk deliveries were dud when we came to examine them. Everyone knew by now that I was out to buy almost any kind of weapon in almost any market, and some of the snidest operators in the East thought I must be easy meat. They matched their wits against mine and once or twice I was led up the garden path with no other motive than plain pillage.

The Casanova was the biggest dance hall in Shanghai and a favorite hang-out of these wise boys, so I wasn't surprised when the manager took me mysteriously into his office, stood me a couple of shots and a fat cigar, and began.

"Say, General, would you be interested in a proposition?"

"What sort?"

"Sewing machines."

"Maybe, but I don't want small stuff. None of your job lots—ten tommy guns and fifty bundooks. It just isn't worth wangling the huchaos."

"I guess you'll think this worth while."

"Let's hear it."

"Three thousand machine guns, ten thousand rifles

with a million rounds, and a hundred thousand hand grenades."

I smelled a rat. Three thousand machine guns is a lot to
be on the market. I'd have been certain to hear about it before he did.

"D'you mean real heavy machine guns or just some sort
of automatic rifle—Lewis guns or some other obsolete junk?"

He hesitated. I could see he didn't know the answer.
The whole thing was a plant, but I strung along to find out
what his game was.

He phoned me again the following evening, shot a line
about the importance of absolute secrecy, and disclosed that
his friend's name was Jess Green, which rang no bell with
me. We met at the Casanova late that night. I shan't forget
it because Jess was wearing what would later on have been
called a "zoot suit." His shoulders were padded inches high
and his coat looked as if he'd pulled the curtains from his
bedroom windows and put sleeves on them. Shanghai had
seen nothing like it in those days. He couldn't have been
more conspicuous if he'd sported a monocle.

I asked his price. He mentioned some silly figures which
showed at once that he had no stuff to sell and knew nothing
about the arms racket. I still couldn't cotton on to his game.
When he said the Casanova was too public for us and he'd
take me to a safe hide-out, I agreed. We got into his
big chauffeur-driven car and he gave the address of Short-
Time Susan's place.

That was the most famous sporting-house in Shanghai
and a center of snide gossip. There was no more certain way
of hitting the half-world headlines than taking a private
room there and throwing a party. Madame evidently knew
him well. He called for two girls by name and they knew
his name—if it was his real name—too. He called for wine

and we took it in turn to order more bottles and drank level, with the girls helping.

There was no more talk about the phony arms deal. I stayed in the dark till there were six empties on the table. He sent for a deck of cards and said, "Let's have a little fun and see who pays for the drinks."

He shuffled, I cut, and then—believe it or not—he dealt me seconds. It had been years since anyone had tried to cheat me. At first I just couldn't believe my eyes. Anyway I lost, and called for the bill. When I paid it, I deliberately flashed my roll. It was a good fat one.

That was his cue.

"Let's have a single-handed stud game," said Jess, "just you and I."

"All right," I replied, looking a bit pie-eyed, "but no limit."

That game lasted all night. I let him win till he was really cock-sure, so that, when I started my tricks, he just thought that the cards were running against him. The girls stayed to kibitz over our shoulders and brought us more booze, but most of my share went into the cuspidor. It was nearly noon when we packed in. Even then we stopped only because I had all Jess's money—to the tune of forty-seven thousand Shanghai dollars.

I took the next boat back to Hong Kong. As we dropped down the Whangpoo, I wondered what I was going to do with the money I'd won. True enough, the man had set out to fleece me and also I'd just made up my mind to start saving up a grubstake against my old age. But I couldn't get away from the fact that I'd won the cash by plain cheating and it was a long, long time since I'd taken money that way. By the time we came in through the Lyemun Pass, I'd made my mind up.

I never heard of Jess Green again. Why he ever came to

Shanghai, why he thought he was a smart gambler, and why he tried to trim me of all people were things I never found out. But the Canton Y.M.C.A. was always short of funds and the old missioner who ran it had set his heart on a swimming pool and there wasn't a hope in hell of building one. If Jess Green reads these words, he may like to know that his name was for many years remembered with gratitude by the Christian Young Men—and the Christian Young Women of South China.

In September 1931 the Japanese moved into Manchuria. I'm told that their pounce came as a surprise to the Western World. To us on the spot it was only one more chapter of a story that began late in the last century. In 1894 Japan thrashed China and took the island of Formosa. In 1905 she thrashed Russia and took Korea and Port Arthur. In 1914 she took Tsing-Tau from Germany and never forgave the Allies who forced her to restore it to China.

Those were just the open and defiant steps in a struggle that went on mostly through commercial, financial and diplomatic channels. The Western Powers may sometimes have been selfish and greedy in their dealings with China, but all they wanted was trade. Japan was set from the first on the complete cultural and political domination of the whole Far East.

When I speak of the Western Powers, I don't include Russia. As soon as the Bolsheviks were securely in the saddle there, they revived the old Siberian expansionist policy of the Tsars and went at it just as violently and just as unscrupulously as the Japanese. The difference between them was this. The Japs weren't nearly as smart as the Communists, but they knew the ground better and were more careful and more consistent. The Communists sometimes over-reached themselves and had setbacks. The Japs just went steadily ahead.

What made them time their jump for that particular moment I don't know, but I've always thought that the Naval Mutiny of September 10th, when the Home Fleet refused to sail from Invergordon, had a lot to do with it. They thought the British wouldn't be too keen on sending their main fleet to the Far East just after that episode. They knew that the States wouldn't make a move. Nobody else was strong enough to be worth worrying about.

Anyhow the Manchurian Incident, as they called it, certainly made me feel happier. Up to then I'd dealt in arms partly to line my own pockets and partly (without too much enthusiasm) to help re-arm the Cantonese armies against their potential enemies in the north. Now, with the Japanese attack, the ranks were closing up once more. I could feel that I was working for China as a whole against a foreign enemy.

I threw myself into the arms business with a new heart. By the autumn of 1932 I'd lined up some real big deals that involved visits to both Europe and the States. That suited me. I'd at last begun to save some of my money. There was enough in the bank to pay for a holiday in England and a little financial help for my family.

That was the first time I got involved with the Japanese police. No sooner had I booked my passage in the *President Coolidge* than my Chinese friends started warning me in their around-the-corner fashion that I was foolish to travel via Japan. I didn't take them very seriously at first, but they went on and on till I asked them outright what they were hinting at.

"We think you may not be *persona grata* with the Nipponites."

"I can see that, but I'll stay on board in the Japanese ports and they won't dare to touch me if I'm under the Stars and Stripes!"

They changed the subject, evidently feeling that they'd

done their stuff. It left me a little uneasy. I went down to the shipping office and got them to make a routine inquiry at the Jap Consulate as to whether a foreign passenger remaining on board a foreign ship came under Japanese police jurisdiction. The answer was a flat uncompromising "Yes." That made me think a bit.

But I couldn't believe that I was running any real risk and to change my plans and travel by Honolulu and the central Pacific meant taking nearly twice as long and wrecking the tight schedule I'd arranged for myself in North America. It was a dull passage up the coast. At Shanghai I palled up with three people who came on board. Two were wise old Roman Catholic priests on some clerical errand. The third was a U.S. naval doctor on his way home from a tour of duty in Peking.

At Nagasaki the police and the immigration authorities came on board. All through the Inland Sea they questioned us. Half the things they asked were just plain silly with no possible bearing on our suitability as visitors. I queued up behind the two old priests and listened hard during their interrogation. I noticed two points. First, that they answered every question, however stupid, very fully and very carefully. Next, that the little Jap official didn't understand half as much as he made out and kept on getting the sticky end of the simplest answer.

I was in high spirits at my approaching holiday and I thought I'd pull his leg. When my turn came I just exuded information at every pore. Each question he put got an answer as lengthy as I could make. If it was miles off the point, so much the better. When it came to my politics he had a nice slab of Shakespeare.

He soaked it all in without batting an eyelid. His pen scratched away and those long vertical lines of jigsaw-puzzle characters covered page after page. At last he finished. He

shut his notebook with a snap and handed back my passport *without* a visa stamp. He grinned politely, he sucked
in his breath and said, "S-s-s-s-ah. I am very sorry for
you. You must not land in Kobe. Thank you. Next please."

That was no disappointment. I hadn't intended to land
in Kobe anyway. All the same I'd a feeling that I hadn't been
quite as clever as I thought.

It was a dull day in harbor. I spent most of it walking
the decks with those two priests and listening to their tales
of mission life in Japanese territory. The American naval
doctor went ashore and came back that afternoon with a
good story. They'd been the usual queue of rickshaws at the
dock gates but as soon as he appeared, one puller left his
place, came up to the top—with no one complaining—and
took him. He seemed a nice willing chap and stronger than
most and he pulled the American all over Kobe. When they
got back to the docks my friend paid him off and then picked
out of his handful of coins three ten-sen pieces, held them out
and said "*cumshaw.*"

The coolie sprang to attention and clicked his heels.
"I am very sorry. I am police officer. I cannot take *cumshaw!*" While the doctor gaped, he picked up his rickshaw
shafts and padded away.

We cleared from Kobe and left the Inland Sea. Our last
port of call was Yokohama. All this supervision and restric-
tion had begun to get my goat. I'd had police trouble before in my life, but that was when I'd done something agin
the law and knew I deserved it. This sort of thing riled me. I
stamped round the decks looking up at the big houses on the
Bluff and wishing we were out in the Pacific.

I was walking the opposite way to the two priests and as
we passed I thought one of them winked at me. Next time
around the same thing happened. On the third round I
stopped and we leant over the guard-rails together.

"You are walking too fast for your follower," he said, "the poor fellow is quite out of breath."

I looked around and there, half hidden behind a ventilator cowl, was a plump little Jap puffing and panting and eyeing me vindictively.

"Yes," said the priest, "the poor fellow has followed you ever since breakfast and now he is tired."

Now, I thought, I'll get my own back. I set off around that ship as fast as I could travel. Up to the boat deck I ran and down to my cabin, into the third-class saloon, and up to the first class smoking-room. He was lagging well behind by now. With a spurt, I got back to the boat deck and dived into the locker where they kept the deck-sports gear.

For about five minutes nothing happened. Then a whistle blew and the fun began. There was a lot more whistling and somebody started to shout. Boots pounded along the decks and a grand volley of Japanese swear-words was shot off as one of them tripped over a combing.

I waited till the row reached its peak, slipped out of the locker, smoothed my hair, straightened my tie, and started a leisurely stroll along the deck. The first plainclothes policeman to see me yelled something and another came running up, then another. In the end I had eight of them following me and muttering to each other.

I led my little procession down the companionway to the upper deck and right around it. I turned and bowed and stepped into the smoking-room. The two priests were there. I sat down at their table. They were in fits of laughter like all the other passengers. The older one said:

"That was very funny, General. I take it you are not returning to the East?"

"Of course I am, Father. What do you mean?"

"In that case you have done a very foolish thing. I only pray that you may never have cause to regret it!"

He'd say no more, and a few hours later we were out of Tokyo Bay and I was watching Fujiyama fading into the sunset.

On this trip home I'd determined that my own family should have priority over everything else. I was thinking about them all the way. As soon as my American business was tidied up and I knew my sailing date from New York, I cabled to tell them.

I landed at Plymouth, and there waiting on the wharf were two of my brothers. It was a typical early winter, West country day, dismal and drizzling. England had put on her typical dead-pan, "don't care who the hell you are" welcome, but there were my own folks to greet me and it made me feel warm all through.

We boarded the train for the long journey up to Manchester. On the way Leslie told me about his draper's shop on Cross Street, which was prospering, and all the other news. When we pulled into London Road Station, there were my father and mother and half a dozen of the family. I kissed mother first, thinking how stooped and frail she'd grown, and just as I did so, one of the *Daily Dispatch* boys took a flashlight picture.

"Lay off that!" I shouted and smashed his camera with my walking stick.

Looking back it seems a silly thing to have done. Usually I haven't minded publicity—in fact, I've liked it. But somehow just at that moment I was right back in amongst my own people—my *mispucha*—and this intrusion from an outsider was damned cheek. The local papers were kind to me and didn't play the story up at all. I don't think I've ever quarrelled with the press again from that day to this.

Altogether the newspaper boys gave me a big hand this time. The *Manchester Evening News* interviewed me and the *Evening Chronicle*, and the *Jewish Gazette* and the Manchester correspondent of the *People* and lots more. Even the heavyweight *Manchester Guardian* thought my views important. It printed an interview with me in which I said that the British policy of conniving at Japanese aggression in Manchuria had aroused the hostility of the Chinese people just at a time when better relations were developing. It was all nonsense, I said, to suggest that Japan needed Manchuria for colonization. What Japan wanted in Manchuria was oil, because if she went to war with a first-class power that was the one commodity she'd have to get from outside sources. For the Japanese to talk about "Manchuria for the Manchus" was as big a joke to people in China as it would be if someone talked about returning America to the Red Indians, because there was just about the same proportion of Manchus in Manchuria as there was of Red Indians in the United States.

By this date the Great Slump had really hit Lancashire. Factories were closing down everywhere and unemployment figures were leaping up. With the Chinese boycott of Japanese goods, especially textiles, becoming more and more effective, it had begun to look as if the Far Eastern market might save the situation when there was no other hope in sight. I'd arrived just at the right time to tell them about it.

A lot of business men were interested. The Manchester Chamber of Commerce gave me a lunch at the Midland Hotel, with Mr. Nathan Laski in the chair. I said my piece and answered endless questions. All this was fully reported in the old *Guardian*, which pleased my father and mother no end. I left Manchester loaded down with catalogues and price lists for the supply departments of the Kwangtung Government. I got some orders too and I'd have got a lot more, if T. V. Soong had been able to float his loan six months later.

Once more my holiday was over. I was on my way to Paris and Geneva to finalize my other business. Back to

China next, and to a situation that seemed to get worse and worse.

The Japanese had swallowed Manchuria. It was their biggest bite yet and they'd got away with it. As a result they felt sure they could get away with anything. They sat back, digested their meal, and prepared for their next pounce. The Communists had established themselves in Kiangsi and Western Fukien. They governed barbarously, but vigorously and efficiently, and they fought well—you had to grant them that. Chiang Kai-shek was always "dispersing" them and "exterminating" them, but they were always there just the same—a poisonous, dangerous growth slap in the middle of the country.

During 1933 Japan took over Jehol, a fourth great province to add to her empire. Meanwhile, the Nineteenth Route Army, which had done well against the Japs in the fighting around Shanghai, was moved down to Fukien for the campaign against the Communists. Its commanders promptly mutinied.

That was the third threat to China—dissensions and disloyalty among the Chinese leaders themselves. It laid the country open to any enemy. Japan knew it. I was only a minor figure on the stage, but I watched the way things were going and wished that Dr. Sun were still alive.

Admitted, I was doing my bit in helping to re-arm the South against the inevitable war, but after all I was being paid for that. I wanted to do something more, if only for Dr. Sun's sake, something that would mean a real sacrifice to me.

CHAPTER XI

Debt of Honor

"Politics," said Morris in his deep, vibrant voice, with the curious Cockney-Canadian accent, "are just *poisonalities*. Tell me who's behind a mob and I'll tell you what they're going to do. Tell me who's heading a movement and I'll tell you what's going to happen to it. If the guy's dumb, it'll break up on internal squabbles; if the guy's yellow, it'll fade out anyway. If he's smart *and* tough, someone's going to get hurt."

The year was 1935, the scene the ballroom of the Peninsular Hotel, and the occasion the annual Reception and Ball given by the Hong Kong branch of the Royal Society of St. George. The band thumped out nostalgically English tunes, and dignified figures, resplendent in white ties, tailcoats, and decorations, their arms around the equally dignified waists of women as unmistakably English as themselves, revolved slowly past the alcove where we sat while Morris talked to me of Chinese manners, customs, and ways of life.

I listened with respect and with gratitude. No one in China was better qualified to speak on such a subject and no one—most certainly no one in unofficial circles—had proved so friendly. Faced in middle life with a difficult, delicate, and totally unfamiliar job, I had found myself floundering hopelessly in the complexities of Oriental affairs and making blunder after blunder. Repeated failure had bred discouragement, and now it seemed quite incredible that a man such as Morris should not only give me his unstinted aid, but also refuse to accept any sort of *quid pro quo*. But Morris, I reflected, was the product of a wildly improbable career.

Twelve years had passed since our first meeting in the carefree, convivial atmosphere of club bars and gunboat wardrooms during the Canton Customs Crisis of 1923. In those years he had developed from a popular and trusted, but slightly comical, character into a figure who could only be described as famous and might almost be called fabulous.

A figure, too, of extraordinary contradictions. His success in the crooked half-world of illicit arms traffic had to be set against his reputation for absolute uncompromising honesty in money matters; his shrewdness in all business deals against his quixotic generosity to anyone in distress and the fantastic lavishness and extravagance of his frequent parties in the great luxury hotels of Hong Kong; the occasional bawdiness of his conversation against his acknowledged role of father-confessor to endless young folk of both sexes and his truly remarkable reputation as a mender of broken—or damaged—marriages.

His name was on most men's lips and, if his real place in Chinese revolutionary history was hard to estimate, his purely military prowess had not gone uncommemorated. One bitter winter morning a few weeks earlier, wandering through a Shanghai suburb in search of an elusive White Russian acquaintance, I had found myself treading the mud and slush of the "Route Cohen."

Time had dealt harshly and yet not altogether unkindly with his appearance. The good-looking youngster had gone forever; he had lost his hair (widow's peak and all) and a huge bald head was his most conspicuous feature; his fine beak of a nose had been partially flattened and bent well to one side of his face, while his cheeks and throat had begun to show the dewlaps of middle age. Yet he remained an impressive figure in any company. His enormous breadth of shoulder enabled him to carry with dignity his ever-increasing weight; his expressive eyes remained unchanged and his whole face radiated optimism and good-humor—the face of a man utterly at peace with the world as he knew it.

For me he was certainly a welcome tonic. His unique knowledge of every figure on the Chinese political scene, his extraordinary insight into character, or "poisonality" as he always insisted on calling it, and his unrivalled experience of Oriental affairs combined to supply exactly the background of which I was in need.

"Say, Morris, did you ever hear of a chap called . . . ?"

European or Asiatic, it made no difference; there would be a pause while one could almost see him flicking over his mental card-index, and then:

"Met him in Nanking about 1924; working for Chang Tso-lin; sold sewing machines for some Swedish outfit; Dr. Sun didn't like him."

Another pause and a flood of further detail would follow, winding up with the query:

"What's he matter to you?"

I would give my reasons, and then, in a few broad and vigorous phrases, Morris would lay bare the unfortunate man's soul, his good points and bad, his strength and his weaknesses, and, above all, his motives—money or malice, drink or women, loyalty to a cause or ambition for himself. He would forecast his behavior in almost any circumstances—and six months later I would see that Morris had been absolutely right.

Furthermore, it was impossible to spend an evening in his company without feeling the better for it. He had known so many vicissitudes that disaster left him unmoved; he had seen so many great men under stress that no action of the great could ever surprise him; and yet he observed the procession of events with the interest and pleasure of a child at its first pantomime.

I saw him but seldom during the next eighteen months, and sometimes found myself wondering whether I had not placed too great faith in his promises. For much of this time he was simply engaged in satisfying himself, by his own leisurely and devious, but nonetheless highly effective methods, that I was genuinely uninterested in Chinese politics, Chinese finance, Chinese defenses, or, in fact, in anything except the armed forces of Japan—and hence that he could help me unreservedly without any danger of disloyalty towards the country he served.

Early in 1936 he severed his connection with Chen Chitong and was once more attached to the personal staff of Sun Fo when the former, having vainly attempted to jockey Chiang Kai-shek into an altogether premature resistance to the Japanese, came out into open revolt against Nanking, was promptly deserted by his warships and aircraft, and obliged to take refuge in Hong Kong, fleeing thither in the inevitable British gunboat.

One hot, dank night of that summer when, replete with rice and shark's fin, we were reposing at ease in long chairs on the roof of a Chinese restaurant, Morris suddenly broke off the flood of reminiscence and anecdote to warn me soberly and seriously that open war with Japan would come within the year. The leading "poisonalities" of China were drawing together in a way that they had never done before. Unification under a strong central government was nearer than it had ever been, and the Japanese simply could not afford to allow such a state of affairs. . . . In actual fact, the first shots were fired within eleven months.

An incident of the same autumn made me realize more than ever with what manner of man I dealt. The Spanish

Civil War had broken out in July and rapidly reached a climax when both sides were in desperate need of aircraft. A plot was laid to get a consignment of fighters released from Czechoslovakian factories ostensibly for sale to the Chinese Government. Once on the high seas the cargo was to be diverted to Barcelona and the aircraft handed over to the Spanish Loyalists.

All that was necessary was an officially chopped, or endorsed, huchao from Nanking, and Morris was asked to procure this. It was, for him, a comparatively simple matter; he was offered ten thousand sterling for his services (five thousand down and the balance on delivery) and the deal was as good as through.

Then he discovered that the aircraft might be going not to the Loyalists but to Franco and his generals. Franco was lined up (in Morris's mind) with Hitler and the persecution of his co-religionists; and Morris haughtily refused to act. Money meant much to him in those days. When he had any, he threw it away with both hands and in consequence he was frequently broke. Yet he was ready to sacrifice a very large sum on the mere possibility that his actions might indirectly assist the enemies of his race.

"So you're going on leave," said Morris at Christmas time. I had, in fact, told no one of my plans, but my passage was booked at the Lloyd Triestino office and Morris had, I remembered, recently patched up a matrimonial dispute in that quarter that had threatened to set our small Italian community by the ears.

"Well, I'm throwing a party at the Peninsular on Chinese New Year's Day and we'll make it your farewell party too. By the way, have you ever heard of Vit-Alexine?"

"What on earth's that?"

"One of those new sex-rejuvenators—Voronoff-monkey-gland stuff—you must have heard of 'em."

"Of course I have, but what's it got to do with me—or you, you old so-and-so?"

"Nothing. I just thought you might be interested. The Japanese Government's in the market for them in a big way."

Morris's face beamed with a childlike innocence, but I refused to be drawn and moodily sipped my drink.

"Yes," he vouchsafed presently, "I've a friend—leastways he's no friend of mine; deals in snow [heroin] and such like and I hate all those guys, but I helped him once and he owes me a break—who's in on a queer sort of deal. The Japanese Naval Air Attaché wants to buy, secretly, six thousand Vit-Alexine treatments. They're expensive too—six pounds sterling apiece—so he's putting down thirty-six thousand smackers—and money talks."

There was a long pause and I settled back in my chair.

"You know that old house surgeon up at the Canossan Hospital. He's a buddy of mine too and I got him talking and he said that some day he meant to investigate the phenomena of black-out in fighter pilots and whether it couldn't be cured by glandular injections. He said he meant to start by playing about with some sort of testicular extracts."

I longed to fire a few questions at him, but knew only too well that this meant having my leg pulled for the next half hour.

"And *he* had another doctor friend who'd done work for the Japs and used to get their Naval medical journal —you know those semi-confidential restricted-circulation papers that they're always publishing."

"Yes, Morris. . . ."

"Well, this second doctor went through those journals and translated bits here and there and it adds up to this. The Jap pilots black-out for seconds longer than Europeans do; they hate high altitudes, they lose sense of direction, and they lose sense of level—and the Japs are as worried as hell about it. They've tried all kinds of odd things—iodine chewing-gum, clothes-pegs on their noses, and God knows what else, but so far they've done no good with 'em. I guess that's why they're trying monkey-gland.

"He says that quite a proportion of their pilots aren't affected like this and they're concentrating on picking those good ones out and training them up and they *are* good. They'll make rings around your boys as long as there're any of them left. But once you've shot down all those real first-line pilots—say, after the war's lasted a couple of years—then the rest'll be no damn good at all."

"Look here, Morris, this is all journalism. Can't you get me something solid and factual? You know the Chinese say the Nips used gas up in the north? I don't believe it, but if they did, they must have had gas masks too—now that would be something worth seeing. They've a whacking great Naval Landing Party in Shanghai; what about promoting a mask from them?"

"Aw, hell, there's no satisfying some people. Anyway, don't you forget my party at the Peninsular next month."

We did not, and indeed it still lives magnificently in my memory. Morris had taken the Roof Garden and the Rose Room and he received us in the latter, a fine old oval chamber, all gilt mirrors and pink lights. As we approached we could hear his booming voice greet the guest ahead of us and remind him of their last meeting at Peking.

"Who the hell was that guy?" he whispered as he took my hand. "How do you like my new tuxedo? Say, promise me you'll stay to the end of the party—the *very* end. I've a couple of magnums up in my room and I'll do some conjuring tricks for you."

We promised and wandered away to the refreshment buffet. Every exotic and out-of-season delicacy was there:

trout from Japan, pheasants from Shanghai, mangoes from Manila. Champagne corks popped and the bartender from the Parisian Grill brandished his shining silver cocktail-shaker. Presently Malini showed his astonishing sleight-of-hand, Joe and Nellie Farren danced, and Susie Leung sang slightly improper French songs.

My wife, who felt for Morris that protective mother-liness which is the attitude of most married women to-wards defenseless middle-aged bachelors, and who knew also something of the usual state of Morris's finances, was horrified at his extravagance. It spoiled our enjoyment of the party and, after the last cabaret act, we drifted away from the throng and ensconced ourselves on long chairs in the Roof Garden to pass the time in patience.

It was a small and somnolent group that eventually assembled in Morris's room as the dawn broke over Devil's Peak, the first Star Ferries left their pier, and the fishing junks hoisted their heavy lateen sails and headed out to sea. My wife found a secluded corner and went straight to sleep, sitting bolt upright and open-eyed as was her wont. I had existed since midnight on black coffee, and now took a stiff drink as the last hope of keeping my eyes open.

Morris was as fresh and bright as ever. He did incred-ible things with a pack of cards, he produced a bunch of freesias from my breast pocket and a live duck from the thin air. One by one the last guests departed and we three were left alone.

"Now," said he, "I'll really show you something."

He crossed the room and towered over my chair; he made mysterious passes with his huge hands above my head and then—apparently from the back of my neck—he pro-duced a gas mask. He held it up by the rubber face-piece, the metal canister dangled limply at the end of the corrugated breathing-tube, and on its side was the unmistakable insignia of the Japanese Naval Landing Party.

"Morris," I said, as we finished our drinks, "your party tonight must have put you into the red and getting this mask can't have been a cheap business. What about my meeting your out-of-pocket expenses for the chap who got it in Shanghai. Just that and nothing more."

He stepped out on to the balcony and looked across the harbor to where the lights of Victoria were going out one by one.

"You two know all about me," he said, and, at the change in his voice, my wife was instantly wide awake and listening. "I've not a drop of English blood in my veins. My father was a Polish Jew and my mother was a Polish Jew and we're descended from the first Rabbis of Israel. And when my father came to London, you didn't exactly lay down the red carpet for him either. He worked darned hard and his family got enough to eat and that was all. But that *wasn't* all. He got a square deal from you English and that was something he'd never had in the whole of his life before. I owe your people something for that and now I've a chance to repay them. It's . . . aw, hell, I suppose you'd call it a debt of honor."

I was still at home when a confused and indecisive engagement around the Marco Polo Bridge ushered in the war that was to last eight years, bring death, destruction and misery to countless millions, and result ultimately in the ruin of both China and Japan.

By the time I returned, Peking and Tientsin had fallen, and the Japanese Navy, insanely jealous of the laurels so easily earned by their Army of Occupation, had embarked in Shanghai on their own private campaign, only to find that they had bitten off considerably more than they could chew.

Canton was under constant bombardment from aircraft based either on carriers or in the south of Formosa, and Wu Teh-chen, having recently become Governor of Kwangtung, had recruited Morris to his staff, officially as A.D.C., but actually in his old Pooh-Bah capacity of "Lord High Everything Else."

Morris had gone to war whole-heartedly. He had lost about 14 pounds in weight, was practicing almost complete teetotalism, and looked twice as fit as ever before. He now cropped his few remaining gray locks in the pseudo-German style affected by certain of the Chinese High Command and, as his own personal gesture of defiance to the Axis Powers, he had grown a small, bristling, Hitleresque mustache. He wore on occasion his general's uniform complete with sword, while his pockets bulged over an armory of revolvers and automatic pistols. With his field officer's cap set squarely on the top of his enormous head, he seemed scarcely human.

But he had grown also in moral stature. Throughout his life he had never wavered in his rather complex loyalties—to England, the land of his birth; to Canada, which had put him on the road to fame, if not to fortune; to China, "which has given me my coffee and doughnuts all these years"; and to Israel, the people of his own race. For the last he had recently made a substantial sacrifice; now was his opportunity to serve the first.

Renouncing his love of the dramatic, he set to work with industry and perseverance at collecting those small, unsensational items of solid fact that, assembled in sufficient number, may—or may not—built up to conclusions of real importance. The first weak and rather ineffective Chinese guerrilla groups were coming into existence and scoring their first small successes against isolated Japanese posts, producing from time to time a few identification badges, patrol orders, and the like. Japanese aircraft crashed fairly frequently in Kwangtung territory, shot down sometimes by A.A. gunners or the few but courageous Chinese pilots, but more often coming to grief by their own haphazard navigation.

These last, if the wrecks could be reached before they had been completely plundered by the peasantry, yielded a rich harvest of maps, instruments, and other material; and Morris was indefatigable in their pursuit. The telephone line between Hong Kong and Canton miraculously held good and his voice would come crashing over it.

"Charles, have you heard? We've shot down a dozen super-heavy Jap bombers near Lokchong! . . . You don't believe a words of it? . . . But, hell, it's official! . . . Oh, well, perhaps it's only six, or maybe three. . . . You've never heard of heavy bombers in the south? . . . Maybe they're medium bombers . . . or light bombers if you like. . . . Oh, well, hell, we've shot *something* down anyway. . . . D'you want to come and have a dekko? . . . Good, I've got a staff car and all the police passes you'll need. And I've taken a room at the Victoria for your wife as well. I've some nice little bargains in silk and jade lined up for her. . . . Yes, you can bring your camera *and* your damn shotgun. Shooting snipe's all you ever think of!"

The big railway bridge at Sheklung had been recently bombed and so we set out in a car, the driver of which had not quite realized what he was in for. Our first leg as far as Waiyeung was plain sailing, but after that most of the road bridges had been scientifically blown, with one adequate hole in the middle span which was not usually visible until you were right on top of it. We wandered unhappily in the hills north of Boklo, crossing the innumerable streams by leaky wooden lighters, which derived their mobility from a minute motor boat tied insecurely alongside, and each of which seemed more rickety and ramshackle than the last.

It was long after midnight before we reached the outskirts of Canton and picked our way cautiously through the rubble-strewn streets till we saw loom up ahead of us the line of banyan trees surrounding the Shameen. Exhaustedly we carried our luggage over the little footbridge and deposited it on the hotel doorstep—to find a truly regal welcome awaiting us.

The head porter, the head waiter, and the head bar-boy were still out of bed and greeted my wife with some ceremony. In the hall was another posse of smiling, bowing servitors who escorted us upstairs to a room filled with flowers as for a bride. They thronged beaming in the doorway and plied my wife with questions: "Missy liking this?" and "Missy liking that?"—all the while pointedly ignoring me.

It had been a trying day and my temper was showing signs of strain when the situation explained itself. In came the old hotel amah, flung herself on my wife's open suitcase, and started to unpack exclaiming as she did so, "Ah, Missy, you belong new piecee missy belong General Mah Kun."

She had been mistaken for Morris's latest blonde bit just arrived from Hong Kong.

He saw me off up-country at noon next day in the promised staff car—our own, we found, had bolted back to Hong Kong at daylight—and it was forty-eight hours before I returned to find Canton displaying its least attractive aspect.

The weather had been overcast for almost a week and Japanese planes seemed to be taking off with a brief to bomb anything that looked like a building. The city itself they could hardly fail to find, but once there they circled aimlessly, fearing very naturally to come down through the cloud to a height at which targets could be identified. The noise of their engines as they flew lower and lower drowned ordinary conversation and was interspersed with uncomfortable thuds and rumbles as, one by one, they decided that they were hopelessly lost and unloaded their bombs at random before heading for home.

Morris was as exuberant as ever and took me off on our usual round of visits: the airport to collect nose-fuses, tail-fins, and any other bomb fragments that looked interesting; the most recently devastated areas to estimate the damage and speculate on what the Japs had been trying to hit; Military Headquarters to pick up any campaign news that might be available; and finally Wu Teh-chen himself, who remains to this day the most impressive Chinese statesman that it has been my fortune to meet.

We wound up with a memorable meal of Shekki pigeon, duck's tongues, and snow fungus at the Tai Ping-kun restaurant, and then his henchman, Hat Ma-chung (answering to the sobriquet of "Hot Dog"), took us to the railway station.

It was bad luck that a stick of light bombs should have fallen across the line ten minutes before our arrival. Our engine had been hit and the usually resourceful station staff were for once at a loss and unwilling to say if another could be got ready for our train. The faithful Hot Dog installed us in a first-class carriage, put a sentry on the door, and rushed off to find Morris, who could be relied on to overcome most obstacles with a wave of his hand—or, rather, with a flourish of the much-stamped and sealing-waxed document he always carried.

But scarcely had Hot Dog left when another and comparatively undamaged engine appeared from its shed and coupled up to our train. The enthusiasm was infectious;

whistles blew, flags waved, signal lights changed from red to green and back again with bewildering rapidity, at least two railway guards discharged their muskets, and it became plain that our departure was due at almost any moment.

Then down the platform charged Morris, followed by the stationmaster and numerous minor officials. His face was completely hidden behind an enormous bouquet of flowers which he thrust into the arms of my wife. He fumbled in his pockets and produced three tiny jade bangles the size of a very small girl's wrist. He panted painfully till he had partially regained his breath and then gasped out, "I got these for your *chi'sai missys.*"

"Morris," said my wife, "you're a darling!"

She chose from her bouquet a crimson camellia, kissed it lightly, and, as the train started to move, leaned from the carriage and tucked it deftly into the lapel of his tunic.

The run down to Hong Kong was lengthy and eventful. One recently repaired bridge showed signs of buckling under our engine and we had to withdraw and wait till it had been further strengthened. Twice, raiding aircraft approached so close that the train pulled up while we sought safety in the surrounding paddy-fields. We reached the frontier next day tired, dirty, and hungry, but throughout that irksome journey I carried with me one unforgettable picture—that of Morris standing alone on the platform, the station staff at a respectful distance behind him, the gallant red blossom in his buttonhole, waving us goodbye, and—blushing like a debutante at her first ball.

The Chinese themselves observed the change in Morris and began to employ him on missions of really remarkable delicacy to be entrusted to any European. A famous elder statesman who had given his country long, devoted, and distinguished service, but was now verging on senility, was living in retirement in Shanghai, and it became known that the Japanese intended to bring him under their influence and build him up into another collaborationist figurehead of the type of "Wang-the-Traitor."

It was essential that he should be removed to a safer spot, and Morris was dispatched to persuade the venerable man to leave the comforts of his home in Shanghai for barbarous Hong Kong. He set out confidently enough, but circumstances were too strong for him. In Hong Kong the old gentleman had maintained for many years an equally elderly concubine of uncertain temper and well known for the sharpness of her tongue.

In spite of all Morris's blandishments, he preferred death, or disgrace, or both to the prospect of life with the terrible old lady; and so he remained in Shanghai where, within the next few months, he was duly assassinated by Chinese "patriots." Morris had failed, but the fact that he could be entrusted with such a mission was sufficient tribute to the confidence imposed in him.

He returned, too, richer by one vivid experience. The story of his failure he told me full and frankly as we sat on the veranda of my Kowloon flat watching the stone-cutters at work on the great gray slabs hewn from the hillocks below Lion Rock. For a few minutes he sat sad and silent, then his face lit up again.

"Say," he said, "something else happened on that trip. D'you remember Irma Snoopoff, the wife of that little rat that works for the Japs? You must know her—all high-heeled shoes, scarlet slacks, and Hays Office sweaters. She was on that same boat going north and so was a nice little officer-boy from Singapore, a lootenant in the artillery. And did she make a pass at him? They ate at the same table and they drank together and had their deck chairs put side by side and they danced together. At the Del Monte they'd have been turned off the floor!

"I felt sure she was pumping the boy and, if he was stationed at those big fifteen-inch batteries at Changgi, he'd have plenty to tell her. I knew I ought to warn him and wondered what was the best way of doing it. In the end I wrote an unsigned note telling him to keep his mouth shut and pushed it under his cabin door. What do you think happened then? She left him and attached herself to me!

"Next morning they were walking round the deck together talking away nineteen to the dozen and she was giving me long thoughtful looks each time we passed. It was tiffin time and I was in the bar having a short one when up came the little lootenant.

" 'General Cohen,' he said very formally. 'My lady friend would much like to meet you. Would you care to join us for a drink?'

" 'Honored,' says I bowing.

"We took our glasses and went over to the table where she was sitting and I bowed again.

" 'Mme. Snoopoff,' says the boy, 'may I present General Cohen?'

(" 'Oh, ho,' I thought, 'so she's using her right name anyway.')

" 'How thrilling,' she says, 'I've often heard my husband speak of you.'

(" 'If that's so, you've heard no language fit for a lady,' I thought.)

"All I said out loud was that we'd often travelled together. They boy paid for a round and I paid for a round and then we went into the saloon.

"After lunch I went up on deck and had settled down

in my favorite corner when I'm damned if the deck-steward didn't come along lugging the Snoopoff's chair and dump it down beside mine. After him came the lady herself with her workbasket. She pulled out a half-knitted jumper and a skein: 'Would you please hold my wool for me, General?'

"Then she was all over me.

" 'How lucky I was to find you on this boat. I've always wanted to meet you, General Cohen. May I call you Morris? You see, although we've never actually talked to each other before, I feel I know you quite well from all the *wonderful* stories I've heard about you. And now I've seen you in the flesh, I can believe *all* those stories. You know, Morris, you've got what they call sex-appeal.'

" 'You must mean Mex-appeal,' I said, but she didn't quite get that and just went on." This is a rather recondite joke. "Dollar-mex" was a Chinese term for spare cash.

" 'Now you'll tell me *all* about the present situation. I'm so ignorant and my husband *never* talks to me about politics. He doesn't really understand me and I feel that you do. Isn't this China Incident *terrible?* Do you believe in Asia for the Asiatics?'

"This gave me a line on her brief. Only the Japs and their stooges used the expression 'China Incident' to describe the full-blown war that was in progress. And 'Asia for the Asiatics' was one of their pet slogans. I took my cue and played up.

"I told her I was a firm believer in Japan's mission to regenerate China and lead all the peoples of the Orient. I told her that British Imperialism was at the back of everyone's troubles from typhoons to trade recessions, and that Yankee Dollar Diplomacy was just one degree worse. I told her that Russia was weak and frightened and that, if she could, she'd sign a pact with Japan tomorrow. I told her

« 261 »

everything that her bosses would like to hear, and last of all I told her that I was staying a week in Shanghai and she could always find me at the Astor House Hotel.

"We got in the next day; I never heard another word from her. Each time the reception clerk had a letter for me, I thought it was going to be a bit of scented notepaper from her and each time my bedside phone rang I expected to hear her smarmy syrupy little voice. I'd lots more to tell her, but she never gave me the chance. The Japs had got all they wanted from her. Perhaps they thought she wasn't too bright. Anyway, they laid her off and, when they did show their hand, it was on a very different level.

"When I came back one morning from another fruitless argument with old Tong Shao-yi, there was a Japanese Legation car drawn up outside the hotel and in the lounge was a uniformed Legation messenger with a note from a diplomat called Suma, who'd been Consul General in Canton for many years and was a pretty good friend of mine. He was delighted to hear that I was in Shanghai. He suggested that I might enjoy talking over old times. What about a suki-yaki dinner any evening that suited me?

"Now the essence of a suki-yaki party is its intimate and confidential atmosphere and old Suma had certainly laid it on in style. He'd taken a room in the best Japanese hotel in the Concession and produced two of the prettiest geisha I've ever seen. But as you know, that doesn't mean much—the most popular geisha are very seldom pretty. I noticed that neither of them spoke a word of English although in Shanghai it wouldn't have been hard to find a couple who did. Whatever Suma was going to talk about was for my ears alone.

"It was a jolly evening at first. Whatever you may say about the Japs, when they want to make you feel happy, they know how to do it. The two geisha cooked for us—big gray prawns fried in oil one by one and laid on sheets of paper, 'kissing-fish,' with their funny pursed-up little mouths, cuttlefish and mullet, followed by the traditional dishes of beef and bean-curd. While the girls cooked they prattled away to Suma and made improper jokes (I could tell they were improper by the sideways glances I got) about me.

"We started drinking saki early on and we drank plenty, finishing up with tea, while one girl played the *samisen* and the other sang little love-songs. All the while there hadn't been one word of business, just old-timers' reminiscences of Dr. Sun and the Revolution and the rest. We were sitting on the usual low stools and my knees were beginning to ache with cramp. I wondered when he was going to come to the point. At last he did.

" 'And what are your duties now, General?'

" 'Why, Mr. Suma, you must know all about me. I'm a buyer of machinery and factory equipment for the Kwang-tung Government. I buy arms and ammunitions, too, sometimes. Not so long ago I signed a big contract for ex-plosives—T.N.T.—with one of your own firms in Kobe, but I doubt if they'll deliver as things are now.'

" 'Yes-s-s, General, but I have long felt—my country has long felt—that you are wasting your talents. The most important, the one essential matter in the East today, is a firm agreement between Japan and China, based of course on the recognition of Manchukuo independence and of the special position of my own country in all East Asian affairs. Together we could conquer—I mean, we could set an example to the whole world. To further such an under-standing would be a task worthy of your great gifts and of the universal respect in which you are held. It would also be extremely well paid. I have been instructed to mention the sum of three thousand yen a month and there would, of course, be a substantial expense account and special rewards for enterprises brought to a successful conclusion.'

" 'Morris Cohen,' I thought, 'this'll teach you never to go pulling a woman's leg again—even when she's as chuckleheaded as the Snoopoff. He's given me a darned good party and he probably thinks he's got me in the bag already.'

"I wriggled out of it somehow. I said that I was only too keen to help in creating a better atmosphere as between China and Japan, but this was hardly the right time to start. Sino-Japanese relations were a hot internal political issue. I'd always kept clear of internal politics and, as a foreigner, I just had to do so. (That made sense at any rate.) I burbled on and soon enough he realized that I wasn't going to play and—strangely for a well-bred Japanese—he took it pretty hard.

"To be rude to me, his guest, would have been right against the rules, but he became silent and began to lower the saki at a rate that made me blink. Presently he switched over to brandy. That's always a bad sign at a Japanese party. I kept up the chatter till the earliest moment at which I could decently make a move. By then the brandy had loosened his tongue quite a bit. We shook hands and he held on to mine and looked me in the eyes:

" 'I'm sorry, General, that you can't see your way clear to come in with us. You know as well as I do that the day of the white man draws to its close. Japan has three enemies, but only one is dangerous. We hate England, we despise America, but we fear Russia!' "

Morris disappeared once more into what we were beginning to call "Free China," bearing in his breast-pocket a list of questions topped by the one word "Gas?" Whatever the Japanese might have done in Manchuria, they had certainly embarked on chemical warfare in the Yangtse valley.

Their commanders in the field had learned to their cost that even the most poorly armed guerrillas were a nasty proposition when ensconced in one of those four-square walled villages that stand like gray forts in the surrounding green sea of paddy. Given a moderate breeze, gas was the obvious solution and, after one or two expensive assaults, gas was certainly being used, but the truth of the matter was hopelessly obscured by a flood of propaganda so foolish and ill-judged as to convince most observers to the contrary.

For long I heard nothing. Then came a cryptic wire from Changsha:

COUGH MIXTURE COMING HOLD YOUR NOSE.

Next morning my telephone rang.

"Kai Tak Airport speaking," gasped a strangled voice, "for God's sake come and take your stinking package away before we throw it in the harbor!"

I came as fast as Star Ferry and Kowloon taxi could take me and turned in at the airport gates, to see that I had achieved a degree of unpopularity that would not soon be lived down. Most of the staff seemed to be standing in a semi-circle outside the manager's office, through the half-open door of which came a sweetish, sickly odor that seared my throat and nostrils, made my eyes water, my head swim, and my stomach evince all the symptoms of severe sea-sickness.

Timorously I peeped into the room and saw on the manager's desk an untidy brown paper parcel perhaps eighteen inches long by nine in diameter. Shuddering and retching I borrowed a canvas air-engine cover, wrapped it around the object, and rushed for my taxi. The driver had fortunately failed to grasp what was happening; he started up his engine and we moved off, as the burly German pilot of the

Eurasia plane that had evidently just touched down came rushing murderously across the tarmac.

Once outside the gates, I opened one door, deposited my bundle on the running-board, and held it there with my foot till we reached the ferry. On board I seated myself right at the stern and thanked the sea-gods for a stiffish breeze down the harbor. Ashore in Victoria it was but a step to my office in the huge white Hong Kong and Shanghai Bank building. I dumped my burden in an empty room, drew a breath of relief, and picked up the afternoon paper.

"Sir-r-r," said a quiet Scots voice at my elbow, and there, regarding me with an expression of prim disapproval stood my youthful secretary, Dorothy Johnston.

In the years of our association Miss Johnston had frequently disapproved of my judgment or my conduct, but never without good reason, and I looked up at her apprehensively.

"Sir-r-r, ye have frequently war-r-rned me that we must never attract attention to our office. I do not know what is in yon parcel, but it smells verra bad and ye must r-r-realize that the air-conditioning system is disseminating that smell throughout the bank building. If ye look out of the window ye will see that people are leaving the main entrance with handkerchiefs to their faces."

One refuge was left—the Government Laboratories. I telephoned, announced my impending arrival, and rang off before anyone could protest. Once there I was in competent hands. The Chief Analyst removed the brown paper covering, closed the split down the side of the canister with putty, and promised a report on the contents in due course.

Forty-eight hours later it arrived. The cylinder was certainly a lethal war-gas weapon, and, though all the components of the filling had not been positively identified, the main constituent was diphenylcyanoarsine.

Full of enthusiasm I seized my phone: his number seemed to have changed but soon I tracked him down.

"I've got your note; may I come down and talk to you about it?"

"Yes, old chap, but don't go to the Labs. My assistant was a bit over-confident in his approach to the job. Some of the stuff's got loose and I've had to evacuate. I'm speaking now from a temporary office in the Central Police Station."

That summer the news was always bad, but Morris's spirits seemed to rise with each reverse, and when opportunity occurred he enjoyed himself as of old. The gas cylinder rated a celebration and we duly celebrated.

We sat down a party of sixteen in an upper chamber overlooking the odoriferous harbor of a little fishing village called, rather surprisingly, Aberdeen. We ate, first lobster, then crayfish, then shark's fin with crab-meat; garoupa and then "seven-day fish," so-called because it will live for seven days out of water; "big fish with sweet and sour sauce"; the three kinds of awabi, or conch-shell; two species of *bêche-de-mer* or sea-slugs; some Swatow scallops and lastly some delicious, though anonymous, soup.

I rose from the table feeling that I never wished to tell a tale, to drink a toast, or to face a fish again. Morris, who had never ceased to eat, talk and to "*gambei*" for three solid hours on end, drove me home and went on to join a poker school. "Some of the boys," he explained, "are farewelling me and they reckon they can trim a bit off me at the same time." (They were wrong.)

Morris was in funds and was flying home, his first visit since 1932. He had recently negotiated a large sale of Vickers anti-aircraft guns on behalf of a foreign firm, only to find the amount of his commission in dispute. His reaction was characteristic; he took the case to court and briefed Eldon Potter, then the leading K.C. in Hong Kong, who subsequently described to me their single interview: "One of the best clients I've known; only took ten minutes of my time; perfectly frank and open and knew exactly what were his rights." The case was settled without litigation for the full amount of his claim and Morris booked his air passage to England.

His father had recently died and his relatives in London and Manchester claimed most of his time and, incidentally, much of his money, since he gave of his abundance to every deserving or unfortunate friend. However, he found leisure to call on my parents and to have tea in our nursery, where he enchanted my children with his conjuring tricks and my youngest daughter proudly displayed to him his green jade bangle on her wrist, but then told him—and with every justification—that he was "an old chatterbox." He was back in Hong Kong within six weeks, having certainly made good use of his time, but his sixty thousand dollars had simply evaporated.

It was a grim and ominous prospect to which he returned. China seemed to be nearing exhaustion; Hankow and Canton were soon to fall and from the Munich Agreement to the collapse of Western Europe, events moved with the inevitability of a Greek tragedy.

Canton had been so frequently threatened that when, early in October, large Japanese troop convoys were once more sighted steaming south through the Formosa Channel, it was impossible to persuade the Kwangtung high command that the situation was really serious.

Morris, together with his loyal friends, Wu Tzi and Ernie Tong, had worked hard, and we reaped at first a rich reward. In the disastrous days that followed, the one bright spot was the flow of accurate, up-to-date information that they provided. A first-rate coast-watcher had been stationed on Fokai Point to the east of the old pirate haunt in Bias Bay; it was a clear, starlit night and for once all the telephone lines worked.

"Japanese fleet deploying off entrance to bay . . . Hachung under bombardment . . . Ou Tau-kung under bombardment . . . first flight landing at Hachung."

A little later they were ashore near Nimshan and then the Chinese claimed to have repulsed at Taipung a landing which looked like a feint. By noon they were attacking Nimshan town on the Waiyeung road, and it was clear that the Chinese were not putting up much of a fight.

By daylight next morning there were seven thousand Japanese in Nimshan, five thousand in Hachung, and, at Ou Tau-kung, a force of unknown strength which was already marching on Tamsui. Our telephone line went dead for ten minutes.

At noon the position was worse; the Japs were storming Tamsui, more than thirty thousand were ashore, and there was still no sign of stiffening in the Chinese resistance. Also our telephone line was failing for longer and longer periods.

The dawn of the 14th found Morris slightly more optimistic. The position was confused; on the Nimshan road the Chinese were at last putting up some sort of a scrap and claimed to have halted the Japanese advance at Pat Shanting hill. The line went dead for two hours, but presently he got through again.

"Say, Charles, things don't look too good. Tamsui's fallen and the column that took the place's going hell-for-leather for Pingshan."

I rushed for my maps as, once more, the line failed. At last I heard his voice again but this time I spoke first.

"Morris, listen. Look at your map. There's a place

called Pingshan north-east of Tamsui and another with the same name south-west of Tamsui and only ten miles from our frontier. In other words, the Japs are either marching straight on Hong Kong New Territory or else straight away from us. Can you tell me which Pingshan you mean?"

"No," replied Morris thoughtfully, "I guess I can't. Isn't war hell?"

With that the line went dead again and this time it stayed dead.

CHAPTER XII

World War Two

THE CANTON CAMPAIGN—said Morris—was a flop from start to finish. True, most of our best troops were already engaged up north and General Hu Han-mou had no more than six or seven newly recruited and weak divisions under his command. True, too, that Bias Bay had always been a disaffected area and that the Japs had spent a lot of money there preparing the way. Some of their formations were actually met on the beach by guides carrying Japanese flags.

All that's true enough, but it doesn't account for our collapse. Canton fell exactly ten days after the first landing well over a hundred miles away. If the Japs had marched the whole distance as fast as they could with no fighting at all, it wouldn't have taken them much less time than it did—and it still makes me sick to think about it.

Waiyeung on the East River was heavily fortified. I thought we were going to make a stand there, but when Waiyeung fell I realized it was all up. Hu Han-mou pulled his military headquarters out the next day and went back to Hot Springs, but Wu Teh-chen wouldn't move.

I wasn't quite sure what was in his mind. He was a level-headed, modern-minded administrator, but underneath still a mixture of the revolutionary veteran and the old-style mandarin. With people like that, personal honor comes first. If he'd felt he was disgraced, he was quite capable of making a final fight on the spot and dying in the ruins of Canton.

Just to be on the safe side, I set about sandbagging his Yamen, mounted machine guns on the roof, and disposed his bodyguard for a final fight. I couldn't see much sense in it myself, but if he felt that way, it was all right by me. I meant to see that we took as many Japs with us as we could.

It never came to that. On the morning of the 20th we heard their guns to the eastward and by the evening they sounded pretty close. During the day we loaded up a convoy of trucks with the government archives and office gear, and after dark we left. We'd cut it pretty fine too. The Japs were already attacking Fatshan as we skirted round the town. We could see the flames of Tsungfa away to the north. Actually they were in Canton just four hours after we'd gone.

Jap aircraft were up at dawn ranging the countryside. We lay up all day in a temple at Yungyuen, and then lit out for Linhsien, a little town in the north of the province where we'd been told to establish a temporary seat of government. It was a desolate area, just dirt tracks winding among mountains with their peaks lost in the clouds. It was those clouds that saved us. In spite of all the enemy planes on the lookout for road traffic escaping from Canton, we were only attacked twice, and got to Linhsien without any more casualties.

We stayed there for a pretty dreary two months. We had plenty to do, reorganizing our headquarters, listening to bad news on the wireless, and, as soon as the newspapers began to arrive, reading all the dirt thrown at us by the vernacular press—and the foreign-language press, too, for that matter. The Japs knew our whereabouts all right. We were bombed most days, but there were some big caves in the mountainside where we could take shelter. The only time they did much damage was one day when they caught a peasant's funeral procession in the open and shot it to bits with their machine guns.

The only break came in the fourth week when Wu Teh-chen was summoned to meet the Generalissimo at a little station up the Canton-Hankow Railway. He asked me if I'd care to accompany him. I said "Yes," though it wasn't the sort of meeting I was going to enjoy. He had to make a report on the new provincial capital, and, as for me, Chiang knew perfectly well that I'd tried to rescue Li Chai-sum when he had him under arrest in Nanking. He also knew that I'd twice refused to serve his nominees. That isn't the best way to get ahead in China. Altogether he must have thought me a pretty obstinate, troublesome sort of devil.

I needn't have been nervous. Chiang Kai-shek is a soldier. He was fighting Japan and he needed both of us. Our front had collapsed, but he wasn't going to waste time in post mortems. He just heard our reports and gave new orders for getting on with the war. He shook hands with me when we left and said "Goodbye." That's the only time I've ever heard him say anything in English. "Goodbye" was all he said and yet I came away feeling two inches taller and another inch around the chest. Chiang may be a stern, ruthless man, but he's a fine leader to follow when you're fighting a losing battle.

We returned to Linhsien, which had been heavily bombed in our absence. Another month went by. One morning there was a stranger sitting in Wu Teh-chen's office, a fine-looking, solemn-faced man I'd never seen before.

"Morris," said my chief, "I've been appointed Minister for Overseas Chinese. This is General Li Hon-wan, the new governor, and he wants to know if you'll join his staff in the same position you've held with me?"

"No, sir," I said. "I'll go with you unless I get a straight order to stay here."

"I see," said Wu Teh-chen solemnly. He looked at General Li, and I'm damned if they didn't both begin to laugh. They went on laughing till I saluted and stamped out.

After that it was all bustle and movement again. Wu Teh-chen had to go up to Chungking (which had become the new national capital since the fall of Hankow) to recruit and organize his staff. Cut off as we were now, that meant nearly a thousand miles of cross-country travel through the wildest parts of China. Our lorry convoy had been dispersed, but we collected ten cars of different makes, mostly very old and decrepit, and rustled up camp beds and mosquito nets and equipment. We could only take half a dozen guards. I strapped on my guns and made a seventh, and we got there somehow. There was a busy three weeks, and then in mid-February we flew down to Hong Kong and set up our headquarters on the first floor of Shell House.

In Hong Kong nothing had changed. The last few months seemed like a bad dream. The hotels were full and the movies were full and the dance halls were full. It was the annual Race Week when I arrived. The whole colony trooped off to Happy Valley every single day. They might hardly have heard about a war. And then Charles was on the doorstep with a little list of sixteen questions he wanted answered.

"Can you tell us any more about this new long-range trench mortar that's supposed to shoot four thousand meters?"

"I'm afraid I can't. . . ."

"Or these new armored landing craft they're said to be using?"

"Well, old fellow, as a matter of fact . . ."

"You must have identified the first formations to land in Bias Bay."

"Maybe we did; but you know there was rather a lot going on just then."

"What the hell *have* you been doing since I saw you last? . . . Picnicking?"

"Yes," I said, "my life's been just one long lovely picnic."

All that spring I sweated away at my old job. China's need for arms was never greater than now, but it was getting more and more difficult to deliver them. Previously there'd been the railway, the road, and the Pearl River, but with Canton in Japanese hands it wasn't so simple. Still the Hong Kong frontier was open—at least pretty well open, as long as one didn't make things too obvious; and in spite of the coastal blockade, there were still a few junks ready to carry my cargoes and take their chance of dodging the Jap destroyers.

As the summer drew on Hitler made it plainer and plainer that he was determined to fight. When Stalin signed his Non-Aggression Pact and war became absolutely inevitable, I really think that it came as a relief to most of us. For myself I had hardly time to think about it. A week earlier a blow had fallen that, for a time, pretty well put me out of business. The Japanese Army suddenly decided to put an end to the arms traffic by occupying the Hong Kong frontier.

They brought with them their Comfort Corps—formations of militarized prostitutes whose movements were always a good guide to the Japs' future plans—which showed that they meant to make a long stay, and I was at my wits' end to know what to do. It meant building up a full-scale, heavy-load smuggling organization straight from scratch. Help came from where I least expected it.

I used to do my work in a hotel room a long way from Wu Teh-chen's own office, so as to run no risk of embarrassing him with the Hong Kong Government. I was busy there one morning when a visiting card was brought in that made me sit up and blink. The name on it was one of those gentlemen with two or three nationalities and four or five passports who are always to be found on the fringe of any war dabbling in my sort of business. This particular chap was well known to all and sundry as the head of a loosely-knit syndicate that worked for the Japs and was absolutely committed to their success. I'd never met him in the flesh, but I knew plenty about him. I thought that his calling on me was just a colossal piece of cheek.

I swept all the papers off my desk into the top drawer, disconnected my phone in case he'd bribed the room-boy to slip in one of those little listening devices, looked out on the balcony, closed the windows, and said, "Show him up."

I remembered that all the dockets off my desk were now lying on top of my loaded pistol, so I pulled open the drawer again and took it out. As I was sitting there with my gun in my hand, in walked our little friend.

It's funny how that sort of guy always manages to catch you at a disadvantage. He took it all in at a glance, grinned and murmured, "Unnecessary, General, I assure you. We meet as friends—at least I hope we do."

I said nothing but just had a long look at him—his face, his clothes, and everything else. He was about the most anonymous bloke I'd ever seen. I've always prided myself on being able to tell a lot from a man's appearance. With this chap you couldn't tell a thing, neither his race, nor his class, nor even his age within twenty years. I guessed he was a Levantine of some sort, but he might have come from anywhere between Gilbraltar and Manila.

In the end I opened the ball.

"Well," I said, "I can't pretend I'm glad to see you here, but what d'you want anyway?"

"General, we are both, I think, in difficulties. You are now unable to get your munitions into Kwangtung and I am having trouble in exporting sugar to Shanghai. But by a strange—one might almost say a providential—coincidence, we are in a position to assist each other. You, with your influence in Hong Kong Government circles, would have little difficulty in obtaining the necessary permits for me from the Department of Economic Warfare. I fortunately am in control of a smuggling organization which could handle all your recent purchases. Gasoline is your principal problem, isn't it?"

"You know damn well it is! The stuff's bulky and heavy and everybody has a use for it. Even if I could get it through the Jap lines in coolie-loads, half of it would be stolen before it reached our dumps. It's my main headache."

"In that case, General, I will put a proposition to you. Obtain on my behalf a permit for the export to Shanghai ex-Hong Kong of one million dollars worth of raw sugar, and I will arrange the delivery in Free China of one million dollars' worth of gasoline. You will have no further worry in the matter. All I shall require is to have access to your go-downs here and the address to which your goods should be consigned. Is it a deal?"

"Wait a minute," I said. "You and I are all right, sitting pretty here in Hong Kong. But a lot of poor bastards are going to risk their necks over this. What happens when they cop it?"

"That has all been foreseen, General. The family of any of my employees who may lose his life in my service will receive five hundred dollars. Such claims will not, however, fall directly on you or me; my whole organization is covered by insurance against hazards of precisely this nature. For that matter I could arrange the insurance during transit of your goods at a very reasonable premium—not more than fifteen per cent, I should fancy."

"But, say, are there *no* strings attached to this? Is there nothing else you want from me?"

"Ah, yes, General, there is just one small matter. I believe, as you may have gathered, in being protected as far as possible against all eventualities. Now, as far as can be humanly foreseen, the victory of Japan is inevitable. But we are only human and liable to err. Supposing by some totally unforeseen accident, China were to emerge from the struggle victorious, then I would be grateful for—in fact, I would rely on—your testimony to the value of my services to that country and the sacrifices I had made on her behalf. Reinsurance, my dear General, reinsurance!"

We shook hands on the deal and he bowed himself out. When the door had shut behind him, I picked up his visiting card again—and I began to laugh. I'd only bothered to read his name before. Now I saw that he described himself as "travelling representative" of one of the largest insurance companies in the Far East.

That was one of the best bargains I ever made. Less than a tenth of my stuff was lost in transit. The rest reached its destination undamaged and pretty promptly, and not one single claim for the five hundred dollars death money did we get. The real secret of his success was, I think, that, although the senior Japanese officers were, of course, incorruptible, many of the juniors could be bribed, and only he had the contacts for bribing them. He had the smuggling racket sewn up tight and it was lucky for China that he had.

The "Phony War" dragged on. Gradually Hong Kong came to realize what had happened. But just about the time they came to realize it the Blitzkrieg broke out, France folded up, and it looked as if the British had had it. At least it looked like that to everyone except the British themselves. All they said in the Hong Kong Club was, "This is going to make it an awful long war." Presently the Battle of Britain was won, and it began to seem that they were right.

Chiang Kai-shek thought so too. His reaction was to send Wu Teh-chen off on a mission to visit the major Chinese overseas communities throughout the Far East and get them thoroughly organized on a wartime basis. He took with him a staff of four—Professor Chang Yuen-yue as his principal adviser, Hwang Tien-cho the Deputy Director of his Ministry, Bing Shui-lee as his private secretary, and myself.

At first I wasn't keen on going. It seemed like escaping from the real war to take a sort of tourist trip. But my arms-smuggling show was running itself by now and I couldn't pretend that I was really needed in Hong Kong. And as General Wu seemed set on having me along, off I went. It was a wonderful journey. Looking back on it is a bit sad. Every single place we visited was in Japanese hands within the next eighteen months.

Our first stop was Manila, where we stayed in the Presidential Palace as guests of Manuel Quezon. I'd known him fifteen years before when he'd trimmed me at poker. He hadn't forgotten his game and he trimmed me again. For ten days we went speechifying all over the Philippines. My boss must have addressed upwards of half a million Chinese. Everybody was good to us. I was given so many presents that I couldn't possibly cart them along with me. I shipped the whole lot back to China.

When we got down to Java the atmosphere was rather different. The Filipinos quite thought that the Japs might attack them one day, but they were a light-hearted lot and they weren't worrying much till it actually happened. The

Dutch, on the other hand, had just seen their home country overrun and conquered and were taking things very seriously indeed. Also a Japanese commercial mission had left Batavia the day we arrived there. They'd been negotiating for oil, but their terms had been much too hard. They hadn't liked the Dutch refusal to sell at all, and, when they departed, had more than hinted that they might be back again soon. The Dutch were thoroughly war-minded and wanted information about our A.R.P. warning system and how we constructed our dug-outs in Chungking.

In Singapore the picture was different again. The British were certainly getting themselves fixed for a war, but they had one full-scale war on their hands already back in Europe, and naturally the Far East, where it hadn't so far spread, had got to take second place. They were doing the best they could, but things weren't moving very fast as yet.

On top of that, there was a fantastic mixture of races in Malaya, not only the three major ones—Chinese, Indians, and Malays—but endless minor groups like the Parsees and the Hadramauti Arabs. All that complicated matters. The Communists were busy there too and I pulled a boner that gave them their chance to foul things up. It wasn't really my fault—at least not much.

A delegation of Chinese Communists wanted to see Wu Teh-chen but refused to call on him at the big private house in Meyer Road where we were staying. He agreed to meet them in a hotel. I didn't much like the idea and went along with my eyes well skinned. It was a scruffy little place in a back street, loud and lively with the clatter of mah jong pieces, the bang of crackers, and the screech of sing-song girls. The deputation were waiting when we walked in. General Wu sat down at the head of the table and the conference was on.

They began asking him questions—the usual "party line" propaganda stuff. While he answered I studied them in turn. The third one I looked at brought me out of my chair as if I'd sat on a tintack. They were wearing thin cotton coolie-coats, and the outside breast-pocket of this man bulged over an object exactly the shape and size of a small automatic pistol.

I slipped around behind him, got my hand on the pocket—it was unbuttoned, by the way—and drew out one of those flat square electric torches!

Everyone jumped to their feet. Wu Teh-chen apologized for my gross discourtesy, though I could see his eyes were smiling. I handed the chap's torch back and almost went on my knees to say how sorry I was.

You'd have thought that they might forget the incident. Not a bit of it. One Chinese-language newspaper in Malaya followed the party line. Next morning it came out with one great banner headline right across the front page: GENERAL MAH KUN MISTRUSTS OUR COMMUNIST COMRADES!

Rangoon, our last port of call, was in much the same state as Singapore—preparing for war as fast as their limited resources would let them, and praying for more time. That was the end of our trip. The other three returned by sea, Wu Teh-chen was in a hurry. He and I drove to Lashio and flew from there to Chungking.

As soon as the plane had settled down on her course heading due north over those nasty-looking saw-toothed ridges, the last six months began to seem just as much of a dream as my first holiday home in England had done, once I was back on the Atlantic.

Our plane circled over the ruined streets of Chungking and came down on that single stone-flagged runway laid on a sandbank bang in the middle of the Yangtse. There was a guard of honor for General Wu and more guards with tommy guns to shepherd our chairs up those winding stone stairways to the road where our cars stood waiting. All around was dust and destruction. We were thankful for the gray overcast that saved us from the usual daily air raid. The South Seas seemed very far off indeed.

My stay in the wartime capital didn't last long. Within a few weeks I was on board a plane bound south for Hong Kong with two lots of instructions in my pocket. One was to start talks with General Grasett, the Garrison Commander, about Chinese military co-operation when the Japs attacked. The other was to help old Admiral Chan Chak in keeping tab on the Fifth Column of Chinese traitors inside the colony.

It was a frustrating sort of assignment. We were hampered at every turn by the British Government's policy (a natural one, when you think how hard pressed they were at home) of no provocation to the Japanese and strict neutrality in the Sino-Japanese War. I'm not the most patient of men. As the months of 1941 passed by, the crash came ever nearer, and we seemed to be making no progress at all. I got more and more worked up about it.

Luckily I was dealing with two good-tempered, level-headed men. General Grasett was a Canadian by birth (which helped matters) and a sapper with a reputation from the First World War. He took the long, broad view and knew how to make me see things his way. Admiral Chan Chak was a tough little fellow with a wooden leg and a body that had been battered in every war and dust-up since the Revolution. He'd played a big part in the building up of the Chinese Navy, which by now had been pretty well wiped out. His philosophy was just to go steadily plugging along regardless of how badly the cards might seem to be stacked against him.

Between the two of them, they kept me on an even keel. The admiral produced a list of twenty-two agents, all active in Hong Kong, with so much evidence that the Hong Kong Police rounded up the whole lot and put them in the jug. They were released again a few days later·

That set us a long way back, but as often happens, the final result wasn't so bad. The leader of the mob had had a nasty fright. As soon as he was free, he hopped it to Macao. Some of our agents were pretty sick of the business. They followed him there, shot him dead outside a fan-tan house, and beat it across the frontier to Shekki where they couldn't be touched. We were in the clear and the Hong Kong Government was in the clear and everyone was happy—except the guy who'd copped it and he was past worrying.

The pro-Japanese crowd soon got their tails up again and became more impudent than ever. At the end of November I flew up to Chungking to talk to Wu Teh-chen, who had now become Secretary General of the Kuomintang and the key man in all top-level political matters. I'd just begun to get my troubles off my chest when on December 2nd a wire came from Hong Kong: "Your presence required here urgently."

It was unsigned, but I knew who had sent it and I could guess what it meant. I rushed down to General Wu's office. The planes were all full but he had someone turned off. I left the same evening. On board with me was the wife of H. H. Kung, going down to see her sister, Mme. Sun Yat-sen.

That was the first of several problems on my hands and—to me—by far the most important. Mme. Sun had established herself in Hong Kong as being the most convenient center from which to run all the charitable, medical, and welfare organizations, grouped under the title China Defence League, with herself at its head. If war was near and it obviously was, then it meant a siege. Mme. Sun must be got out.

As soon as we touched down, I went to her house. There I bumped up against the hardest of all brick walls—the obstinacy of a really good woman. Up to the day of the Great Doctor's death she'd always done what he said was right. Since then she'd always done what she thought was right. She saw no reason to change now. It was no good trying to argue with her.

"Morris Cohen," she said, "do you believe that the British will defend Hong Kong?"

"Sure," I replied, "they'll fight all right, but there're not very many of them and there're an awful lot of Japs, and it mayn't last very long."

"If there is fighting here, there will be wounded, there will be refugees and children will suffer. Perhaps I may be able to help them. I shall stay right here!"

That was all. It was quite enough. The days went by. I called on her every morning and sat down in her drawing-room and talked my head off. All she did was to smile and repeat, "My duty is to stay here."

I saw Moss, the Superintendent of Kai Tak Airport, who was a personal friend of both sisters, and begged him to keep in close touch with them, and, if the worst came to the worst, bundle them on to some outgoing plane somehow or other. He promised to do his best. That was all I could fix up, and I was just worried to death. I felt that this might be the last service I could ever do for Dr. Sun. I was determined not to fail him.

The second week-end of that month was a nervy time for all of us. It was no surprise when, at eight o'clock on Monday morning, I heard the familiar sound of ack-ack fire and bombs as the Jap air force made their first raid on Kai

Tak and, incidentally, knocked out every plane on the ground.

I played my last card. I went once more to Mme. Sun and told her that she must realize she was a sort of national heroine to the Chinese people. If she stayed here while the fortress fell (as it had to fall, sooner or later), a lot of Chinese would take arms to defend her person to the death. She'd be the cause of a lot of unnecessary slaughter. That was an argument she could appreciate. I only wish I'd thought of it before. She promised to leave as soon as a plane was available.

The following night a few transport planes got in from the north. I took the two sisters across to the mainland and saw them off. It was a pretty grim farewell. We all knew that it was likely to be our last. For once I found myself absolutely tongue-tied. I couldn't think what the hell to say. We shook hands, and I just blurted out, "We'll fight to the bitter end, anyway."

She stopped on the steps of the ramp, looked down at me and said, "We'll fight, too, Morris, but not to the *bitter* end. The end, when it comes, will be sweet!"

The door shut behind her, they wheeled the ramp away, the plane taxied off across the tarmac, and I was left with just those words to hold onto for comfort.

Could I have gone with them? Yes, Wu Teh-chen wanted me back and there was a seat for me on that same plane. Why didn't I? There were a number of reasons. For one thing, I was sold on the idea of Hong Kong being relieved by an attack of the Chinese armies on the rear of the Japs. I'd been trying to fix up the liaison for that all the summer. Even if I didn't quite believe it was ever going to happen, I'd have looked several kinds of a rat if I'd quit just when it was due.

There were a whole lot of fellows in Hong Kong—of every kind and color—who'd worked against the Japs under my banner. They were for it when the fortress fell. I couldn't very well leave them to face the music without me. Was I a fool? I think I was. I had plenty of time for thinking in the next two years. Anyway my mind was made up. I recrossed the harbor and went back to my room in the Hong Kong Hotel.

We got the sisters out only just in time. Next day Kai Tak came under direct fire. The R.A.F. demolished their installations and evacuated. The day after, we were driven clean out of Kowloon and back onto the island.

The next fortnight was one disaster after another. The Japs crossed the harbor at Lyemun Pass, established themselves on the island, and gradually drove us back to the westward. Shelling became heavier and heavier. The end couldn't be very far off.

I was too busy to worry much. It was now open war between my boys and the fifth columnists—and our hands were no longer tied. They were in their element. They went around popping hand grenades through the traitors' windows while they were at supper. It was a good technique. We paid off some long-standing accounts like that.

By Christmas Eve the position was desperate. Ammunition was running short, the water supply had failed, rice distribution had broken down, and the civilian population were panicking. I spent most of Christmas Day helping with the organization of an escape by boat for Admiral Chan Chak and some other tough nuts. They were shot up as they left. The Admiral's boat was sunk, but he swam like a fish —wooden leg and all—and got clear. That was the last bit of good news I had for a long time.

On Boxing Day we knew it was all over. In the afternoon the news of our surrender was broadcast. There was nothing more for me to do. I sat in the lounge of the Hong Kong Hotel waiting to be picked up. I thought of all the different things the Japs might have against me. I began to feel frightened—more frightened than I'd ever been in my life.

CHAPTER XIII

Stanley Prison Camp

I DIDN'T HAVE TO WAIT very long either. No one knew what was going to happen next. We dozed off in chairs or on the floor of the hotel lobby. Diamond, the manager, had been made responsible that no one came in or went out, and T. B. Wilson, who was a pal of his, took night duty at the reception desk for him.

About midnight there was the hell of a rattling and banging on the doors. In stalked a Jap officer holding a big automatic pistol, and followed by two soldiers with their rifles at the "ready." He marched straight up to the desk, dug his gun into Wilson's ribs, and barked, "Is General Cohen here?"

I could see Wilson hesitate. He was a loyal bloke, even when it was no good being loyal. I stepped out and said, "I'm General Cohen!"

"You will come with us."

"Here it is," I thought, "this is my pen-and-ink, my death warrant." I took a last look around the spot I knew so well and followed the officer out with the two men behind me. I tried hard to put a bit of swagger into my walk, so that the people who saw me go would tell my friends. If my shoulders were square and my chin up, my heart was way down in my boots.

And, after all that, nothing much happened. They took me to the temporary headquarters they'd established in an office block. There I was lined up before three more officers who were obviously fairly important. They were formal and correct, not friendly but perfectly polite. They wanted to know just one thing—the whereabouts of a longish list of prominent Chinese characters they believed to have been trapped in Hong Kong at the surrender.

I was very polite, too, and just said that I didn't know, which was no more than the truth. Those who hadn't managed to escape disguised as coolies, which wasn't so difficult at that time, had gone into hiding all over the place. I knew how to get in touch with them, but, quite honestly I hadn't the slightest idea where their hide-outs were located.

They asked me a few more questions and then the senior officer said, "We are sorry that you cannot help us, General. You may return to your hotel, but do not leave it without permission."

I'd thought of all kinds of unpleasant possibilities. To be released again was the only one that hadn't occurred to me. I walked out of that building in a daze. I wandered down Pedder Street, taking no notice of the turmoil around me, thinking, "Morris, this is too good to be true!"

I pulled up with a jerk. That was it. It *was* too good to be true. I was a conspicuous figure and a sitting bird for them to pick up again whenever they wanted me. The reason they'd let me go was simply so that I'd lead them to the other people they were after.

I reckoned they'd leave me alone for a while to lull me into a false sense of security. I had just a few hours' grace. I worked fast. Before daylight I'd got messages off to most of my Chinese friends that I was "hot"—they must cut out all contact with me for the sake of their own skins. I went to sleep and I didn't sleep so badly either. I'd done all I could. The rest was in God's hands.

The next five days were pretty hard to take. I hung around the hotel till I was nearly frantic. It was almost a relief when, one morning, we were herded out and assembled on Murray Parade Ground, together with all the civilian nationals of countries at war with Japan. It struck me as being rather like Judgment Day. All my past life in China seemed to be there, friends of yesterday and other friends I hadn't seen for years and had almost forgotten, business friends and wartime friends and drinking and poker-playing friends. One or two enemies too.

We stayed there most of the day. Finally they broke us up into groups, on no particular principle that one could see, and sent us off to temporary prisons in different parts of the town. I drew it unlucky and found myself in a low-class joint at West Point that might have been called a Chinese hotel but was better known as a brothel. I had to share a tiny cubicle, containing only one cot, with a lady (she'd been secretary to the taipan of Butterfield & Swire) and her child.

I stuck my neck out and asked if I couldn't be transferred to a near-by cubicle which I knew was occupied by men only. That was my first taste of the Jap military mentality. They said "No," and they were angry. Most of all they were amazed at my cheek—at the idea of a mere civilian prisoner-of-war daring to ask for anything at all.

We got hardly any food, but kind old Mme. Weill sent me some parcels which I shared around with the other inmates. For the rest, I was busy with my own thoughts. They weren't particularly pleasant, but they were going to be mighty important for my future—that is, if I was going to have any future. I realized only too well that the brief questioning I'd had on the night of the surrender had been only a preliminary in the hope of making some quick arrests. There was lots more to come. I just sat and sat in that tiny squalid room thinking of questions I was bound to be asked and working out plausible answers.

We were there about three weeks before the soldiers

bustled us out into the streets, down to the Bund, and into a flotilla of launches. They cast off and headed out west under Mount Davis. We knew then we were bound for Stanley, a promontory on the south side of the island where the big civil prison stood. It was the obvious place for the main internment camp.

This looked good to me. It seemed to show that the Japs were treating me as a civilian internee, and not—which they might well have done—as a combatant officer of the Chinese Army. It was no luxury hotel when we got there, but it was better than my crowded cubicle. I settled down to make the best of things. On February 2nd (I'm not likely to forget the date), the Kempeitai came for me again and took me off to their own private prison in the old Magistrate's Court at Kowloon.

Once more I gave myself just a few hours to live. Once more nothing much happened at first. They locked me up alone in a little room that had formerly been the office of the magistrate's clerk. They left me there for two nights. Then they took me out and put me in another room with Seymour Major, a quiet, shrewd, soft-spoken chap I'd known quite well when he was in charge of the Special Branch of the C.I.D. It was a relief to have someone to talk to, but we had to be pretty careful, in case there were any listening devices around.

In the next few days the room gradually filled up till there were eight of us crammed in there. Three of them were also officers of the Special Branch—Elston, Shaftain, and Rex Davis. I was sorry to see Elston because he had a high forehead and a big moon-face like Charles. If the Japs thought he really was Charles, it made things pretty bad for all of us.

On the 10th they took me out of that room and moved me down to a cell in the basement, a real prison cell, the sort that newly arrested prisoners were popped into while they cooled down. It had a floor, a ceiling, three solid walls, and a fourth wall of iron bars. That was all—no cot, no furniture at all, unless you count an empty gasoline tin in one corner for my lavatory.

Even then it wasn't till the next day that they started in on me. This, I think, was where they made their big mistake. They worked to the rules and the rules said that a prisoner left alone and knowing that he's in for a severe interrogation will work himself into a state of nerves and be that much easier to soften up. That might be true for most people, but we Jews have had our share of persecution and imprisonment and general ill-treatment, and maybe we react to it differently. I know I did. I'd felt frightened all the time, but that hadn't prevented my brain working on my problems. By now I'd worked out pretty well all the angles and all the answers. It was lucky for me I had.

Four men were in the room where I was taken. The first thing that struck me was that they were a much lower grade than the group I'd met before. There was an officer who asked the questions, an interpreter, and two ugly-looking customers who just stood and said nothing. The officer began with a persuasive little speech explaining how much I had to gain by co-operating and being frank and helpful. He went on to say how much they already knew about me. They knew plenty.

They started right back at the time I'd made monkeys of their colleagues on board the *President Coolidge* in Yokohama harbor. I remembered how that wise old missionary had warned me I was being foolish to do it. They went on to the time in Shanghai when I refused to help old Suma—only they had it all wrong and accused me of promising to work in with him and then double-crossing. It went on like that.

They had masses and masses of information, but most of it was cock-eyed and some was just plain hooey.

The officer got around at last to my wartime activities and to the people, Chinese and British, I'd worked with. I realized by now what an awful mess his files must be in, and I got a little more confident. I just denied everything and swore I knew nothing at all. Quite suddenly the officer lost his temper.

"Get down on your knees!" he shouted. The two strong-arm men closed in on either side of me.

"Now tell the truth!" One of the men kicked me in the ribs—hard.

He repeated his question. Each time I opened my mouth to speak they kicked me again—no matter what I answered. "Keep your temper," I said to myself, "keep your temper, or you're a dead duck!"

One of them slashed me across the shoulders with a bamboo. That was too much. I got to my feet and socked him on the jaw. It was a good sock, too. I found out later that I'd skinned my knuckles, but it was the end for me. The officer joined in, and the three of them let me have it with fists, boots, and bamboos till they were tired. They dragged me back to my cell and left me alone on the cold stone floor.

That was the first thing I noticed when my brain began to work again—the cold. I was shivering. I just lay there and shivered all that day and through the night. In the morning the guard brought me a bowl of rice. Behind him came the interpreter with a pencil and a writing pad. He pushed them into my hands and said, "You must write down the exact position you held with the so-called Chinese National Government. You'd better tell the truth or it will be the worse for you."

I was still feeling pretty bad, in no sort of shape to think clearly. I thanked my stars that I'd worked this one out while my brain was clear. My hand was a bit shaky, but I managed to form the letters. I wrote (every word is still clear in my mind):

> I came to China in 1922 at the request of Dr. Sun Yat-sen and I was his aide-de-camp till he died. After that I was connected with the Central Bank of China. I served as aide-de-camp to Marshal Li Chai-sum and after that I was on the staff of General Wu Teh-chen. But for the last few years I have been retired on a pension and have devoted my time entirely to raising funds for the sick and wounded.

He read it slowly, mouthing the words as if they tasted bad. Then he gave me a nasty smirking look and said, "You must tell me the names of three people in Hong Kong who can confirm your story."

I was glad I'd thought that one out, too, beforehand. My brain was still only firing on one cylinder, but I had my answer: "Wang Ching-wei, Chen Kung-po, and Mr. Taketo."

The first was the well-known head of the Japanese "Puppet" Government of China. He'd been a friend of mine long ago when he was one of Dr. Sun's bright boys. He was on the wrong side now and usually called "Wang-the-Traitor," but I knew he'd help me if he could. The second was just a figurehead in the Puppet Government, a genial old boy who liked his liquor and singsong girls. We'd been on parties together and I knew him for a good fellow at heart. On the third I took a risk. Taketo had been Manager of the Bank of Tai Wan in Canton, and later on in Hong Kong he'd been in on various under-cover deals. We'd always been buddies. I'd done him one or two good turns, and now I just banked on his gratitude.

The interpreter went away saying nothing. I was left alone the rest of that day. Next morning they took me out and, without asking any more questions, just beat me up again. I can't tell you what it was like. Even now I hate to think about it.

They threw me back into my cell. I lay there weak and shivering. For the first time in my life I really wanted to die. Somewhere in his book Lawrence of Arabia tells how he felt after being beaten by Turkish soldiers, "The citadel of my integrity had been irrevocably lost." That isn't the sort of language I've ever learned to use, but that was how I felt that day.

I was tired, too, just ordinary plain dog-tired. During the night I must have dozed, because when I came to again I was a bit warmer and the cell was full of people. While I slept, Major and the three other Special Branch Officers had been put in there. One of them had covered me with a blanket. That was the turning point for me. I just couldn't let them see how bad I was. I had to pull myself together whether I liked it or not.

The one thing they wanted was a smoke and they had no cigarettes. I was wearing a quilted Chinese coat and I'd foreseen something like this. During my few days in Stanley, I'd sewed a dozen fags into the lining on one side of the skirt and on the other a dozen matches, or rather match-heads broken off short. I bestirred myself, unpicked the stitches and handed them out. Their thanks did a lot to make a man of me again.

We began to take notice of our guards. All of them belonged to that damned Kempeitai outfit and wore a badge that looked like a chrysanthemum. That was a word I could never manage to get my tongue around and I called them "Corinthians." The others ribbed me about it.

The officers and N.C.O.'s were real swine. The privates

who did sentry-go outside our cell seemed a bit more human, and I started to work on one of them. First, I caught his attention by using my hands to throw animal shadow-shapes on the wall of the corridor outside our cell—duck quacking and dogs barking and rabbits, that sort of thing. When I'd got him interested, I did little conjuring tricks—games you play to amuse a child, like pretending to pull off your thumb. Soon I had him grinning and signing to me to go on and do more of them.

By this time all my cigarettes had been smoked and we were just crazy for the smell of tobacco. I did smoking in dumb show and held my hand through the bars of the cell. I'm darned if he didn't drop two or three fags into it. How we enjoyed them! But still we had to be careful. Two of us stood by the cell bars looking one each way up and down the corridor in case anyone came along, while the others formed a circle at the back taking a couple of puffs each, blowing the smoke out through a little ventilator and then passing the fag on. It would go around and around till there was nothing left but a scrap of paper and a few shreds of baccy. Elston called it "The Feast of Excited Insects." This was the name of a famous Chinese festival.

After a bit the sentries became quite friendly—at least three of them did, but they warned us not to try anything on with the fourth, who was a mean sort of guy. They were terrified of the commandant. He used to creep around wearing carpet slippers to catch them on the hop. One by one all my cell-mates were taken out for questioning. They weren't maltreated, except for poor Elston, who was kicked in the mouth. Bit by bit we got our tails up. Then there was a really horrible episode.

The next cell to ours was absolutely crammed with Chinese. They stood there jammed together—there wasn't room to lie down, or even to sit. There must have been upwards of seventy of them. Every morning a coolie would come along to take away their latrine tins. One day he left the door of the cell open. Four of the prisoners saw their chance, ran out, knocked over the sentry, and bolted into the courtyard.

The sentry was taken by surprise and didn't attempt to use his rifle or bayonet. He just yelled. We heard shouts and shots. In a very few minutes all four were dragged back down the corridor and flung into the cell again.

After a little while every Jap in the building came running down the stairs to the basement with bamboos, rifles, sword-scabbards, lengths of rope—anything they happened to lay their hands on. They dragged everyone in that cell out into the corridor. Everyone! Not just the four who'd tried to escape. They started to beat them right in front of our eyes. It was horrible. You read of gutters running in blood and perhaps it doesn't mean much. I tell you that blood really ran down the floor of that corridor.

At the end of it they just threw the broken, moaning bodies back into the cell, all except the four fugitives. Two of them had been killed in the beating. The other two were taken out into the courtyard. We heard that filthy soft crunchy noise that means a beheading's been bungled.

Our four sentries were changed. From the next lot we got nothing but black looks and abuse. The corridor was constantly patrolled by N.C.O.'s. When one of them had said something to the guard I noticed that Rex Davis, who understood Japanese, was looking rather grim.

"What's matter?" I asked him.

"That guy was saying that you and I are going to lose our heads on Tuesday!"

I'd thought my number was up so many times by now that this really didn't worry me so very much. All I did was to unpick the hem of my coat again and hand over to Major a couple of five-hundred-dollar bills that I'd sewed in there with the fags.

A day or two later they took me out again to the interrogation room and made me kneel down. The officer who'd asked all the questions and was the biggest beast of the lot, jerked his great two-handed samurai sword out of its scabbard, swung it up, and said, "Put your head forward!"

I muttered, "*Shema Yisrael, Adonai Elohenu, Adonai Ehad* [Hear, O Israel, the Lord is our God, the Lord is One]." Aloud I said, with what I really thought would be my last breath, "Get on with it, you lousy bastard!"

All I got was a kick in the ribs that knocked me clean over on my side, and I was told to get up and go back to my cell. When I got there I realized that this time I hadn't felt very much afraid. I'd gone through too much already to have a great deal of fear left in me.

The next thing that came along was that we were released. That sounds rather bald, but it was just how it happened. One morning early there was a rumor that the Special Branch boys were going back to Stanley. About noon, a group of guards headed by that same officer came down to the cells. The doors were opened, and, as the names were called, the prisoners walked out.

I hung back, scarcely bothering to listen. I never dreamed that I'd be among them. I saw that same swine of an officer beckoning and, as I came forward, he said, "You, too, for Stanley Camp."

They formed us up and marched us along Nathan Road. Half way down we were bustled into a side street and told to wait. Rex Davis asked the guards what was up and said:

"It seems that the new Military Governor of Hong Kong is arriving and it's not for the likes of us to look at him."

"Goody!" I exclaimed, "he must be the Japanese Lady Godiva!"

"You're a tough devil, Morris," said Elston, "you never stopped joking even in that filthy cell. Does nothing ever worry you?"

If only he'd known. . . .

Nobody could have called me tough by the time we got to Stanley. I just flopped out on a straw mattress and stayed there for a fortnight while the doctors worked on me. My friends started to look in. The first thing they confessed was that they'd been so sure I'd never come back they'd divided between them the little store of baccy and cigarettes and canned fruit I'd left behind. God knows I didn't grudge it to them.

Presently I began to get around again. I found myself taking pleasure in a whole lot of things I'd never noticed before. To be able to walk up and down in the open air, to sniff the smell of the sea, to have the sky overhead with clouds and rain showers and stars at night—even things like sunrise and sunset that had always seemed a bit sissy to me, now I found myself noticing them. Nobody could enjoy life in Stanley Camp. What I was enjoying was just being alive at all.

After about a month of going around in that kind of vaguely happy mood, I was jerked back to reality. There were two Japanese Supervisors at the camp, both former residents of Hong Kong, not bad blokes either. Yamashida had been head barber at the Hong Kong Hotel and knew me pretty well. Nikazawa's father had kept a tailor's shop at West Point and he himself had risen in the world and become manager of the Japanese Club. He walked into my room one day and said, "General Cohen, you are wanted at the Camp Headquarters in ten minutes' time, please."

I thought of those damned Kempeitai with their boots and their bamboos. I wondered what the hell I could do. I could only think of one thing. That was to unpick my coat-hem once more and hand over those same five-hundred-dollar notes to someone whose expectation of life looked a bit longer than mine did.

I said goodbye all around, went over to the Camp Head-quarters, marched inside—and there, holding out his hand and smiling all over his face, was Mr. Taketo.

"My dear General, I am glad to see you looking so well. I have heard of your unfortunate experience with our gendarmerie, but believe me, I was powerless to help you."

He was all over me. He gave me three cartons of cig-arettes, he gave me a bottle of White Horse whisky, and then I'm damned if he didn't ask me to collaborate with the Japs and offer me my freedom as the price of outright treachery. They're a funny race—that's about all you can say of them.

There was a time when I'd have lost my temper, thrown his cigarettes in his face and said some nasty things. I'd learned better by now. I just told him in very simple lan-guage and short, easy sentences, that I'd served China for upwards of twenty years and I wasn't going to betray her now in the hour of her adversity and her greatest need. To begin with, he just couldn't understand. I kept my temper and went on telling him again and again until at last he hoisted it in.

He didn't seem very upset about it. He remained just as friendly. He advised me to do nothing to make myself con-spicuous in the camp or attract the attention of the Kempeitai (and that was a warning he needn't have bothered with). He said we would always be buddies. He promised to do anything he could to help me. In the eight-een months that followed he certainly kept his word.

Throughout that tricky, troublesome time he did everything that was humanly possible. He sent me bits of advance news. He sent me little presents of food and fags and even drink. Three times did he come out to see me and ask if there was anything he could do to help. Perhaps his greatest service was to secure the sacking of a Chinese contractor called Cheng who was stealing our precious rice rations and selling them on the side.

Through Taketo I was first to hear the most exciting news imaginable—that there was a move to repatriate some of the prisoners, but probably only Americans and Canadians, and of them only those with quasi-diplomatic status. This was no philanthropic business but simple straightforward horse-trading. After Pearl Harbor, the U.S.A. had interned a hell of a lot of Japs, and Canada had caught quite a fair number too. Hardly any had been nabbed by poor old England. The Japs wanted some of their big boys back and wanted them at once. They were ready to bargain, but only for folk from those two countries.

Taketo told me this. He also said that McLean, the Canadian Trade Commissioner (the same man who'd held my five-hundred-dollar notes the second time I'd got rid of them), was certain to be on the list. That was a hot tip. I knew how to use it. Off I trotted to his room.

"Say, McLean, if I tell you the one bit of 'gen' you're dying to hear, will you give me your mattress as soon as you've no further use for it?"

"Sure I will."

"You're going home with the Yanks!"

He kept his word. His bedding saved my old bones a lot. I'd slept on *Mimi Lau's*, camp slang for bricks and concrete, for a good six months, and it was getting me down. The only trouble was it was a full-size mattress and took up more than my share of floor space in the tiny room I shared with four others. They were good guys and didn't mind.

Another couple of months passed. In June, I think it was, the great day came and we all turned out to say goodbye to them. T. B. Wilson hadn't spent all his yen (the Japs allowed us each about twenty-five a month) and he offered them to me. I thought there were others who needed them more. Just then two kids passed by looking as hungry as we all felt and I asked them, "You had any sweets from the canteen today?"

"No, worse luck," they said. (Of course I knew damn well they hadn't.)

"Here," I said to Wilson, "you can give me ten yen after all."

He handed over the notes and I gave them to the kids. The look on their faces made me forget how empty my own belly was.

One favor I did ask Wilson. That was to get a message through to my sister in South Africa and my family in Manchester. He did that for me and a good thing it was. They'd swallowed the broadcasts and press reports about my execution and they all believed I'd had it—and come to think of it, they'd damn nearly been right.

The lucky ones sailed out through the Lyemun Pass and we were left to make the best of it, for just how long nobody could tell. To make the best of it was all that any of us could do. It was wonderful to see the different ways different people tackled the task. On the whole, folk ran true to form. A good guy in the Hong Kong Club was still a good guy in Stanley Camp. I could name lots of 'em. A louse at liberty was a louse just the same when he was locked up.

There were surprises, some pretty startling ones too. Ladies who'd lived all their lives in every sort of luxury and never lifted a finger to help themselves got right down to it and worked like slaves, not only for their own families, but everybody else's as well. On the other hand, there were men, and women too, who were absolutely beaten by the lack of baccy. It wasn't that they'd been particularly heavy smokers, but some weakness in their characters made life impossible for them without a cigarette, and they'd go to shocking lengths to get hold of one.

The worst of all our troubles was hunger, and the worst part of it was seeing the children go hungry and their mothers go hungrier still so as to give them a bit more to eat. It made me feel bad to watch them. Luckily that was just the one way that I could help.

I had to take Taketo's warning seriously and make myself inconspicuous, if I wanted to keep clear of trouble with the Kempeitai. That "included me out" of a lot of things. I dared not try to aid with the escapes, or to join in protesting against the filthy conditions under which we were made to live, or even to sit on committees and help in running the camp organizations.

The one thing I could do was to scrounge. I'd learned that game as a boy in Stepney and taken a post-graduate course as a sapper in France, and I'd never forgotten the tricks of the trade. So I scrounged. Twice a day we queued up for our ration of half a pound of low-grade rice, and once a week maybe we got a morsel of stinking fish as well. I set to work to supplement that and I didn't do so badly.

I'd stuck to my money and those much-handled and hidden five-hundred-dollar bills came in useful. I had good Chinese contacts, including one of the "puppet" Chinese camp superintendents. I even managed to bribe an Indian guard, though that was a tricky business, and I lost some sleep over it. One way and another I filled a lot of empty bellies every now and again.

Old Taketo remained my stand-by. Through him I brought off my biggest coup. He actually sent me two dozen eggs, and fairly fresh ones too. I bought a bag of flour and had it smuggled in by the Indian guard and threw a real party. We'd fixed up a brazier in my room and I made pancakes—gave them plenty of fire so as to kill the bugs in the flour—and asked all those folk I reckoned needed a square meal the most. Forty of my friends ate my food that day. I was prouder of that party than of any I ever gave at the Peninsular Hotel.

Months went by. The muggy, steamy weather got worse, as it always does towards the end of the hot season. I'd given up my snappy suitings long before. Now my morning dress was a dirty pair of shorts and that was all— except for a bit of once-white towel I wore tucked into my belt to wipe the sweat off my bare chest.

My money began to run short. I had to borrow from an old missionary friend, the Reverend Spence of Winnipeg, and pay him back when our monthly yen came along. Then the "puppet" Chinese camp superintendent (he was really a hundred per cent loyal) decided to bolt to Free China. I wished him luck and was glad to hear he'd got clear away. With him went one of my best outside contacts. Things were getting tougher.

I got down to my last fifty-dollar note. I clung to it for a long time. Then one day I met Mrs. Ferrier, the same White Russian girl who'd translated those Soviet Consulate documents for me in Canton more than twelve years back. She'd been caught at the time of the internment with two dollars in her pocket and one dress on her back and nothing else. On top of that her husband was shut up in a different camp. She'd had it pretty hard all around.

I blew that last bill the same evening. I gave her six packets of cigarettes and I gave her a party—my last big one. I could only get a dozen eggs this time and there was no flour to be had. I couldn't make pancakes but had to fry them instead. That meant they didn't go so far. She came along and brought a hungry friend, as I'd told her to do. She repaid me too. She got that filthy rag of towel I carried and soaked it and boiled it and scrubbed it. The dirt was so ingrained that, when it came back, it was a darkish gray. Even that was an improvement. I can't think of a kinder action.

Summer turned into autumn. It got cool and then it got cold. We knew it because the buildings were leaky and drafty and we hadn't enough clothes, and what we had were pretty well worn-out. With winter came the first Allied air raids and that was good for our morale, but it made the Japanese guards meaner than ever. We'd had one rux with them for spoiling their propaganda pictures by sticking our thumbs up and making the V-sign with our fingers. Now they got really nasty and forbade us to look up at our own planes, or even to look out of our windows while a raid was on.

It began to get warm again. Another summer loomed up ahead with its heat and its sickness and its everlasting hunger that one could never quite forget. The only thing that buoyed me up was a rumor that there might be another repatriation scheme, and that this time all Canadians were going to be freed. And there was the behavior of Mr. Taketo, who was being very mysterious indeed. He didn't just ask to keep myself out of sight of the gendarmerie, he simply *begged* me to lie low, and I damn well did. At the same time I couldn't quite believe that the Japs would let me go, considering all they knew of my past, and all they must still think I could tell them.

Gradually the rumors solidified. It became certain that another exchange scheme was under way. There'd still be no English in it, but the remaining Canadians and Americans were certain to go. I was assured that I was in the party. I still couldn't quite believe it, and determined to forget about the whole idea till I actually found my feet on the deck of a ship.

One morning in mid-September all North Americans were summoned to the Camp Headquarters. Even then I was afraid to go. I felt sure the Kempeitai would be there to pick me out and haul me off to Kowloon again. I sent scouts ahead. It was only when they came back to say that there was just one Japanese official present, and he was Mr. Nikazawa, that I plucked up my courage and went along.

He told us we were due to leave in a few days' time, then he made quite a speech. He asked us not to spread adverse reports about the Camp, as this would only make matters worse for those still inside. He implored us not to criticize the military administration, as he alone was responsible for everything that had happened (which, of course, was absolute nonsense). He warned us not to try to take out notes or papers of any kind, as we would certainly be searched before leaving. In fact, he made two things perfectly clear. First, that the Japanese Government had a pretty bad conscience. Second, that they meant to play on our fears for the friends we were leaving behind as a means of preventing us from telling the truth to the outside world.

Most of this I was told afterwards. At the time I hardly heard a word of what he said. I knew that, when he'd finished talking, he was going to read out the names of those who were being released. I was waiting to hear if my name was there or not. At last the lecture finished and he picked up the list. I leaned forward and listened as I'd never listened in my life before.

He took his time about it too. He adjusted his spectacles and scanned the sheet of paper in his hand. He said the first words to himself as if to be sure that he pronounced them right. He drew in his breath with that long Japanese hiss, and he began. The very first name was, "M. Cohen, Canadian"!

On the evening of September 22nd we heard that the *Taia Maru* was in Hong Kong harbor. We were only allowed to take two small parcels each. That didn't worry me much as I'd given away everything I could possibly spare. One of my parcels held the suit I'd been wearing when we were locked up. Now it was at least three sizes too big for me. It hung in folds all around. The other parcel held two shirts and a pair of shoes.

All the same I looked pretty snazzy, because of my shorts. My old ones had worn out. They'd been patched and patched till at last they'd fallen to pieces. The remnants had become my towel. Then Mrs. Ferrier had gotten an old window-curtain and made me a new pair out of that. It was a beautiful job as regards the cut and fit, but they were colored a bright crimson and they certainly caught the eye. It was lucky I hadn't to bother any longer about keeping myself inconspicuous.

Next morning I got up early and said goodbye to the grand old mattress that McLean had bequeathed me fifteen months before. I'd thought a lot about who would want it the most. I carted it over to the rooms where the Hong Kong police officers slept and gave it to Seymour Major, who'd been in that Kempeitai prison cell with me.

It was a dreary, drizzly day—typical monsoon weather —but nobody minded that. At eleven we were told to line up with our luggage in the open. So many of our friends gathered to see us off that the Jap guards became nervous in case some of the crowd should slip away among us. They herded us into the former Prep School building and allowed nobody inside except those who were leaving. Our friends sat on the wall of the cemetery, waving and shouting and spinning out the farewells to the last possible minute.

At last—it must have been about six o'clock—we were marched down to the launches and taken to the *Taia Maru*, where we found internees from Shanghai and Canton already on board. It was our first meeting with the outside world. Though they were only folk from other prison camps, it was a thrill. We were still exchanging news and gossip when the ship weighed anchor and put to sea.

She was filthy dirty and already badly overcrowded. We called at San Fernando in the Philippines, at Saigon, and at Singapore. At each place we took on board another group of repatriates. The overcrowding got worse and worse, but nobody cared. The men and boys slept on deck or in the cargo holds, the young women and girls slept in improvised dormitories. The cabins were kept for elderly ladies and the sick.

The food was putrid and there was very little of it. We soon found that the Japanese stewards were stealing supplies and selling them back to the passengers. That was a racket it was hard to break. I nosed around till I discovered a locker where bags of onions were stowed. I'd slip along there after dark and we'd pass the night eating onion sandwiches—and did they taste good! The Japs had taken the *Taia Maru* from the French with her liquor stocks almost untouched. We'd had nearly two years' compulsory teetotalism. Now there was champagne to be drunk. We drank it.

The rest of the time I just lazed around and reflected on my luck at being still alive. The old tub wallowed her way across the Bay of Bengal, rounded the south of Ceylon, and chugged up the Indian coast to Goa, where we lay for a few days waiting for the *Gripsholm* with the Japanese who were being exchanged.

When she came in it made us rather bitter to see how healthy, well-fed, and well-dressed the Japs looked compared with the skinny scarecrows we'd become. We forgot all that as soon as the exchange had been made, and we learned what life on board the *Gripsholm* was like. It was the tops. Fine clean cabins, bunks so comfortable that you could hardly rouse yourself out of them to meet the next meal, lots of entertainments, and wonderful food.

I came down to the saloon for our first meal behind a party of missionaries. When they saw the tables and the dishes on them, they stood gaping for a moment. Their leader cleared his throat and began, "Now Thank We All Our God." They sang the hymn right through to the end.

We were out of the hands of the Japs at last and at liberty to do as we liked. That was how I felt till we got to Port Elizabeth. I had relations there and they all came to meet me, my sister, my niece, her husband, and their two children. The very first thing they said was, "Come off your boat and stay with us here for a while." There was nothing I'd have liked better. But a wire came from the Canadian High Commissioner:

ALL EXCHANGE PRISONERS OF WAR REQUIRED BY INTERNATIONAL LAW GO DIRECT CANADA WOULD PREJUDICE FURTHER EXCHANGE IF COHEN LANDED HERE FURTHERMORE REQUEST HIM NOT MAKE PUBLIC STATEMENT OF ANY KIND OR GRANT PRESS INTERVIEW AND ON NO ACCOUNT REFER JAPANESE CIRCUMSPECTION IMPERATIVE FOR SAFETY.

That pulled us up sharp. It made me realize that the Japs still had us on a string, even if it was a long one. Our next port was Rio. There I simply had to go into hiding to dodge the newspaper men and the radio men and the rest of them. I knew damn well that, if once I started shooting my mouth, I'd say enough about those Kempeitai brutes to ruin any hope of further exchanges for the rest of the war. We steamed up past the Statue of Liberty and docked in

New York. Here the Yankees were in the clear all right, but we poor Canucks weren't. They kept us on board till the others had landed. Then we were taken ashore under bond, put into guarded buses, taken to the Grand Central Station, and loaded onto trains bound for Canada. It wasn't till next day, when we pulled into Montreal, that I picked up my parcels and stepped down on the platform—a free man.

There were weeks of reunions and interviews and receptions and junketings of all sorts. I still kept pretty quiet as to what went on in Hong Kong. But when I was summoned to Ottawa to meet the military authorities I opened up and gave them the true, ugly picture. When I'd done, we chatted for a while and they asked me if there was anything they could do.

"Yes," I said. "A quarter of a century back I served in the Kaiser's War as a sapper. Lots of guys are wearing medals they won then. I've never had mine yet."

Bells rang and officers came running. In less than ten minutes I was holding a neat little case. I opened it, and there were the British War Medal and the Allied Victory Medal. A little slip of paper in it read: "279259 Sgt. M. Cohen."

EPILOGUE

THE FALL OF HONG KONG left me with many missing friends, and of them all it was on the memory of Morris that I least liked to dwell. I learned presently that he had not been killed and later that he had been released; but at the same time I heard—and from a reliable source—that he had been kept for many days in close confinement with frequent interrogations and had been severely beaten at least twice.

Morris was nearer sixty than fifty; his life had been a hard one in every sense, and, when a man of his type is tried too far, the collapse can be complete and final. I pictured him, his bubbling optimism gone for ever, broken in body and with shattered nerves, creeping—probably penniless— into some corner to end his days.

But how little had I realized his resilience in the extremes of adversity. One morning soon after V.J. Day my telephone rang and I flinched from the receiver as a well-remembered bellow assailed my ear.

"Charles! This is General Morris Abraham Cohen and I want you to meet my wife!"

In Canada he had met and married Judith, a strikingly handsome middle-aged lady of his own people, the owner of the largest dressmaking establishment in Montreal and the leading couturière of that city.

Our wives liked each other at sight and as quiet, respectable, middle-aged couples we disported ourselves in London. Morris and Judith are perfectly matched and in those dreary days it was a rare pleasure to see any two people so wholeheartedly happy.

Judith had only one worry, but it was well founded. Those who have once served China can never feel free of her service. Black though the outlook was, her future remained unpredictable. The time might come when China would again have need of him and Judith knew that, when that day dawned, Morris would go back to China.